ORAL HISTORY OF THE YAVAPAI

This book belongs in every American History classroom.
—**Ernest Jones, Sr.**, President
Yavapai-Prescott Indian Tribe
and Tribal Board of Directors

Not enough is taught in our schools about what happened to the American Indians. We are glad this book has brought our side of history to the public. As the State of Arizona celebrates its one hundred birthday in February 2012, my hope is this book sheds new light on the subject with greater understanding for all peoples, including the original inhabitants of Arizona.
—**Raphael Bear**, President 2004-2008
Fort McDowell Yavapai Nation

I am pleased to join the praise of this fine book, *Oral History of the Yavapai* by Yavapai elders Mike Harrison and John Williams and by Sigrid Khera, anthropologist, and Carolina Butler. This historical work will benefit not only the Yavapai and other Native Americans but all Arizonans and far beyond even our borders.
—**Dennis DeConcini**
United States Senator from Arizona
1987-1995, Retired

Using insightful accounts, this engaging oral history provides a timely understanding of the Yavapai, their history and culture for Arizona's Centennial.

—Donald Fixico, Ph.D.
Distinguished Foundation Professor of
History & Affiliate Faculty
of American Indian Studies
Arizona State University

I was delighted to see this long-awaited project reach completion. This volume is a significant addition to Yavapai history and a lasting contribution to the full story of the Southwest.

—Peter Iverson, Ph.D.
Regents' Professor of History
Arizona State University
and author of *Carlos Montezuma and the Changing World of American Indians*

This book is a valuable resource for not only the Yavapai people but for anyone who wants to know and understand American Indians. It provides an accurate recounting of Yavapai history and a detailed portrayal of the Yavapai culture and way of life through the eyewitness words of two men whose lives and memories encompass the transition from the old ways to modern times after the clashing interaction with white people.

—Leon Speroff, M.D.
and author of *Carlos Montezuma, M.D.*

This book deals with the history, stories, traditions and life-ways of the Yavapai as narrated by two respected Yavapai elders, carefully recorded and lovingly preserved by their friends, Sigrid Khera and Carolina Butler. Mike Harrison and John Williams wanted people to know that the Yavapai are a separate people, distinct from the Apache, with whom they have historically been confused.

It is a rare book in that it recounts the history of Yavapai-Euroamerican relationships during the 1800s from the Yavapai perspective, as told to Mike and John by their parents' generation.

This makes *Oral History of the Yavapai* an important volume for anthropologists, historians, and the Yavapai people themselves, since that generation was the last to have lived a traditional lifestyle before Yavapai culture was decimated by war and forced incarceration outside their homeland.

It will provide readers with an account of the "Apache" war period and the Long Walk to San Carlos that is not found elsewhere. It is also a first-person narrative about a Yavapai man's life in the 20th century. *Oral History of the Yavapai* is a significant addition to the meager literature that is available about the Yavapai, their culture, and history. It should become mandatory reading for anyone interested in the Yavapai, the Apache, and the Indian Wars period in Arizona.

— **Peter J. Pilles, Jr.**
Forest Archaeologist
Coconino National Forest

Carlos Montezuma of the Yavapai tribe was the fascinating focus of my research. In the course of that work, I was lucky to have met some special Fort McDowell Yavapai. Late afternoons by the lovely Verde River, we would sit, talk, be silent together, talk some more. Not only about their fascinating history but about their beliefs, the Spirits of Four Peaks, creation, and a wonderfully mischievious trickster spirit whose clever and well-timed pranks kept folks on the proper path.

In that meaningfully rich context, it is a joy to commend this work. Reading history in the Native folks' own words, sensing their feelings, and probing their hearts and minds seldom occurs. This book is a welcome event not just for Native America, but for all peoples everywhere.

—John W. Larner, Ph.D.

Editor, *The Papers of Carlos Montezuma, M.D.*

As an historical consultant to the Government of Canada, I work closely with the primary documents associated with aboriginal peoples on both sides of the Canada/United States international boundary. Consequently, I am intimately acquainted with the significance of having access to the *Oral History of the Yavapai* and with the importance of those historical records even existing.

—Pamela Y. Stanton, Ph.D.

Mayne Island, BC, Canada

[Editor's note: Ernest Jones, Sr., Prescott Yavapai, is a great-grandson of the great Yavapai medicine man Jim Mukhat. Raphael Bear, Fort McDowell Yavapai, is a grandson of famed basketweaver Bessie Mike.]

ORAL HISTORY OF THE YAVAPAI

◆

Mike Harrison & John Williams
Sigrid Khera, Ph.D.

Carolina C. Butler, Editor

Acacia Publishing

The University of Arizona Press
www.uapress.arizona.edu

© 2012 by Carolina C. Butler
All rights reserved
First published 2012 by Acacia Publishing, Inc., Gilbert, Arizona

ISBN-13: 978-0-8165-3254-4 (paper)

Cover design: Carla Olson, www.bluefrogjump.com
Cover photos: *Wigidjassa* (Four Peaks) 7,657' elev., by Elias Butler,
www.eliasbutler.com; John Williams and Mike Harrison photo
by Melissa Jones

Library of Congress Control Number:
2012941000

Printed in the United States of America
♾ This paper meets the requirements of ANSI/NISO Z39.48-1992
(Permanence of Paper).

Dedicated
to the bravery of the Yavapai

The basket shown on each of the five Part I-V section pages was woven in 1974 at the Fort McDowell Reservation by Yavapai basketweaver Emma Johnson (1904-1976). Basket is in the collection of Carolina Butler.

In 1955, Karl Heider, a Harvard anthropology student, interviewed Yavapai elders Nellie Quail and Warren Gazzam at Fort McDowell about Yavapai pottery.

Karl Heider: "Were there any decorations?"

Nellie Quail: "May be some times. Arrow point. The diamond shape is our tribes'."

Warren Gazzam: "Some designs go way back to the cliff dwellers."

Nellie: "But that's ours—the diamond shape. They could use just the point or the whole of it. But it's the same."

Thus, we have used the diamond shape, which has also been used extensively in Yavapai basketweaving, to decorate the title page, the contents page and each of the chapter title pages.

Emma Johnson, Fort McDowell Yavapai, September 1975. Photo by Sigrid Khera.

CAUTION

Make safety your top concern when enjoying Arizona's outdoors. Take water, food, cell phone, and extra water in your car. Wear protective shoes, hat, clothing, etc. Tell someone where you are going and when to expect you back.

Inform yourself at Arizona's Office of Tourism or at a Visitor Center or park ranger station for safety tips for the place you are visiting. Call 911 for emergencies.

Inform yourself on the laws protecting Arizona's plants and animals. Vandalism can be reported to park rangers or law enforcement. Help protect and preserve the environment.

Neither the editor nor publisher endorse the consumption or any use of Arizona's wild plants mentioned in this book. Do not touch cactus needles or poison ivy.

Please respect ancient Indian ruins and petroglyphs and related items. They are protected by law. Report vandalism to the Law Enforcement Officer at the nearest Ranger District.

Keep children from climbing the ruins or touching the petroglyphs. Do not move rocks; they may be archaeologically significant. Enjoy seeing all items from the past such as arrowheads, pottery shards, pioneer items, old structures, etc.—but leave them for others to enjoy. Take a picture instead.

We assume no liability for personal injury related to being in Arizona's outdoors. The above is not a complete list of precautions. We present this minimum list as a courtesy.

Contents

━━━━━━━ ◆ ━━━━━━━

Editor's Preface

In his 1891 classic, *On The Border With Crook*, U.S. Army Captain John G. Bourke, who served on the staff of General George Crook from 1870-1886, wrote, "For years I have contemplated the project of writing the history of these people based upon the Indians' own story."[1] This book is just that: The Yavapai Indians' own story—history from the other side.

In March 1974, anthropologist Dr. Sigrid Khera (1934-1984) started working with Mike Harrison (1886-1983) and John Williams (1904-1983), two tribal elders living on the Fort McDowell Reservation in Arizona, recording their Yavapai history. The three continued their collaboration for years until their work was completed. Today, the remains of the three lie in peace at the reservation cemetery at Fort McDowell.

Before her sad passing, Dr. Khera left me all her research material, including a completed manuscript of Yavapai history, fully documented in more than 200 audio recordings of her interviews with Mike and John, a claim no other author on the Yavapai can make. I also have obtained signed permissions from the families of Mike Harrison, John Williams, and Jim White, which is another claim no

i

other author of Yavapai history and songs can make. The 200 audio recordings contain additional Yavapai stories and many Yavapai songs, Yavapai pronunciation of Yavapai words, and other cultural riches to add to our nation's treasure of American Indian history. The recordings of these Yavapai songs have been converted into a series of 16 CDs.

Upon publication of this book, the Dr. Sigrid Khera Yavapai Collection will be donated to the Labriola National American Indian Data Center in the Arizona State University Libraries at Arizona State University in Tempe, Arizona. Those who wish to read Dr. Khera's complete original unpublished manuscript on the Yavapai, (December 1982, *Souls on the Land*) exactly as she wrote it, will find it at the Labriola Center.

The materials collected and assembled by Dr. Khera are beyond today's measure. Only study, research and time will reveal all their gifts. I cannot say enough in admiration of the sacrifices she made when doing her research on the Yavapai, while also fulfilling her responsibilities as a wife and mother, making her many trips between Scottsdale and Fort McDowell, spending hours taping the interviews, and, at a time before computers, typing her work on a manual typewriter, and more. Thank you, Dr. Khera.

In editing Dr. Khera's manuscript, the eight Yavapai oral history chapters remain unchanged and are in the Yavapais' own words. The Yavapai oral history is the heart of this book. Their history is the heart of the Yavapai. Many Yavapai had feared that the history of their tribe would be lost but it has been saved, thanks to these three inspiring individuals—Mike Harrison, John Williams, and Dr. Khera. And more Yavapai songs have been saved thanks to their collaboration with Jim White.

I tightened up Dr. Khera's story about how she met the Yavapai. Let me now address the rest of her original manuscript. Because much of her ethnographic outline of the Yavapai had already been published in Volume 10 of the Smithsonian Institution's *Handbook of North American Indians, Southwest*, 1983, I needed to take a different approach and at the same time fulfill Dr. Khera's goals.

I have attempted to put the reader in awe at the size and extent of the aboriginal Yavapai Indians' ancestral land. If the reader learns the Yavapai Indians' ancestral territory, he or she will no longer mis-name the Yavapai. In my research I delved into the normal studies but re-read others less known. Also, I delved into the findings of the Indian Claims Commission, based on its years of evidence gathering, field hearings, deliberations, and testimony from plaintiffs, defendants, and experts on both sides. There is no better evidence than this to document this book.

It was also Dr. Khera's goal to show that there were White people's academic, military and civil documents to support her Yavapai informants' oral history. I decided to fulfill and fit in Dr. Khera's goals while guiding the reader through the history of one American Indian tribe, the Yavapai, whose beginning in Arizona is approximated at 1250 A.D., and set the Yavapai in the timeline of events which would impact their lives beginning with Christopher Columbus' discovery of the New World in 1492.

When Dr. Khera died in 1984 and left me her manuscript, I placed it in my bank safety box. It's taken me a long time because I've had a busy life. When I met Sigrid in 1974, I was already helping the Fort McDowell Yavapai save their land which the government wanted for the Orme Dam. The Yavapai were victorious in 1981 but the dam's powerful political supporters kept trying to revive it for years afterwards and I dedicated my time to pushing them back. In 1987, I was a leader in the defeat of the $3 billion Rio Salado Project—formerly one of the arguments made for the Orme Dam—in a Maricopa County election.

After that, I helped the San Carlos Apache oppose the Vatican's observatory atop the Apaches' sacred Mount Graham. Throughout, I was active on water issues—in Arizona, testifying in Washington, working with California water activists and working with in- and out-of-state journalists. My activities can be traced in many books by others.

For 41 years since 1971, the Yavapai have been my friends and I theirs, at Fort McDowell, Camp Verde and Prescott reservations. For 41 years I have learned from the Yavapai, read their scientific studies, learned from Dr. Sigrid Khera and other academics, and learned from other tribes. I have strived to document everything in this book.

Carolina Castillo Butler
February 14, 2012

PART I

BACKGROUND

Chapter 1

◆

Arizona

Arizona, the "Grand Canyon State," is in the southwestern part of the United States. It is bounded on the north by Utah, on the east by New Mexico, on the south by Mexico, and on the west by California and Nevada.

Though thought of as a young state, for the native people and the land area which is Arizona it has been a longer history, much longer than the arrival of the first outsiders. The Spanish explorers first entered Arizona in 1528 (de Vaca) and in 1539 (de Niza). Spain claimed control until 1821 when Mexico won control. In 1848, after the Mexican-American War, all of present-day Arizona lying north of the Gila River became the Territory of New Mexico, part of the United States. In the 1854 Gadsden Purchase, the land south of the Gila to the present border with Mexico was purchased from Mexico. In 1863 Arizona separated from the Territory of New Mexico and became

Arizona Territory. Forty-nine years later, Arizona gained statehood on February 14, 1912.[1]

Arizona's land area is 113,417 square miles.[2] It measures 392 miles from north to south and 338 miles from east to west. It contains three distinct topographic areas: (1) a high plateau region (Colorado Plateau) in the northeast part of the state, (2) a mountainous area (Mogollon Rim) which runs diagonally southeast to northwest through the state's midsection, (3) the deserts (Sonoran, Mohave and Chihuahuan) and "Sky Island" mountains in the central and south. These diverse topographic areas all have different climates.

Land ownership in Arizona is: Federal 42.2%, Indian Trust 27.6%, State Trust 12.7%, Private 17.5%.[3] Some decry that only 17.5% (19,848 square miles) of Arizona is private land but that is bigger than the combination of Rhode Island, Delaware, New Jersey and Massachusetts. There are 20 Indian reservations in Arizona.

Elevation of the city of Yuma is 138 feet above sea level and the highest elevation in Arizona is 12,633 feet at Humphrey's Peak near Flagstaff. Mountains are found throughout the state, with over 3,900 peaks statewide.

Arizona is an amazing state with diverse terrain and dramatic natural beauty. The world's greatest natural wonder, the Grand Canyon, lies in Arizona. A few other stunning natural places include: Antelope Canyon, Canyon de Chelly, Petrified Forest, Sunset Crater, Sedona, Oak Creek Canyon, Devil's Canyon, Chiricahua National Monument, Coronado Trail, Saguaro National Park, Kartchner Caverns, Colossal Caves and Organ Pipe Cactus

National Monument. The world's largest contiguous ponderosa pine forest surrounds Flagstaff.

There are also over 100 outstanding wilderness and wildlife areas such as Paria Canyon, Granite Mountain, Four Peaks, Superstition Mountains, Aravaipa Canyon, Gila Box, and Mount Graham. Many wilderness and wildlife areas are located in the Yavapai Indians' aboriginal territory.

The Colorado River in Arizona carved the Grand Canyon and forms the state's western boundary with California and part of Nevada. Many of Arizona's waterways are usually dry, except when it rains significantly.

The Gila River crosses Arizona's waist like a low-slung belt. It enters Arizona at Duncan from New Mexico and heads west for more than 300 miles and into the Colorado River at Yuma. The Gila is usually dry but when it rains, she rolls.[4]

The Verde River runs north to south like a body's aorta in the middle of Arizona. It is about 175 miles long and it carries water. It begins below the dam that holds water from the Big Chino Wash and Williamson Valley Wash creating Sullivan Lake which sits just south of Paulden in Yavapai County. The Verde River's tributaries include Tangle Creek, Granite Creek, Sycamore Creek, Wet Bottom Creek, East Verde River, Fossil Creek and Oak Creek.[5] Areas up and down the river are described as the Upper Verde Valley, the Middle Verde Valley, and the Lower Verde Valley. From north to south, the Verde River runs through the middle of the Yavapai Indians' ancestral land.

The Verde River ends where it enters the Salt River about an hour's drive slightly northeastward from downtown Phoenix. The confluence of the Verde and Salt rivers was to be the site of the proposed Orme Dam which would have forced the relocation of the Yavapai tribe of Fort McDowell. Fortunately, the dam plan was defeated in 1981.[6]

Verde River at Fort McDowell, 1975. Photo by Sigrid Khera

Chapter 2

◆

Indian Claims Commission

On March 24, 1965, the Indian Claims Commission, a special judicial body, found that the United States took 9,238,600 acres of land from the aboriginal Yavapai Indians on May 1, 1873, without payment of any compensation. The Commission's description of that area is shown on the following pages.[1]

The final judgment in favor of the Yavapai was entered by the Commission on March 13, 1969, in the amount of $5,100,000.00.[2]

15 Ind. Cl. Comm. 193

BEFORE THE INDIAN CLAIMS COMMISSION

THE YAVAPAI and the groups and bands thereof, ex rel. Calloway Bonnaha, Harry Jones, Fred Beauty, and Warren Gazzam;	)))))
THE YAVAPAI-APACHE INDIAN COMMUNITY;	))
THE FORT McDOWELL MOHAVE-APACHE COMMUNITY;	))
Petitioners,	))
v.	) Docket No. 22-E)
THE UNITED STATES OF AMERICA,	))
Defendant.	)

ORDER AMENDING FINDING OF FACT

Additional facts having been brought to our attention with reference to the award areas in Docket Nos. 283, 295, and 319,

IT IS THEREFORE ORDERED that the description of the award area in Docket No. 22-E as set forth in Finding of Fact 34 of said docket be and it is hereby amended to read as follows:

Beginning at the intersection of a line between Black Peak and a point on the south bank of Bill Williams River which is three miles upstream from where the said river enters the Colorado River, and a line between the N.W. corner of Section 19, T. 3 N., R. 26 E., SB Mer., California, and Mineral Hill, Arizona, which line marks a boundary of a portion of the award to the Mohave Tribe of Indians; thence east southeasterly along the award line to Mineral Hill; thence northwesterly on the award line between Mineral Hill and Crossman Point to the intersection with a line between the previously described point on the Bill Williams River and Mohave Springs; thence northerly to Mohave Springs; thence on a line easterly to Aubrey Peak; thence on a line in an easterly direction to the southeast corner of T. 13 N., R. 13 W.; thence on a line to the northeast corner of T. 11 N., R. 11 W.; thence on a line to Camp Wood; thence on a line in a northeasterly direction to a point on highway #89 three miles south of where said highway intersects highway #66; thence easterly on a line to Bellemont, Arizona; thence on a line southwesterly to the southwest corner of T. 12 N., R. 3 E., thence on a line in an

6

15 Ind. Cl. Comm. 193

easterly direction to the juncture of Fossil Creek and the
Verde River; thence on a line in a southeasterly direction to
the crest of the Mazatzal Mountains; thence in a.southeasterly
direction following the crest of the Mazatzal and Pinal
Mountains to Signal Peak; thence on a line to Sonora,
Arizona; thence northwesterly on a line to the juncture of
the Salt and Verde Rivers; thence northwesterly on a line
to the most northern edge of Lake Pleasant; thence in a
westerly direction on a line to Morristown, Arizona; thence
on a line in a southerly direction to the northernmost edge
of the White Tank Mountains; thence on a line in a westerly
direction to Burnt Mountain; thence on a line in a southerly
direction to Yellow Medicine Butte; thence on a line in a
southwesterly direction to Thumb Butte Tank; thence southwesterly on a line between Thumb Butte Tank and Long Mtn.
to the intersection of a portion of the boundary of the
award to the Quechan Tribe of Indians, said point of intersection being in T. 7 S., R. 19 W., G & SR meridian, Arizona,
this point also being approximately 4 miles northeast of
Long Mtn. on said line; thence northwesterly along the award
line to the intersection of a line connecting Long Mtn. and
Mohave Peak; thence northwesterly along the latter line to
Mohave Peak; thence on a line in a northerly direction
towards Moon Mtn. to the intersection of the Quechan Tribe
of Indians award line in the southwest corner of T. 1 N.,
R. 21 W., G & SR meridian; thence northwesterly and northerly
and westerly along award line to the intersection of line
connecting Mohave Peak and Moon Mtn.; thence along the latter
line to Moon Mtn.; thence in a northeasterly direction to
Black Peak; thence on a line in a northeasterly direction to
the point of beginning.

Dated at Washington, D. C., this 24th day of March, 1965.

Arthur V. Watkins
Chief Commissioner

Wm. M. Holt
Associate Commissioner

T. Harold Scott
Associate Commissioner

Oral History of the Yavapai

Chapter 3

◆

Maps

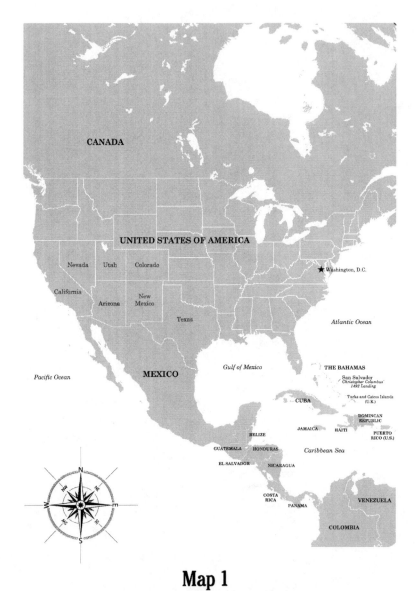

Map 1
Location of Columbus' 1492 landing in the New World.
San Salvador Island, The Bahamas

Map 2
Arizona Counties and Selected Cities, 2012.

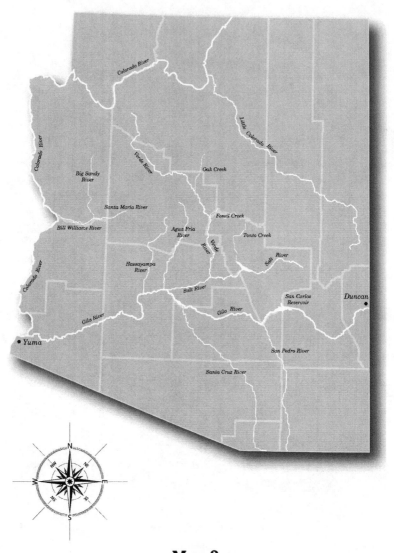

Map 3
Arizona: Selected Waterways.

Map 4
Arizona: Selected Mountain Ranges.

Map 5
Arizona: Selected Military Posts, 1849-1900.

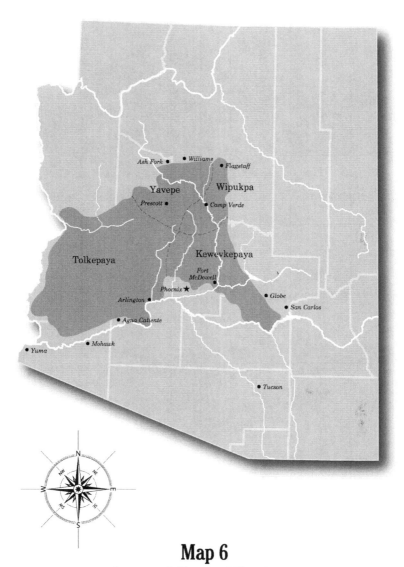

Map 6

Ancestral Yavapai Territory.
*The land taken from the Yavapai Indians, subtribes shown,
on May 1, 1873, by the United States.*

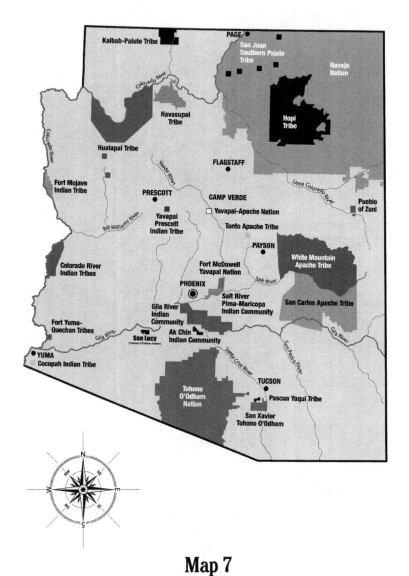

Map 7
Indian Reservations in Arizona, 2011.
Courtesy: Inter Tribal Council of Arizona

PART II

TRIBAL ELDER MIKE HARRISON ASKS FOR YAVAPAI HISTORY

Sigrid Khera's manual typewriter. Photo by Susheila Khera.

Chapter 4

━━━━━ ◆ ━━━━━

Anthropologist Meets the Yavapai

In February 1974, only a few weeks after I had moved to Phoenix, somebody from the Anthropology Department at Arizona State University in Tempe showed me a letter which caught my attention immediately. The letter said that an elder of the Fort McDowell Mohave-Apache Reservation wanted somebody to write down their history as they themselves knew it. The letter was signed with "Carolina Butler, Committee to Save Fort McDowell Reservation." [1]

Since the recording of Indian oral history had been part of my research with northern Ojibway for the National Museum of Canada for many years, I was immediately interested in this task.

Attached to the letter was an article from *The Times* of London dated June 25, 1973, entitled "Last Stand of the Yavapai." The article and a short note by Carolina Butler told the reader that the Indians of Fort McDowell, a small tribe of some 350, were threatened by a dam project, Orme Dam, which would flood most of their 24,680-acre reservation.

A tribe threatened to lose its land by a dam? I asked other people what was going on. Nobody seemed to be quite sure. There were the phrases usual in such situations. A dam? Probably lots of money involved. In such case there was nothing one could do about it. Small groups, Indians and others, stood no chance against big-money interests. So better to forget about it. The whole thing was too political anyway.

I also could not figure out who the Mohave-Apache were. I was an anthropologist but at that time the Southwest was not exactly my area of specialization. I knew that the Western Apache lived a long distance east from Phoenix. What kind of mixture between Mohave and Apache were the Mohave-Apache supposed to be?

I contacted Carolina Castillo Butler. She told me she was a many-generations Arizonan, Mexican-American, and that in a tribal council meeting at Fort McDowell on November 6, 1973, tribal *members* had voted unanimously for her to help them keep their land against the dam.[2] And she told me she was expecting her fourth child.

A few days later we made the half hour drive from her home in Scottsdale to Fort McDowell. It was mid-March 1974. I cannot remember what my first impression of the reservation was. I remember only that I was very hot and that the mesquite trees gave little shade because their leaves were not out yet. On the other hand I remember most vividly the first meeting with the two old men who had asked Carolina to find someone who would write down what they had to say.

There was a brush shade with a dusty table, rickety chairs, a rusty iron bedstead and two hungry dogs who jumped all over us. A tall, thin old man in a T-shirt and with thick eyeglasses disappeared into a little shack next to the brush shade. After a little while he came out again but dressed with shirt and tie and a straw hat on his head. This was Mike Harrison (1886-1983), then 88, the oldest man of Fort McDowell. He shook hands with Carolina and me and Carolina joked a little with him in Spanish. Mike spoke some Spanish and he seemed quite proud of it. It was Mike who had decided that the non-Indian world should know who his people were and had asked Carolina to write their history. Together with his cousin John Williams, Mike took the initiative to have this knowledge recorded.

And then there was John Williams (1904-1983), then 70. Unlike Mike Harrison, John was of husky build. He wore a broad-rimmed cowboy hat and he had the gait of a man who had spent more time in the saddle than on the ground. His knowledge of the past gave John Williams, who had never gone to school and who could not speak "standard" English, extraordinary strength and confidence. One of his close cousins later said about him, "When he was young, all of the old people told him things all the time. It looked as if they wanted him to carry on what they themselves had seen and knew so that it would not get lost. They had picked him out to pass the knowledge on to the next generations."

"This is Sigrid Khera," said Carolina. "I have brought her so you can tell her about the history of your people. Maybe she can write a book of it, maybe just a few pages. But whatever it is, she will write it down for you."

Mike Harrison and John Williams at Mike's place, Fort McDowell,
1975. Photo by Sigrid Khera

I unpacked my small cassette tape recorder and told them if it was all right with them, they could start talking about what they wanted to say and at home I would type their recorded speeches on paper. Once we had a lot written down, we could try making a book out of it.

Now I expected questions about myself. Some checking of my credibility, something more about what should be done with the recorded material. Instead, Mike took the microphone and gave a speech in Spanish and then in somewhat hard to understand English. He said that the White people had come as uninvited guests, they had killed his people at many different places, and they had killed many of them at a cave in the Salt River Canyon. Then they had sent the survivors to San Carlos and had kept them there for 25 years. They had given them the Fort McDowell Reservation and now they wanted to flood them out by building a dam.

Then John Williams talked into the microphone and his English was quite clear. He also talked about the killings in the cave and about other killings. He said White people talked of "Indian Wars" but he could not see much of a "war" when it was only the Indians who got killed.

"And they say 'Apache War'—but we are not Apache. We are Yavapai. There were no Apache around here, only Yavapai when the White people came."

He said that his people had been killed even though they had not wanted to fight the Whites and that they had been removed from their homeland for 25 years.

This was the very first message which the two men had to give and it was the most important one which they would repeat throughout the coming years when they told their people's history.

The two men were ready to talk on for a long time. But Carolina, who had little children, had to go home.

"When are you coming back here?" I was asked by each one of them.

"Next Wednesday, maybe in the morning, maybe around ten?"

"You come back. We wait for you."

From then on we met at least twice a week for three, four, and more hours. Meantime, Carolina wrote and apprised the tribal council about our work.[3] First, I would pick up John and then he and I drove to Mike's, who lived far off from everybody else toward the north end of the reservation. Mike was very old, almost blind, and he lived alone. But he was still a man who was very particular about his personal appearance. If Mike expected us he was already sitting at the table under the brush shade with tie and straw hat. If we came unexpectedly like the first time, he quickly disappeared in his little house to come back after ten minutes, properly dressed for the occasion. Mike's orderliness went beyond his personal appearance. In his kitchen shack, pots, pans, jars and boxes, all had their places on shelves. In his bedroom, clothes were neatly arranged on hangers and hooks, the bed was always made and the floor was swept. He did all this by himself.

We were hardly seated when the talking began. Usually John had already started to talk about a particular topic in the car and he often continued it once we were at Mike's. Mike listened and then he spoke about it in Yavapai. When he had finished, after maybe ten minutes, John translated it to me. Then Mike would go on for another round and John would again translate it. However, by then John usually carried on about what he himself knew about the topic. Finally, after some time he would say, "Mike knows about that better." Then again Mike would talk about it for a while in Yavapai, John would translate it and eventually continue with his own knowledge. Interviewing the two Yavapai elders together gave high value to their information with one checking the other as opposed to a single informant with no checks. At home I would replay the audio recording of each session and type everything down exactly to the word. One hour recording generally took three hours to transcribe.

I also recorded Mike and John singing Yavapai songs. Mike played the flute and John the gourd rattle. I took many photographs of the people, housing, historic Yavapai objects they showed me, fairs and other community events. Later when we started our field trips I photographed places such as Skeleton Cave, San Carlos, Camp Verde, Date Creek, Montezuma Well, the sacred caves around Sedona in the Red Rock country and many other places significant to the Yavapai.

Somewhere in between all the talking and recording at Mike's we had coffee, sandwiches and cookies which I had brought along. Mike in particular consumed these with visible delight. During the eating it was quiet. But afterwards the talking was resumed with renewed vigor.

One day John brought another old man along to the sessions, introducing him to me as one of his relatives. Several times during that session, whenever we had started a particular topic, John turned to his relative saying, "Now, you tell it how it was!" The man said a few sentences, then turned to John, "You go on."

The next time when I met John he said, "You see, he didn't believe that I know it. So I asked him to come along. Maybe now he believes me I am saying the right things."

This was the first time that I experienced that another person in the community challenged John's relations about the past. Soon I noticed that almost everybody else in his age group challenged it too. When I got together with other old people they would say, "How does John know (about such and such event)? My grandmother (or grandfather, etc.) had been there, and she (he) had told me about it."

Then the person who had expressed the doubts would tell the story as he or she knew it and usually there was no difference to John's story or at the most a few small details.

In the long run it became quite obvious that Mike and John had the widest knowledge about the past and this was generally admitted. However, this did not mean that the others ceased to be on the lookout for any possible mistakes which the two old men might have made.

Thus, I quickly learned that in a small society history is not simply a "common good," a convention which everybody accepts without much questioning. History is very much the "private good" of each individual member of the society. Each person's relatives had been involved in the events of the past and they had passed on to their descendants the knowledge about what they themselves had experienced. Thus, if someone talked about an event, one who knew about it from his own older relatives would watch out sharply what was going to be said about it. If there were differences to what he knew, these would have to be discussed—and sometimes in a most critical manner. Under such watchfulness there is little chance for "cheating." A person who is deliberately bending history has to face the kind of criticism which would impair his standing in society. And in a small society where there is no "escape" from all the others, nobody wants to risk severe criticism.

I had come to the Fort McDowell Mohave-Apache Community without even knowing that they were Yavapai. The Whites thought the Yavapai were Apaches but they were not. The Yavapai are a different tribe and have a different language. Once I knew who these people were I checked what literature existed about the Yavapai. However, I decided at that point not to read anything previously written. I wanted to listen to what the Yavapai themselves had to say. I wanted to experience how they explained things to me without my being influenced by second- and third-hand information.

Mike and John talked and most of the time I kept quiet and just listened. Nothing was told only once. Everything they told was repeated many times. Those stories and topics which they considered most important were told most often.

In relating the history of their people, Mike and John gave priority to certain events. The killing of a whole band of Yavapai by the U.S. Army in a cave above the Salt River Canyon—later called Skeleton Cave after the remains of the victims—was the event they related first and with the deepest emotions. It was retold innumerable times as the greatest tragedy for the Yavapai and the narrators in specific. They had lost many important relatives of their parental and grandparental generations. To them as the descendants it meant that they had to live a life in which many social ties were denied to them. The devastating loss of loved ones in the Skeleton Cave massacre was followed by other events where the Yavapai were senselessly and cruelly killed by Whites; the removal of the Yavapai from their homelands and their confinement at San Carlos; their return 25 years later; and the pains they underwent to get and keep their reservations.

Our work had been going on for over a year when John began showing me places important to the Yavapai, important because of events that had happened there and others because of their natural resources—good water, abundance of edible plants or game. Besides John and his wife Minnie (1920-2001), participants in these many field trips sometimes included some of their children, other elders such as Emma Shenah (1917-2011), Carolina with her children, my children, students from Arizona State University, and others. Mike Harrison was never able to come along because the trips required several hours driving in the hot car and also walking over rough territory.

Our first field trip brought us to the area in the central Arizona highlands south of Flagstaff which the Yavapai call the "Middle of the World" because it was there that life began and the present world order had been established. Montezuma Well, a sunken lake in the limestone plateau of the Middle Verde Valley is one of the most important places as the first people had emerged from there. Other important places are throughout the red rock mountains around Sedona. The Yavapais are greatly alarmed that private land and development of their revered area, so rich in beauty and spiritual essence, will shut them out or hinder their ability to visit their special places where they can pray and conduct rituals and gain strength.

Healing ceremony at Fort McDowell, summer 1976. John Williams and Jim White (Cocopah). Jim White was taught by Yavapai medicine man Mike Nelson. Photo by Melissa Jones.

In the summer of 1976 the sessions with Mike Harrison came to an end. He was brought to a nursing home. Working with Mike had been very special.

Mike and John had told me about prayers, songs, dreams and sacred places but for a long time I was left ignorant of the fact that rituals were held at Fort McDowell when a medicine man from another tribe visited John and his family. John had told me many times about his Cocopah friend from Somerton, Jim White (1903-1978) who had helped Minnie, with her sugar (diabetes) and had helped Minnie walk again (arthritis). When I first saw Jim White, then 73, in 1976, he appeared frail but his tireless concern for people and his sharpness of mind and keen humor made one overlook that he was a very sick man.

Mike Nelson, a Yavapai medicine man, had taught Jim White. Mike Nelson (1880-1955), a *Yavepe* (central Yavapai), had been struck by lightning and was suddenly inspired to become a medicine man. Near the end of his life he announced the day he would die.

Like his teacher, Jim White had become a popular healer. I saw him when he visited Fort McDowell throughout 1977 conducting rituals to heal, to ask for rain, to assure the growth of all living things, for the well-being of people and to help the forces of life to continue. He ended his last visit with the dance that asked all the forces of the universe to protect the Fort McDowell reservation. With Jim's visits John was encouraged to talk and shared more about the Yavapai belief system.

Mike and John had told that before the Anglo-Americans entered the aboriginal Yavapai Indians' territory in the 1860s, the Yavapai prayed all the time, held rituals, taught the people daily how to live right and were faithful to the practice of their religious beliefs. Every morning the Yavapai greeted the living sun as it filled them with new life. Theirs was a way of life with an undeniably strong connection between the land and their religious beliefs. They felt that the religious beliefs of the

Yavapai had served the Yavapai well and had provided them with a solid foundation.

Sacred places included where events occurred when everything began and the world was destroyed, located in the Middle Verde Valley and in the Sedona Red Rock country, and where certain rituals took place. Also, certain archaeological sites throughout Yavapai land are sacred as well as Granite Mountain, Four Peaks, Superstitions, McDowell Mountain (Mount McDowell) and other places important to the protective Mountain Spirits. These include Fort McDowell, located along the life-giving water of the Verde River, and its places for rituals and dances. To the Yavapai, dance is prayer to the earth and to other cosmological forces. An unknown number of burial places on sacred ground outside the cemetery exist in the Fort McDowell reservation.

All these revered places mean specific kinds of protection for the Yavapai—coming from the powers activated by rituals; coming from protection from the spirits of the people who had lived there before; protection coming from the Mountain Spirits; and the awareness of the constant presence of these protective forces provides a feeling of fundamental security and safety crucial for the upkeep of the social order and for the wellbeing and mental and physical health of the tribe's members.

When the military post was set up at Fort McDowell in 1865, the Yavapai could no longer use this place for rituals which had been held there regularly. Under confinement and control of the military, they lost their religious freedom. Outside organized religions began almost as soon as Fort McDowell reservation was established in 1903. In 1905, Yavapai dances and other rituals were again held at specific places despite explicit prohibition by authorities. In 1920, the Holy Ground Church was set up at Fort McDowell with more traditional Yavapai religious practices in which much of the community participated regularly for many years. It is impossible to sum up all the changes forced on the Yavapai and their beliefs since the 1860s but perhaps it is best stated by John: "I know that my people know what God is to them."

I recorded John and Jim singing many more Yavapai songs that year and Jim encouraged me to use my recorder during the rituals and to write down everything. He said when he was not around we could listen to it and it would make us feel better and help us to think the right way. He allowed Melissa Jones, my former student, to photograph the Yavapai rituals.

Late in 1978 I accepted a position outside Arizona but kept up my close contacts there. I was kept informed in particular about all the events concerning Orme Dam and the threat hanging heavy over the Yavapai of again losing their land and of another forced relocation. However, in November 1981, after years of opposition, an alternative for the Orme Dam was chosen by the United States Secretary of the Interior James Watt. [4]

Sigrid Khera, Ph.D.
December 1982

PART III

THE YAVAPAI:
A GENERAL ETHNOGRAPHIC
OUTLINE

Chapter 5

———— ◆ ————

Ethnic Identity, Language and Territory

The Yavapai are those Indians who in aboriginal times hunted and gathered over a large portion of west central Arizona. From earliest historical times they had been referred to by a variety of names but nevertheless were a distinct group in their native situation and identifiable as Yavapai.[1]

Their vast ancestral territory measured some 20,000 square miles (more than one-sixth of Arizona, which is 113,417 total square miles), roughly 200 miles in its east-west dimension and 100 miles in its north-south dimension. Generally bounded on the south by the Gila River valley, on the west by the Colorado River valley, on the north by a chain of mountain peaks extending from Crossman Peak in the Mohave Mountains eastward to San

Francisco Mountains and on the east by the summit ridge of the Pinal, Mazatzal and Mogollon Mountain ranges.[2]

The territory of the Yavapai Indians remained relatively constant in its boundaries from the time of early Spanish contact up until the 1870s. There is no evidence that the Yavapai expanded in any direction in historic times nor is there anything to indicate that any of the neighboring Indians took over Yavapai territory. As to the length of time the Yavapai had occupied this territory, Albert H. Schroeder, anthropologist and historian, said, "...though these data are not conclusive at present, due to lack of sufficient survey and excavation, they suggest that the Yavapai have occupied the same general territory from at least 900 A.D." However, more recent work suggests A.D. 1250 is more likely. [3]

The early Spanish explorers, beginning perhaps in 1539 (de Niza) and 1540 (Coronado and Alarcon), gave the Yavapai many different names. Later, the Yavapai Indians were also erroneously referred to as Apaches, Apache-Mohave, Apache-Yuma, Apache-Tonto, etc.

Yavapai is a Yuman language. Upland Yuman is spoken by the Yavapai, Hualapai and Havasupai. Apache is an Athapaskan language shared by Western Apache, Chiricahua, Mescalero, Jicarilla, Navajo, Lipan, Kiowa-Apache.[4]

For too long and up to the present, the Yavapai Indians have been confused with the Apaches. The best way to determine correct Yavapai identity when reading a book, article, documentary material, etc., is to know the boundaries of the Yavapai Indians' aboriginal territory. [5] The description of it is given in Chapter 2 of this book by the Indian Claims Commission, March 24, 1965, who after years of deliberation, 970 pages of testimony, extensive documentary evidence, 780 numbered exhibits, and challenges by seven other tribes, found that the United States took 9,238,600 acres from the aboriginal Yavapai Indians on May 1, 1873, without payment of any compensation. On March 13, 1969, the Indian Claims Commission granted an award in the amount of $5,100,000.00 in favor of the Yavapai. [6] Following is further detail on the award area and activities of the aboriginal Yavapai Indians.

The southern part of the Yavapai territory included the specific locales or parts thereof of the Castle Dome Mountains, Eagle Tail Mountains, Palomas Mountains, the north end of the Gila Bend Mountains, the Big Horn Mountains, Goldfield Mountains, Superstition Mountains, Bradshaw Mountains, Kofa Mountains, the lower courses of the Hassayampa River, Agua Fria River, Cave Creek, and Castle Dome Hot Springs.[7]

Perry Tank Canyon. Bradshaw Mountains in background, 2000. Photo by Elias Butler

Large cracked boulder with petroglyph, west of Gila Bend, 2000. Photo by Elias Butler.

The Yavapai hunted mountain sheep in the Gila Bend, Castle Dome and Kofa mountains. They hunted deer in the Bradshaw and Superstition mountains. Rabbits and deer were hunted between the Agua Fria and Hassayampa rivers. The Yavapai gathered saguaro fruit in the summer at Castle Hot Springs, at Cave Creek, from the lower hill slopes of the Salt River, between the Agua Fria and Hassayampa rivers and in the Kofa and Superstition mountains. The Yavapai also gathered paloverde beans at Cave Creek, mescal in the Castle Dome Mountains and mescal, prickly pear, mulberries and squawberries in the Kofa Mountains. They used the Palomas Mountain area to gather mescal, prickly pear, paloverde beans, mesquite

38

and ironwood. The Bradshaw Mountains were a source of acorns, walnuts and mulberries. The Yavapai hunted various types of game at New River and gathered grass seed and prickly pear in the Superstition Mountains.

Oak Creek at Red Rock Crossing, *Wipuk* (Sedona), 2001. Photo by Elias Butler.

Yavapai rancherias or camps were located in the Castle Dome, Kofa, Palomas, Goldfield and Superstition mountains and along the Hassayampa River.

On the west, the Yavapai Indians were found in parts of the Colorado River Valley from early times up into the 1860s. They inhabited the mountainous areas to the east of the Colorado River Valley, the Kofa and Castle Dome mountains already mentioned plus the Harcuvar, Harquahala and Dome Rock mountains. All these mountain areas contained Yavapai rancherias. The Yavapai gathered mescal and prickly pear in the Harcuvar and Harquahala mountains. Water was scarce in their western territory but there were a number of natural water tanks and springs in different parts of this area so the Yavapai could use it for hunting and gathering. The Yavapai also obtained salt from the hills facing the Colorado River and shells from the area near Parker, Arizona.[8]

The northern boundary of the Yavapai territory included parts near the San Francisco Mountains, the headwaters of the Verde River and its tributaries, the Hells Canyon area, the Black Mesa country, the south end of Williamson Valley, Bill Williams Fork and the headwaters of the Bill Williams and Santa Maria rivers to within a short distance of the mouth of the Bill Williams River. Documentary data suggest that the Yavapai made extensive seasonal use of the area between the San Francisco Mountains and Oak Creek Canyon.[9]

Yavapai rancherias were located in the San Francisco Mountains, Bill Williams Mountain, Sycamore Canyon, Black Mesa, Hells Canyon, Skull Valley, Kirkland Creek, Date Creek and along the Bill Williams and Santa Maria

Fish Creek Canyon, February 1975. Photo by Sigrid Khera.

Agua Fria River, Agua Fria National Monument, 2011. Photo by Elias Butler.

rivers. The Bill Williams and Santa Maria river areas were also a source for gathering prickly pears, mescal and grass seeds. Acorns were gathered in Skull Valley. Williamson Valley provided walnuts and juniper berries. The Yavapai gathered mescal and juniper berries and hunted deer along Sycamore Creek and in the Black Mesa and Hells Canyon territory. They also hunted deer in Cottonwood Canyon and gathered piñon nuts in the San Francisco Mountains.

On the east, the Yavapai gathered acorns and piñon nuts on the westernmost slopes of the Mazatzal and Pinal mountains. Yavapai area included all the drainages below the Mogollon Rim, north of Clear Creek. They had rancherias, hunted quail, rats and rabbits and gathered grass seed, acorns and prickly pears in the general area between the Superstition Mountains and Fish Creek. Yavapai rancherias were also located near present-day Miami, Arizona. They had rancherias and gathered mescal near Pine Mountain. The Mingus Mountain and Black Hill areas were a source of juniper berries, piñon nuts and acorns and the Yavapai also had rancherias, farmed and hunted rabbits and rats in this area. The Verde River was a resource rich area for the Yavapai where they had rancherias, hunted deer and quail, gathered mescal, prickly pear, berries, and utilized the yucca plant and mesquite.[10]

In the interior of the Yavapai Indians' aboriginal territory they hunted deer and antelope in Chino Valley. They had camps and grew maize along Big Bug Creek. They had camps in the Date Creek Mountains, Peeples Valley near Turkey Creek and Black Canyon and along the Agua Fria River. Here, they hunted antelope, deer and rabbits and gathered saguaro fruit, walnuts and mesquite beans. Sunflower seeds, acorns and piñon nuts were gathered in the Sierra Prieta. Acorns, manzanita, mescal and walnuts were gathered near Granite Mountain. The Yavapai gathered acorns and berries in the Weaver Mountains and the prickly pear in Peeples Valley.[11]

The Yavapai Indians ranged over this large territory, moving from one camp to another from season to season, their moves dictated by the time of the year the various wild foods ripened and by the locale of the game they hunted. The Yavapai remained in their aboriginal state until 1860. From time immemorial until March 1875 when they were removed to the San Carlos Reservation, outside their own country, and confined there for 25 years, the Yavapai Indians had exclusive use and occupancy of their vast ancestral land.[12]

Chapter 6

———— ◆ ————

The Spaniards Save History

*I think that Columbus is the baddest
man in the world. I think they should
have killed him when he first come here.
If they do that, maybe there are more
Indians around here.*

— John Williams

Following Christopher Columbus who sailed across the Atlantic for Spain and "discovered" America in 1492, Spanish explorations of the New World spread out with objectives of claiming new lands for Spain, planting Roman Catholic roots, and seeking gold and silver. Their treatment of the native peoples was with rare exceptions cruel and barbaric and they were arrogantly dismissive and scornful of the natives' spiritual beliefs. But so were the later European arrivals of the 1600s and beyond. Only 30 short years after Columbus, Spaniards conquered the Aztec Empire in Mexico in 1521 and the Inca Empire in Peru in 1532 and made other conquests.

In Arizona, the Spanish explorer Fray Marcos de Niza passed through an edge of southeastern Yavapai territory in 1539 and he guided Francisco Vasquez de Coronado through the same route in 1540. Also in 1540, Hernando de Alarcon made his first trip up the Colorado River where he was told that the chief of a tribe, the "Cumanas," (Yavapai) was threatening to wage war because they had entered his country. On Alarcon's second trip, the same Indian told him that two "Cumanas" had come to inquire about the Christians. A little farther upstream two "Cumana" Indians arrived. Alarcon asked these two "to give their master a cross" which they promised to do. Thereafter, "Cruzados" was a name given by the Spaniards to some Indians (Yavapai) reported using cross-shaped adornments. Was this started by Alarcon's cross? In Spanish, cross is cruz.[1]

In 1583, Antonio de Espejo's expedition traveled into the Middle Verde Valley and surrounding areas. Diego Perez de Luxan, who accompanied Espejo, said Indians encountered there wore crowns of painted sticks. Is this perhaps the origin of the Yavapai's Crown Dancer's headdress? These Indians (Yavapai) also showed the Spanish the way to their mines near present-day Jerome.[2]

In 1598, Marcos Farfán de los Godos' expedition visited these mines which he described as eighteen feet deep with brown, yellow, blue and green ores which the Indians (Yavapai) used to paint themselves and to paint their blankets.[3]

In 1583, the Spaniards encountered Indians who wore crowns of painted sticks. The above figure was carved at Fort McDowell in 1974 under the instruction of Yavapai elder John Williams. Photo by Sigrid Khera.

In 1604, Juan de Oñate and Escobar explored in Yavapai territory and Father Geronimo Zarate Salmeron interviewed them on their return, recording additional details about the Yavapai.[4]

During the 1600s, Spanish accounts of the Yavapai continued in sparse writings and picked up with the 1768-1776 explorations of a Franciscan missionary, Father Francisco Garcés. While the Declaration of Independence was adopted by delegates to the Second Continental Congress in Philadelphia on July 4, 1776, Garcés was exploring Arizona.[5]

Though the Spanish explorers did not correctly name the Yavapai Indians as they journeyed through their territory and in some cases did not even travel into Yavapai territory, they nevertheless saved history. The Spaniards were inquisitive and wrote down their observations. They wrote not only about the Indians they encountered and about their locations but of Indians living elsewhere reported to them by others.

Much of the strength of the Yavapai Indians' successful case with the Indian Claims Commission is because of Spanish historical documents.[6] Because the ancient Yavapai did not have a written language and their custom was to cremate the dead and burn the deceased's shelter and belongings, this did not leave easy clues as to the size and boundaries of their ancestral territory.[7] The written chronicles of the Spaniards saved Yavapai history.

No Spanish missions were built on Yavapai land.[8]

Chapter 7

◆

Prehistory

Yavapai origin myths do not mention the displacement of previous inhabitants from their territory. In their oral history the Yavapai do not have a migration story. Because of their practice of doing everything possible to forget the dead—cremating the body, burning the deceased's shelter and personal possessions, and not mentioning the name of the dead—it has been difficult to obtain information pertaining to the time prior to that of the grandparents of the surviving people.[1] Even among themselves they have guarded information.

This silence can work against Indians as in the case of the government's attempt in the 1970s to relocate the Yavapai from Fort McDowell for the proposed Orme Dam. Powerful political and business interests argued that Fort McDowell was not part of the Yavapai Indians' ancestral land.[2] Telling who your parents, grandparents, and ancestors are and where they were born is important information to give in order to establish tribal identity and territory. Otherwise others may give false information instead.

Also, burning the deceased's possessions made little difference in a paperless world but this practice now works against Indians. At Fort McDowell reservation the Yavapai always maintained that their real boundary should be bigger, that President Theodore Roosevelt (1858-1919) had given them a map showing the military boundary line as theirs. John Williams told that his father got a map with the military border line, "But when he died, my cousin's wife come over there and they burned everything and they burned all the papers in it. That's what they did when people died. But everything is gone."

Archaeological studies done in the Yavapai Indians' aboriginal territory can be found through Arizona's three major universities: University of Arizona in Tucson, Arizona State University in Tempe, Northern Arizona University in Flagstaff. Archaeological work is also done by the community colleges, the U.S. Forest Service offices in Arizona, etc., and private firms. All the sciences can contribute to filling in the picture of the prehistoric Yavapai Indians' way of life.

Chapter 8

══════ ◆ ══════

Population

It is supposed that the Yavapai Indians were never a very populous group.[1] Early available written sources provide very little specific data. A 1744 report by Fray Carlos Delgado includes his comment, "...the nation inhabiting the Sierra Azul (located in the Middle Verde Valley near present-day Jerome)... is a very large nation, with people as numerous as ants."[2] In the 1860s and 1870s, population estimates were made at a time when the Yavapai were stunned by warfare, disease, and displacement by White settlers. Varying estimates of 1,500 and 2,000 and other similar figures were given by Army posts.[3] Historical circumstances were such that the population of the Yavapai Indians cannot be clearly established.[4]

But the Yavapai Indians' ancestral territory still holds hidden history. Perhaps more could be learned about the population of the prehistoric Yavapai from past records and research now that their recognized ancestral territory has defined their identity. Still more can be revealed by specialists not only in archaeology and anthropology but in demography, geology, hydrology, biology, botany, etc., and from the Yavapai themselves. A conference on just the Yavapai that brings all the disciplines together with the Yavapai to present current studies would be ideal.

Most of all, it should be recognized that today the population of the Yavapai is delicate. The fact that it is a small tribe puts them at high risk. Ordeals like the threat of relocation which the now-defeated Orme Dam brought to the Fort McDowell tribe are devastating. Studies show these stresses increase illness, mortality, family and community disintegration. And what if another deadly disease like the 1918 flu epidemic struck? Everything that can be done should be done to ensure that the Yavapai will thrive and reach a robust population.

Mike Harrison and Hiawatha Hood. 1975 Photo by Melissa Jones.

Chapter 9

◆

YAVAPAI:
Tolkepaya, Wipukpa, Yavepe, Kewevkepaya

The early Spanish explorers distinguished three Yavapai groups and named those in the western part "Tejuas," northeast "Cruzados," and southeast "Nijoras."[1] E. W. Gifford (1932:177, 1936:249) who published the major ethnographies on the Yavapai, wrote of three subtribes: *Tolkepaya*, the Western Yavapai; *Wipukpa* and *Yavepe*, the Northeastern Yavapai; and *Kewevkepaya*, the Southeastern Yavapai.[2]

Modern Yavapais recognize four regional subtribes with minor dialectal differences: (1) *Tolkepaya* (Western Yavapai). (2) *Wipukpa* (Northeastern Yavapai). (3) *Yavepe* (Central Yavapai). (4) *Kewevkepaya* (Southeastern Yavapai).[3]

The *Tolkepaya* (Western Yavapai) ranged from the Colorado River to the western slopes of the Kirkland Valley.

The *Wipukpa* (Northeastern Yavapai) lived in the Middle Verde Valley, the Bradshaw Mountains, the Sedona Red Rock country as far north as the San Francisco Peaks.

The *Yavepe* (Central Yavapai) occupied the area around present-day Prescott and Jerome Mountain.

The *Kewevkepaya* (Southeastern) lived in the Bradshaw Mountains, the Verde Valley, as far north as Fossil Creek, the Tonto Basin, and the Superstition and Pinal mountains.[4]

Fort McDowell. Mike Harrison, John Williams and Carolina Butler, 1975. Photo by Melissa Jones.

Chapter 10

◆

Bordering Tribes

The Yavapai recognized themselves to be a people distinct from all their neighbors.[1] From the Spanish period onward it was noted that the Yavapai were bordered on the east, south and west by Indian tribes or groups clearly separate and different from the Yavapai in speech or culture. On the south, the Yavapai were bordered by the Pima and Maricopa who depended more upon agriculture than did the Yavapai whose primary source of food was in hunting and gathering over a wide range of desert and mountains. Hostile raiding characterized their relations.[2]

On the west along the Colorado River, the Yavapai were bordered by the Cocopah, Quechan, Mohave and Chemehuevi, and these relations were relatively peaceful. Each of these Yuman-speaking tribes spoke a language different from but intelligible to the Yavapai and each maintained a culture different from the Yavapai. Some

Cocopah families trace their ancestry to *Tolkepaya* (Western Yavapai). It is not clear however if they had joined during the 1850s and 1860s due to White impact on their territory or if they had joined for some other reason at an earlier period.[3]

On the north, the Yavapai were bordered by the Hualapai and Havasupai. The Hualapai were a mountain people with a culture almost the same as the Yavapai. Both the Hualapai and Havasupai spoke a language very similar to the Yavapai but hostilities with these two northern tribes occurred from time to time. Adding to the hostility in 1869 were bands of Hualapai Indians that joined Army troops in their campaign against the Yavapai.[4]

On the east, the Yavapai were bordered by the Apache. The Apaches were of a different ethnic origin and spoke a language belonging to the Athapaskan stock totally unrelated to the Yuman language spoken by the Yavapai.[5] It was between 1747 and 1788 that the Apaches were first recorded near the southeastern border of the Southeastern Yavapai's territory.[6] The Apaches entered the Tonto Basin region after 1750, an area that evidently was occupied in 1540 by the Yavapai.[7] However, the Yavapai continued to make use of the same area.[8] Pressures on the Apache from the 1770s into the 1870s may have forced them westward against the Yavapai.[9]

Relations between the Yavapai and Apache groups to the east were generally friendly; however, it was understood that the summit ridge of the Pinal and Mazatzal Mountains was the boundary between Yavapai territory and Apache.[10] Except for the Apache in the east, none of the neighboring tribes entered Yavapai territory for subsistence from the land. They entered only for purposes of trading, raiding or warfare. [11]

Warfare was not national in character among the Yavapai. As a result of a battle between Yavapai and non-Yavapai Indians over a gathering or hunting area, the relatives of those who were killed or captured would gather a following of young warriors from several Yavapai bands for a retaliatory raid. After the raid was completed, the warriors returned to their own bands.[12]

Each Yavapai group bordering on a neighboring non-Yavapai people recognized a "no man's land" or line between themselves and their neighbors. The Yavapai groups did not recognize such a "no man's land" between themselves.[13] In defending against their enemies or in raids against Indian and White enemies, Yavapai Indians from different family units, bands and groups, joined together in the common cause. No record has been found of Yavapai family units, bands or groups who made war against one another. [14]

There is no record of one Yavapai group fighting another of their own people. [15]

Chapter 11

———————◆———————

Anglo-Americans Enter

This, then, was the setting of the Yavapai Indians, who anthropologists and historians agree remained in their aboriginal state up to 1860.[1] They could not read. They did not receive mail. They did not read a newspaper. And unbeknownst to them, Columbus had crossed the ocean in 1492, which had started wave after wave of foreigners into the New World. Countries had gone to war with domination of territories changing hands and the Yavapai did not know this either.

It would be in the 1820s when Anglo-Americans started entering the Yavapai Indians' aboriginal territory which would bring violent changes to their world. Up until then the Yavapai and their families had built lives with a future for their children and their children's children. Up until then, the Yavapai had to work hard every day to find food for their families but they enjoyed it and did it well. As Fort McDowell tribal elders Mike Harrison and John

Williams say in their oral history, "We have no trouble before the White people are around. In those days there was nothing bad. Nothing to be afraid of."

1607   115 years after Columbus, the English crossed the ocean and founded Jamestown in Virginia.

1620   13 years later, the English (Pilgrims) crossed the ocean and settled Plymouth Colony in Massachusetts.

1775-1783—Revolutionary War. There are now thirteen British colonies and they win American independence from Great Britain.

1810-1821—Mexican War of Independence. Mexico won its independence from Spain.

1821-1848—The Yavapai under Mexico.[2]

1826   Anglo-American trappers start entering the Yavapai Indians' country.[3]

1848   January 24, gold found near Sacramento starts California Gold Rush.

1848   February 2, Treaty of Guadalupe Hidalgo marked the end of the Mexican-American War (1846-1848) and Mexico ceded to the United States—California, Nevada, Utah, Texas, New Mexico, Arizona north of the Gila River, and more. Yavapai territory thus passed to the United States.[4]

1849   Fort Yuma established (1849-1885) at the Colorado River, the California-Arizona boundary.[6] The U.S. military was quick to start protecting the gold seekers.

1851   U.S. Army surveyors started entering the Yavapai Indians' territory, exploring for wagon roads and a transcontinental railroad route.[6]

1854   Gadsden Purchase. The U.S. purchased from Mexico the land in Arizona south of the Gila River to its present-day border with Mexico for the purpose of the U.S.'s construction of a transcontinental railroad route.[7]

1859   Fort Mohave established (1859-1890) at the Colorado River.[8] More protection for the invaders.

1863   Gold was found in the Yavapai Indians' territory: at the Hassayampa Creek, at Lynx Creek near Prescott and on Rich Hill northeast of present-day Wickenburg. Henry Wickenburg discovered gold, the Vulture Lode, southwest of Wickenburg.[9]

1863   January 1, President Lincoln signed the Emancipation Proclamation declaring that slaves in rebel states were free. Out West in Arizona they had started killing Yavapai Indians.

1863   Arizona Territory established on February 24, 1863, divided from the Territory of New Mexico. Bill signed by President Abraham Lincoln.[10]

PART IV

WHAT THE WHITE PEOPLE'S DOCUMENTS SAY

Chapter 12

◆

Extermination Policy

U.S. Army letters, annual reports, and other documentary materials of the 1850s, 1860s, 1870s, etc., support the oral history told by Fort McDowell Yavapai elders Mike Harrison and John Williams. Again and again they said that their people are Yavapai, not Apache. Because of this mistaken identity given to them from the start by the White people, the Yavapai were classified as hostile. Mike and John also said again and again that the Yavapai were not the White people's enemy, they never had been. Their chiefs had told them not to kill White people. In recounting the brutal encounters with the U.S. Army and White settlers, Mike and John repeatedly told of their people's defenselessness using bows and arrows against pistols and rifles. Documents also support the Yavapai's oral history of a long, continuous struggle for survival ever since the White people started moving into their ancestral land. The Yavapai have had only short respites from battles with the White people and, thus, little chance to thrive.

In November 1860, Abraham Lincoln (1809-1865) was elected president of the United States. There were 33 states in the Union and the population was 31 million. The Civil War between the states began in April 1861 and ended in April 1865.

Out West, right after establishment of Arizona Territory in 1863, the first group of federal officials appointed by President Lincoln traveled to Arizona. They included Arizona Territory Governor John Noble Goodwin (1824-1887), Superintendent of Indian Affairs Charles D. Poston (1825-1902), and federal judge Joseph P. Allyn.[1]

For Arizona's Yavapai Indians in the 1860s, they would lose their lives, their freedom, their land and theirs and their future generations' lives would be changed forever.

With their way of life as hunters and gatherers disrupted by the arrival of White trappers, miners, ranchers, soldiers and settlers, the Yavapai could not feed themselves and turned to raiding livestock. This alone was enough to demand the extermination of all the Yavapai in the central part of Arizona.

Judge Allyn (1833-1869) served as judge of the district court at La Paz, Arizona Territory. He hated the Indians and was eager for Arizona's development.[2] From December 1863 to May 1865 he wrote 24 letters to a friend and editor in the East who published them in the *Hartford* (Connecticut) *Evening Press*. Judge Allyn used the pen name Putnam.[3] His letters give vivid testimony of the attitudes and dealings toward Indians.

It is sickening to read passages from Judge Allyn's letters such as one dated February 6, 1864, from Fort

Whipple:"These repeated depredations have so thoroughly aroused the animosity of the settlers that a war of extermination has in fact already begun. Indians are shot wherever seen, and quite recently a party of whites went into the country east on a scout, and failing to find the Indians at a safely accessible place, invited them in to a council, gave them food, and while they were eating, at a given time fired on them, killing some thirty." One White man was killed with a lance.[4] This was the infamous Pinole Treaty led by King S. Woolsey (1832-1879), owner of a large ranch on the Agua Fria River near present-day Mayer.[5]

A later letter dated Nov. 30, 1869, from W. S. Terrpo [?], Headquarters Detachment en route to establish Camp Reno, accused Woolsey and his party of "murdering them (the Indians) in cold blood."[6]

Entering Salt River Canyon where the Yavapai lived in caves and were hunted down and killed in the 1860s and 1870s. *Wigidjassa* (Four Peaks) in background to the north. Photo by Carolina Butler, 2011.

Judge Allyn's February 6, 1864, letter also stated that "...the governor (Arizona Territory Governor John N. Goodwin) in a brief speech took all by storm by advocating the extermination of the Indians."[7]

A March 5, 1864, letter from the Office of the Secretary of the Territory of Arizona at Fort Whipple, addressed to Indian Superintendent Charles D. Poston, included, "The sentiment here is in favor of an utter extermination of the ruthless savages who have so long prevented the settlement and the development of the territory."[8]

A March 9, 1864, article, "Indian Troubles," in the *Arizona Miner*, Prescott, tells of King Woolsey's ranch robbed of all its stock, saying, "He is one of our most daring and skillful Indian fighters, and believes fully, as he has good reason to, in the extermination policy." The article ends with, "The first step demanded by all the interests of the Territory is to hasten the extermination of these copper-skinned villains. Let every effort be made to clean them out. It is idle to talk of soft measures with such inveterate and brutal plunderers and assassins."[9]

The Indian hunter King S. Woolsey even brushed away criticism that he also killed Indian women and children, writing, "We would have killed more women but owing to having attacked in the day time when the women were at work gathering mescal." (Woolsey letter, March 29, 1864, to General James H. Carleton.[10]) Shamefully, today there is a butte in the Grand Canyon named after Woolsey as are other Arizona landmarks.

This was the 1860s and the westward expansion had reached Arizona and extermination of the Indians had been the policy for many from the beginning. By the

1860s, how many tribes had been completely wiped out? Before any researcher or interested traveler could pay much attention to them and to their culture or to their names, their beliefs, their songs, everything—entire American Indian tribes had perished and no one was left to tell about them.

Oral History of the Yavapai

Chapter 13

◆

Mistaken Identity

Again and again, in recounting their history, Fort McDowell Yavapai elders Mike Harrison (1886-1983) and John Williams (1904-1983) said that their people are Yavapai, not Apache.

The wrong identity given to the Yavapai began in the 1500s with the Spanish explorers, then continued with the arrival of Anglo trappers in the 1820s, then with Army expeditions starting in the 1850s and continued thereafter throughout countless Army records, letters, newspapers, citizen letters, journals, etc. The Yavapai are wrongly identified in most of these writings.

The Yavapai have been given so many different names that several pages in anthropologist and historian Albert H. Schroeder's 1974 report for the Indian Claims Commission are devoted to listing them in his "Chronological List of

Names Applied to the Yavapai Groups" covering the years 1540-1942.[1]

Writings of the bloodiest chapters for the Yavapai in the 1860s and 1870s mostly misidentify them as Apaches or Apache-Mohave or Tonto-Apache or Apache-Yuma. During their 25-year confinement at San Carlos (1875-1900) the Yavapai were mis-labeled in the census as Mohave-Apache or Yuma-Apache (per Karl Heider's 1955 interview with Yavapai Warren Gazzam).

The gravestone at Fort McDowell cemetery of the famous full blood Yavapai, *Wassaja*, Carlos Montezuma, mistakenly reads: Mohave Apache Indian. This is because the Masons led Montezuma's funeral service and designed the gravestone which prominently features a Masonic symbol.[2] The gravestone also reads 1869-1923, but when baptized in Florence (not far from Fort McDowell) in 1871, his age was estimated and 1866 was written on the baptismal certificate as his birth year.[3]

Much has been written about this full blood Yavapai because he had an unbelievable life and left an inspiring legacy. *Wassaja* was not born into a world of peace. In 1866 there was an extermination policy on Indians. His mother gave birth to *Wassaja* on the ground somewhere in *Kewevkepaya* (Southeastern Yavapai) country, probably within view of Four Peaks or the Superstition Mountains. For his aboriginal parents, he was the new generation and the continuation of their native race.

But at about age 5, *Wassaja* was captured, sold to an Italian adventurer, taken to Chicago and educated. Carlos Montezuma became a prominent doctor, helped found the Society of American Indians, became a champion of

Indian rights, was recognized as a national leader and was consulted by the prominent and powerful.

He grew up without his mother or father or sisters or his tribal community and yet did not let these challenges bar his way from contributing to the lives of others. Even with his humble birth, he proved that every human being contains within himself the gifts and the spirit given to all.

Similarly, *Hoomothya*, Mike Burns, is another Yavapai—born perhaps in the same year and general locale as Carlos Montezuma—who left his mark in history by his many published interviews and books. Mike Burns' birth year has been estimated as 1865 or 1866. He died in 1934 and is buried at the Fort McDowell cemetery.[4]

And now to return to examples of mistaken identity.

The devastating 1872 Skeleton Cave massacre of Yavapai Indians has been written about in countless articles, most of which misidentify the victims as Apache. This misidentification of the Yavapai is particularly painful.

An example is in one of the most valuable books on early Arizona history, *On The Border With Crook*, published in 1891, written by Captain John G. Bourke, and he, too, misnames them. Bourke served on the staff of General George Crook from 1870 to 1886 and took part in the U.S. Army's attack on the Yavapai at Skeleton Cave. In his book, Bourke gives a descriptive account of what happened.[5]

The Skeleton Cave massacre took place in a cave high above the Salt River where it flows toward Phoenix. The large, shallow cave was a longtime shelter for the Yavapai in the rugged and majestic canyon. The White soldiers urged the Indians to come out but—like the ancient Jews

trapped at Masada centuries ago and so symbolic today—
the Yavapai chose to die rather than surrender. Unable to get
direct shots into the cave, the soldiers aimed their carbines
at its roof where the bullets ricocheted, killing the Yavapai.
Other soldiers positioned at the crest over the cave rolled
huge boulders down on the Yavapai, creating noise, dust,
and utter destruction. Finally, the soldiers charged into the
cave. Bourke wrote, "I hope that my readers will be satisfied
with the meagrest description of the awful sight that met
our eyes; there were men and women dead or writhing in the
agonies of death, and with them several babies, killed by our
glancing bullets, or by the storm of rocks and stones that had
descended from above."

Aerial view of Salt River Canyon in center. *Wigidjisawa* (Superstition
Mountains) in foreground, *Wigidjassa* (Four Peaks) in background. Photo
by Elias Butler, 2009.

Bourke also wrote admirably with a general sentiment of sorrow for an old medicine man whom the soldiers had observed during their attack, defending his people, and defying the approach of death. They found his still-warm corpse beneath a huge mass of rock which had also killed a "squaw and young man who had remained by his side."

No soldier was killed but 76 Yavapai died. For the Yavapai their losses at Skeleton Cave were worse than a Pearl Harbor or a 9/11 attack because the percentage of their total population killed was so much greater. Mass violence, as survivors anywhere know, traumatizes the whole society for generations.

Another valuable first-person account of the 1860s is in John Nicolson's book, *The Arizona of Joseph Pratt Allyn,* which contains all 24 letters written by Judge Allyn (pen name Putnam) from December 1863 to May 1865. Though much of Judge Allyn's experiences take place in the heart of Yavapai territory, he calls them Apache.

Perhaps because of the mistaken identity given to the Yavapai by the White people calling them Apaches, they were classified as hostile. But no doubt this was convenient for the many who wanted the Yavapai Indians out of the way of their own ambitions. Bourke included in his book a telling message written May 17, 1885, to General Crook from a frustrated Lieutenant Britton Davis, who says in closing, "Greed and avarice on the part of the whites—in other words, the almighty dollar—is at the bottom of nine-tenths of all our Indian trouble."[6]

Fort McDowell Cemetery. Mass burial of Yavapai victims of the Skeleton Cave massacre is marked by a circle of rocks next to the fenced grave of *Wassaja,* the famed Yavapai Carlos Montezuma. On May 25, 1985, the Yavapai conducted a ceremony and dedicated a formal marker for the mass grave. 1975 photo by Sigrid Khera.

Chapter 14

———— ◆ ————

Bows and Arrows
against Pistols and Rifles

Fort McDowell Yavapai elders Mike Harrison and John Williams said again and again that the Yavapai were not the White people's enemy; they never had been. Their chiefs had told them not to kill White people, that only more would come and then they would do bad things to them. The Yavapai's weapons were clubs and bows and arrows.

The Yavapai's lack of effective weapons is noted in a January 25, 1864, letter from Arizona Territory Governor John Noble Goodwin at Fort Whipple, to General James H. Carleton: "The Indians (Yavapai) in this country are unarmed. They will steal, but they don't kill while the Apaches are well armed and fight desperately."[1]

Yavapai style projectile points. Photo by Peter J. Pilles, Jr., archaeologist, Coconino National Forest.

The Army's superiority kept the Yavapai on the run unable to hunt, unable to gather their seasonal wild foods, unable to plant, unable to feed themselves. And they also destroyed the Yavapai's food reserves, their wikiups, their belongings, everything they made by hand.

Fort McDowell. John Williams holds a war club. Photo by Sigrid Khera, 1975.

In a November 25, 1869, report from William Edward Price, Camp Mohave, Arizona Territory, to Bd. Maj. General F. Wheaton, Commanding Sub. District Upper Arizona, Price tells of one expedition where he and his forces came upon three Yavapai camps. "The (first) camp consisted of 21 wikiups... We captured and destroyed 180 buckskins, 81 large baskets, 33 water ollas, 2000 pounds grass seed and dried deer meat, 50 lbs. seed cake, 13 iron and tin pots, 7 bows, 130 arrows and 600 arrow points, 12 yards of new white muslin which indicated that they had either been to or communicated with the reservation, quantities of paints, bullets and bullet moulds and many minor articles useful to Indians... Then we took breakfast in their camp and burned it up."[2]

Next day the same expedition, "...destroyed 30 freshly abandoned wikiups and three caches of seeds. We camped at base of Bill Williams Mountain." Then marched 30 miles the next day and again (third camp), "...destroyed 16 more wikiups with bundles..." The Price expedition returned to its starting point at Camp Toll Gate, established in May 1869, 40 miles northeast of Prescott on Walnut Creek.[3]

Yavapai elders Mike Harrison and John Williams frequently said, "White people talk about Indian War. That's no war when only Indians are killed." In Albert H. Schroeder's 1974 report, *A Study of Yavapai History*, for the Indian Claims Commission, he provides several pages tabulating more than 100 "Army Encounters with Various Yavapai Groups" for the years 1864-1878. He lists how many Yavapai were killed, wounded, captured, the date, location, and Army unit.[4] Unfortunately, he does not list how many soldiers were killed. Many times it was none. Individual citizen and Army reports reveal this. Some of the encounters in Yavapai territory reported by Schroeder are shown below with White casualties noted when known.

Jan. 1860   13 Indians killed in Prescott country by a party led by Jack Swilling.[5]

Dec. 1863   20 Indians killed near Fort Whipple after a peace had been made.[6]

Jan. 1864   30 Indians killed in Salt River Canyon by a party led by rancher King S. Woolsey. One White man killed, lanced.[7]

1865   28 Indians killed working on a toll road for Indian Agent John C. Dunn.[8]

Jack Swilling, miner, Phoenix settler, 1860s. Arizona State Capitol Archives photo.

Mar. 1866   20 Indians killed at Palos Blancos and Ft. McDowell.[9]

Aug. 1866   33 Indians killed at Grapevine Spring, Skull Valley massacre.[10]

Apr. 1867   50 Indians killed at Black Mountains and Rio Verde near Black Mountains.[11]

Nov. 1868   15 Indians killed near Squaw Peak.[12]

Sep. 1869   18 Indians killed at Red Creek.[13]

Jun. 1871   56 Indians killed, East Fork River, Mazatzal Mountains and Wild Rye Creek. No soldiers killed.[14]

Sep. 1872   40 Indians killed at Muchos Canyon, Santa Maria River. No soldiers killed.[15]

Dec. 1872   76 Indians killed in a cave (Skeleton Cave) in Salt River Canyon. No soldiers killed.[16]

Mar. 1873   33 Indians killed at Turret Mountain.[17]

Oct. 1873   25 Indians killed at Mazatzal Mountains, Sycamore Springs or Sunflower Valley.[18]

May 1874   38 Indians killed at Four Peaks.[19]

Sep. 1874   14 Indians killed at headwaters of Cave Creek.[20]

Hakaonwa (Date Creek). Although Schroeder lists encounters at Date Creek, he lists no Yavapai casualties—but for the Yavapai their losses at Camp Date Creek were heavy and bitter. April 1978 photo by Sigrid Khera.

Chapter 15

═══════ ◆ ═══════

Under Military Orders
for 40 Years

With their increasing entrance into the Yavapai's area in the 1800s the Anglo-Americans were expanding their holdings and the Yavapai Indians were attempting to protect theirs. The U.S. Army quickly established several military posts to get the Indians out of the way — one way or another — for the White settlers. Troops were sent out to track down, attack, kill and capture Indians found off the Colorado River Reservation and not living attached to one or another military post.[1] Arizona military posts which impacted the Yavapai were established in:

1863   Fort Whipple (1863-1913), near Prescott.[2]

1864   Camp Date Creek (1864-1874), 60 miles
        southwest of Prescott.[3]

1864   Fort Verde (1864-1890), near the confluence of the Verde River and Beaver Creek.[4]

1865   Fort McDowell (1865-1890), on the Verde River near its junction with the Salt River.[5]

1865   Colorado River Reservation, established March 3, 1865.[6]

1871   Rio Verde Reservation established near Camp Verde by Executive Order of Nov. 9, 1871, extending 40 miles along the Verde River, 10 miles on each side, was set apart for them as their permanent home.[7]

1873   San Carlos (1873-1900), in southeastern Arizona.[8]

1875   Two months after the Yavapai were walked 180 miles from the Rio Verde Reservation to San Carlos Apache Reservation, President Ulysses S. Grant (1822-1885) revoked his previous 1871 order and restored the Rio Verde Reservation to public domain by Executive Order of April 23, 1875. [9]

The Yavapai alternated between periods of submission on a reservation or at a military post and periods of return to their former way of life.[10] Under the military, there was not enough food nor enough protection from their Indian enemies, or from White soldiers and White citizens.

In a November 21, 1866, report, Colorado River Reservation agent John Feudge wrote to Commissioner of Indian Affairs D. N. Cooley in Washington, D.C., asking what was he to do about the lack of food and the Indians' hunger, "These friendly Indians (Yavapai) finding themselves, at the commencement of winter, in a most wretched state of destitution, without food, or clothing of any description, except a breech-cloth of calico, worn by the men, and a short petticoat, made of bark strings, by the women."[11]

In September 1873 when the Yavapai were on the Rio Verde Reservation there were so many sick or dead that many of the dead were left unburned because of the inability of surviving relatives to carry wood for the funeral pyre.[12]

The suffering the Yavapai endured in the 1860s and 1870s is immeasurable. Further, mass violence traumatizes the whole society for generations. Killing of the Yavapai started in 1860 and the campaign against them ended in 1900 when the Yavapai were released from military confinement at the San Carlos Apache Reservation. The Army's 40-year campaign against them is detailed in Timothy Braatz's 2003 book, *Surviving Conquest.*

More of the military orders over the Yavapai were:

Dec. 21, 1871—General George Crook ordered that all "roving Apache" (Yavapai) were to be on a reservation as of February 15, 1872, or be treated as hostile. But the Yavapai were on their own land. To them, the invaders were the hostile ones. The invaders were the aggressors.[13]

April 1873—Most Yavapai surrendered.[14]

May 1873—The removal of the Yavapai Indians to the Verde reservation on May 1, 1873, marks the date on which the United States, without payment of compensation, took from these Indians the lands aboriginally used and occupied by them.[15]

May 1873-1875— Soon they were producing successful harvests on the Rio Verde Reservation until a group of Tucson contractors, competitor suppliers, pressured the government to transfer the Yavapai to the San Carlos Reservation, outside their country.[16]

Feb.-Mar. 1875—Despite their opposition, the Yavapai were marched 180 miles over the roughest terrain, crossing swollen streams in the cold. Special Commissioner of Indian Affairs Levi Edwin Dudley (1842-1913) refused to allow them to be moved along the dirt road around the mountains, where teams and wagons could have been used, saying, "They are Indians—let the beggars walk."[17]

Capt. John G. Bourke later wrote, "It was an outrageous proceeding, one for which I should still blush had I not long since gotten over blushing for anything that the United States Government did in Indian matters."[18]

1875-1900—Removed forcibly and relocated to a strange land and with a different tribe of Indians, the Yavapai were confined at the San Carlos Apache Reservation in southeastern Arizona for 25 years. Warren Gazzam, a Yavapai born in San Carlos, later said, "We were a captured people."[19]

San Carlos. Overlooking where Yavapai were confined outside their homeland for 25 years, 1875-1900. Fort McDowell Yavapai (L to R) John Williams, Kimberley Williams, Andrew Johnson. October 6, 1976, photo by Sigrid Khera

Oral History of the Yavapai

Chapter 16

◆

One More Armed Invasion in the 20th Century

The Yavapai confined at San Carlos since 1875 yearned to return to their own homeland. Shortly before 1900, some were released, some appealed and went to Washington, and some started drifting back to places corresponding to the location of their aboriginal groups —*Wipukpa* (Northeastern Yavapai), *Yavepe* (Central Yavapai), *Kewevkepaya* (Southeastern Yavapai). Today, most of the Yavapai live on three reservations.

Fort McDowell Yavapai Nation

The Fort McDowell reservation was established on September 15, 1903, by Executive Order signed by President Theodore Roosevelt (1858-1919). The 24,680-acre reservation, long and narrow, straddles the Verde

River at the site of the old military post and is located less than an hour's drive northeast of Phoenix. Enrolled members in early 2012 are 925.

Yavapai-Apache Nation

Located off of I-17 between Phoenix and Flagstaff, the combination Yavapai-Apache have a scattered cluster of reservation land totaling approximately 635 acres: 458 acres at Middle Verde, 40 acres at Camp Verde, 58 acres at Clarkdale, almost 4 acres at Rimrock, almost 75 acres at Interstate 17 Visitor Complex, established in 1909, 1914, 1916 and 1969. Enrolled members in early 2012 are 3,300.

Yavapai-Prescott Indian Tribe

This reservation was established with 75 acres on June 7, 1935, at the former Fort Whipple, adjacent to Prescott. On May 18, 1956, 1,320 acres were added. Enrolled members in 2011 are 176.

Today, the total acreage of all three Yavapai reservations is approximately 26,710 acres. This is less than 3/10ths of one percent of their original ancestral land, which was 9,238,600 acres.

The *Tolkepaya* (Western Yavapai) who were the most numerous subtribe before entrance of the Anglo-Americans in the 1800s never got a reservation. Some remarkable *Tolkepaya* were: Yuma Frank, Warren Gazzam and Sam Eh-ti-sa (Etchesaw) (1866-1960), last of the Yavapai scouts.

Warren Gazzam (1880?-1967) was born in captivity in San Carlos. In 1891, he and 50 other Indian children were taken in seven wagons, each pulled by eight mules, from San Carlos to Bowie and from there by train to a boarding school at Grand Junction, Colorado. After seven years there he was sent to Carlisle Indian School (which existed from 1879 to 1918) in Pennsylvania, where he took up music. Warren Gazzam played in Carnegie Hall in New York City and at the White House in 1900. He played for President William McKinley (1843-1901) and his whole cabinet.

He returned to Arizona to see his mother in Agua Caliente, settled there along with some *Tolkepaya* still living there in 1901 and in Palomas and Mohawk. He moved to Fort McDowell in 1914.[1] Warren Gazzam was a plaintiff in the Yavapai's land claims case.

Wassaja Carlos Montezuma, early 1900s, photographer unknown. Butler personal collection.

The Yavapai's struggle for survival continued through the 20th century as government policies and others more powerful dictated their lives. Important events include:

1910   Barely seven years after getting their reservation, George Dickens, a Fort McDowell Yavapai, wrote on March 20, 1910, to Dr. Carlos Montezuma in Chicago, "Dear Cousin...we are to be moved to the Pima Indian Reservation. We oppose to this... ...we need your help." The Yavapai's land and water rights were at risk. Montezuma gained a congressional hearing and the removal attempt failed.[2]

1912   Arizona gained statehood on February 14, 1912, becoming the 48th state of the United States, bill signed by President William Howard Taft (1857-1930).

1921   Removal of Fort McDowell Yavapai to the Salt River Reservation (Pima) was attempted again. With help from Montezuma's attorney Joseph W. Latimer and the Friends of the American Indians, removal attempt failed again.[3]

1924   The Indian Citizenship Act of 1924 granted U.S. citizenship to American Indians, signed into law by President Calvin Coolidge (1872-1933).

1932 and 1936—The anthropologist E.W. Gifford
published major studies on the Yavapai. His
research during earlier and timely visits at Fort
McDowell and at Mayer resulted in an impressive
collection of ethnographic data. His informant at
Fort McDowell was Mike Burns (1865?-1934) who
later left his own manuscripts.

In Gifford's later study he worked with thirteen
informants: Jim Stacy (Watarama); Jim Miller
(older brother of Jim Stacy); Johnson Stacy (son
of Jim Stacy); Jim Mukhat, the medicine man;
Susie Miller (wife of Jim Miller); Jim Theinka;
James Sign; Mike Burns; Sam Ichesa (Eh-ti-
sa); the woman Shampura; Chico Martinez;
the woman Ketchi; and Captain Coffee (Gifford
1936:248-249). Gifford's informants had been
children and young adults when the Yavapai were
conquered and made captive.

The experts on both sides in the Yavapai's case
before the Indian Claims Commission, historian
Alfred B. Thomas, and anthropologist and
historian Albert H. Schroeder, relied on Gifford's
1932 and 1936 ethnographic published reports.[4]

Raising the Flag on Iwo Jima, by Joe Rosenthal/Associated Press.

1945   On February 23, 1945, Ira Hayes (1923-1955), a Pima Indian from Arizona, was one of six (5 Marines, 1 Navy corpsman) who raised the U.S. flag on Iwo Jima's Mount Suribachi during World War II. On that day, United States Marine Pfc. Ira Hayes did not have the right to vote in Arizona.

1946   President Harry S. Truman (1884-1972) signed the Act of 1946 creating the Indian Claims Commission to hear and determine claims by Indian tribes. It may be that no side was completely satisfied but this may be one law where the U.S. taxpayers' money was well spent for the "scholarly fallout was stunning indeed. The materials presented included a concentrated body of ethno-historical research data and adversary findings unique in the record of cultural histioriography and... in the annals of jurisprudence." Published in 118 volumes, the Garland American Indian Ethnohistory series presented original documents on the history and anthropology of many American Indian tribes and groups who were involved in the Indian Claims actions of the 1950s and 1960s.[5] Records of the Indian Claims Commission are at the National Archives in Washington, D.C. and also have been digitized and made available on the Internet by Oklahoma State University.

1948   A successful lawsuit brought against the State of Arizona by a World War II veteran, Frank Harrison (1911-1986), and Harry Austin, both Yavapai from the Fort McDowell reservation, won an Arizona Supreme Court decision on July 15, 1948, written by Levi S. Udall, granting Indians in Arizona the right to vote.[6] Harrison and Austin were represented pro bono by Phoenix attorneys Lem and Ben Mathews.

1952   Disastrous U.S. government policies for American Indians directed toward termination, assimilation, and ending supportive government programs, were enacted in the mid-20th century. Hiawatha Hood (1912-1991), a Yavapai born in Camp Verde, accepted relocation to Chicago in a 1952 Bureau of Indian Affairs Urban Indian Relocation Program.[7] He returned to Fort McDowell in 1975 to fight for his land, to save it from the Orme Dam. Hiawatha was passionate, a strong leader and an eloquent spokesman. He served as tribal chairman in 1977. On February 22, 1977, he spoke against Orme Dam in a nationwide CBS-TV Reports program, *Arizona: Here We Come.* In a July 23, 1977, Phoenix KTVK-TV program, Hiawatha used humor to reply to Senator Barry Goldwater, who wanted the Orme Dam, and had written an unkind letter published in the July 1977 *Audubon* magazine.[8] To the end of his life, Hiawatha Hood was tireless in working for the dignity and honor of his people.

1965   The Indian Claims Commission issued its findings of fact determining the extent and boundaries of aboriginal Yavapai land which they had used and occupied, from time immemorial, to be 9,238,600 acres. This finding may not have returned any land to the Yavapai but it reclaimed their rightful place in history. The Commission's final judgment was entered on March 13, 1969, in the amount of $5,100,000.00.[9] That comes to 55 cents per acre.

1968   President Lyndon B. Johnson (1908-1973) signed Public Law 90-537 authorizing the construction of the Central Arizona Project for carrying water uphill from the Colorado River to Orme Dam, which was to be built at the confluence of the Salt and Verde rivers, located a few miles northeast of Phoenix. The dam's reservoir would flood most of the Fort McDowell Reservation and force relocation of the tribe. Further, the government could take their property through eminent domain proceedings if the Yavapai rejected the deal. Fortunately, this small tribe, about 350 at the time of this battle, was victorious in 1981. The final impact study concluded, as the Yavapai themselves had said from the beginning, that if relocated once again, they would cease to exist.[10]

1983-1984—After starting their work in 1974 of recording Yavapai history, Fort McDowell elders Mike Harrison and John Williams died in 1983. Their friend, anthropologist Sigrid Khera, died in 1984.

1988   The Indian Gaming Regulatory Act signed by President Ronald Reagan (1911-2004) on October 17, 1988, enacted legislation to help the Indians economically.

1992   In a surprise attack, on May 12, 1992, FBI agents, fully armed with M-16 rifles and wearing flak jackets, stormed onto the quiet Fort McDowell Yavapai reservation and with moving vans and equipment, seized hundreds of gambling machines from the Fort McDowell Gaming Center because Arizona and the tribe had not come to a gaming agreement. In response, tribal members quickly used their cars, their pickup trucks and their huge sand-and-gravel trucks to block the roads.[11]

David King (1936-) then a Yavapai council member, told an FBI agent pointing an M-16 at him, "Use it or get it out of my face." David, a minister of his church, had been a U.S. Army paratrooper with the 82nd Airborne, the 101st Airborne and 11th Airborne. David is also the artist who designed the tribal seal.[12]

For three weeks, the Fort McDowell Yavapai kept a 24-hour blockade at the entrances to their reservation, refusing to surrender their machines. A settlement was worked out and signed in November.[13]

The moving vans the FBI had rented and parked at Fort McDowell had big letters on their sides reading MAYFLOWER, the name of the ship which brought the Pilgrims from England to Massachusetts in 1620 to colonize the New World.

American Indians like David King are proud to serve their country in the U.S. military and American Indians represent the highest per capita enlistment of any ethnic group in the United States.

Fort McDowell. Annual Memorial Day ceremony at the cemetery. Students from the Phoenix Indian School march, May 17, 1975. Photo by Sigrid Khera.

Oral History of the Yavapai

PART V

ORAL HISTORY OF THE YAVAPAI

The following eight oral history chapters, Chapters 17-24, by Mike Harrison and John Williams (above) are in their own words and appear exactly as heard and originally transcribed by Dr. Sigrid Khera, anthropologist (below). No attempt has been made to standardize grammar, spelling and punctuation. Their words remain unchanged from Dr. Khera's original manuscript. Words in parentheses have been added for clarity.

Chapter 17

━━━━━━ ◆ ━━━━━━

The White People Meet the Yavapai

O ver there in that cave on the Salt River these people, my people, died in there. That was the first time the White people meet the Yavapai and they kill them all in there. There was only one girl that came out of this shooting in the cave. Only one. That girl jumped off the bluff and she got out. The rest of them, they killed them. This was up in the Salt River Canyon.

My mother's two brothers and one sister died at that killing. And my grandmother's brother and two sisters died in there. My grandfather died in that place. All my relatives died in there. That is why I don't like to talk about it. But anyways.

When the White people come, lots of Yavapai get killed. This here is our home. But when the White people come, they take it away from us. They start mining out of these big rocks. We know nothing about these things.

White people come here and they get gold, they get silver, they get copper, they get iron, they get lead out of these rocks. If the White people would not kill the Indians, it would be all right. But they kill them, kill them, and I don't know why they do that.

Before the White people live here, we have no trouble at all. At that time we all stay together, not like now, all separate. Now there are few of us left and that is why we are scattered out. Each family group when they stayed some place they had a chief, a *mayora*. The chief tells the people how to get along and how to get things. And when we kill a deer or some other animal, we all eat it together. Anything we get, we eat it all together.

In summer we stay in the wikiup. It stays cool. In wintertime the Yavapai went back to the mountains to the caves. There they built a fire and it kept them warm. A whole bunch of them stayed at one place. People stayed together like quails. That is why the soldiers killed all of them in one place.

People stayed together in the cave at the Salt River, and they sent a boy to some other people at Saddle Mountain. The chief sent him to tell the others to come and share deer meat. But the Army scouts got this boy, and he showed them the cave. Otherwise the soldiers would not have found it. The soldiers went up to the cave and they could shoot right into it.

When the soldiers got that boy, some Yavapai were up on a mountain and they watched it. They knew now the boy is going to show the soldiers where they live. So they tell the chief in the cave, "They are going to get us. Let's get out of here." That chief was my grandmother's father.

He was the best medicine man and he knew everything. He knows what is going to be. So he tells them, "If I go out, they don't let me go. They look for me and kill me wherever I go. So I'm not going to go out. I'm going to stay right here. Right here. Rest of you, if you want to go out, go out. They are not going to forget us. They are going to do the same thing to us all the time."

Lots of people stayed with him. My grandfather stayed there with him. My grandmother tried to get him out. "No," he said, "you go ahead and go." My grandfather stayed in there and he died in that cave. My grandmother's daughter and two boys died with him. She wants to take them out, but they don't want to go. The father is there, and that's why the kids don't want to go out. My mother was a baby then, so my grandmother took her out. And she took out some of her sister's children. Two boys and one girl. The older children of her sister stayed behind.

A bunch of people went out from the cave before the soldiers came. Women with babies, boys and girls. When they left, my grandmother's father said to them, "You go out. Maybe you save a few days. But maybe they kill you over there, when they kill another bunch of our people."

My grandmother and the others went out from the cave to go to Saddle Mountain. When they go over the hill they hear the shooting, 'pang, pang, pang.' They know what happened. But they never did go back after that.

The soldiers didn't really come up to the cave. They were right across the cave. It is open all the way and the people can go no place. The soldiers shoot them down, shoot them down, shoot them down. Kill them all. One girl jumped out, off the cliff and got saved. That's only one. But she was not in good shape. She must have hit the rocks. She broke her hip. And that is the only one that got out of there.

In 1923 we went with Carl (*Carlos*) Montezuma (also known by his Yavapai name, *Wassaja*) to get the bones from the cave. In that cave, on the wall, it looked like oil sprayed on. Down on the floor it looked like oil. There is that 'oil' all over. It is the blood. When the bullets hit the bodies, the blood got scattered all around. Looks awful. We found many bones. Lots of little bones also. When we bring the bones, Montezuma is standing there crying. And we all start crying right there. We see that blood on the wall. It is too bad for us. It is here that all our people died. For nothing. And when I got back to Prescott and told my grandmother, my grandmother sure cried.

Those who left the cave before the soldiers came went to Saddle Mountain. They fled from the cave and went up to Four Peaks from the east side. They crossed between two of the peaks and then went on to Saddle Mountain. When they were going to climb down from the Four Peaks, my grandmother left her grinding stone in the brush there. They had to walk fast and it was too heavy. It was a green grinding stone. Like turquoise. I asked my grandmother, "But that little one on top (*mano*), you still got this?"

"No," she said, "I lost it." Then she said, "If you go up there some time, go and look for it. It is between two peaks, almost at the bottom there. I throw it away there." I never found it.

Skeleton Cave. 1976 photo by Sigrid Khera.

On the way to Saddle Mountain the soldiers come near. They heard the soldiers talking. People were hiding in the brush and the mothers were holding the little babies' mouth, so the soldiers can't hear them. Pretty soon a baby died. Got choked.

When they came to Saddle Mountain they stayed there for a while. One night they hear something crying. They hear it another night. It comes from a pile of brush below the place where they stay. The chief said, "It sounds like *mìéh* (ghost)." After the third night the chief sent out four boys to look what is crying. "Four of you guys go over there and find out."

They go over to that place and one hollers, "What are you down there?" It is the woman who jumped down the bluff.

"I'm from over there, that cave where they kill us. I jumped off the bluff. I'm hurt. I can't walk. My hip is bust. But I made it over here."

The boys went back to the camp and told the chief, "It is a human over there, a woman."

"Can she walk?"

"No, she looks like she is hurt. That's why she stays there."

Then the chief said, "Well, get a buckskin. Put her on top and bring her over here."

So they took a buckskin where the legs are still on. They put her on it and bring her over to the camp.

At that time the people pray for the hurt woman. They sing over her and she got all right. She healed all right, but she can't walk straight. Looks like a hip is out of joint. It makes a noise when she walks, but it doesn't look like it hurt her. One leg is short. Maybe the muscle had been pulled back. But she sure can do anything. Gather things. When they get out to get something to eat, she takes the burden basket and packs it with anything they find. But later she got killed at Bloody Basin.

My grandmother saw this woman. She looked kind of bad when they brought her in. Her legs were full of stickers. She can't walk, just crawl. We don't know how many days she goes up to Saddle Mountain. We don't know how she made it. She had no food with her. Water is hard to get. There are some canyons with water, but it is hard to get down there when you are up high.

Hard country for crippled people to go. All the other people around had taken off when they heard about the killing. So nobody could have helped her.

From Saddle Mountain the people went to Bloody Basin. We call that place *Atasquaselhúa*. That is, "Sycamore with yellow leaves in fall." Maybe the chief told them to go there. They know there is lots of mescal there. The women had a place up there where they cook mescal. They call that place *màtkáma*. That's where they cook the mescal all the time. They don't use any other place for that. The one over there at Bloody Basin is a big one. People from all over used to come together there. They put the mescal in the ground three nights, and then they got it out and eat it.

That killing in the cave happened in the winter time. It must have been in the spring when they went over to Bloody Basin to cook mescal. In the spring when the stalks come out, that's when they are sweet. That is the time when we cut it out and cook it. We call this time *boéme*. It means "in the spring."

Atasquaselhua (Bloody Basin). 1979 photo by Sigrid Khera.

Three tribes of Yavapai got together at Bloody Basin. *Kewevkepaya*, *Wipukpa* and *Yavepe*. Three of them. They get together and cook mescal, cook deer. Get together and eat, dance and have a good time. But the soldiers met them there and killed them. Then the White people called the place Bloody Basin. Called it after our blood.

Some of the people had gone out to the hills to gather more food. These were the ones who were still out when the soldiers started shooting. They watched the soldiers from the hills, and when they left, they came down. When the soldiers had killed all the people, they found two babies in their cradles alive. The soldiers hung them in a tree in their cradles and left them there. When the Yavapai came back they found them. They took them down and raised them.

The mescal heaps are still there. When I was working in Bloody Basin at the ranch, I went to that place *màtkáma*. The mescal heaps were still covered with dirt. The people had left it when it was still cooking. Now all is covered with weeds and grass. I tried to get some out. Cleaned the dirt away from underneath the grass. The mescal was still there.

All the dead bodies, the people piled them up and burned them. Piles of brush and piles of wood. Put the bodies on top and burn them.

But that cave in the Salt River Canyon, they don't come back to it. That is why the bones are still there. And that is the same way up in Skull Valley.

When I was a cowboy around Skull Valley, I see lots of bones there. Sometimes a head, sometimes a leg, sometimes an arm at a rock pile and under the brush. I ask my grandmother, "I see lots of heads over there. Where are they coming from?" My grandmother don't tell me. She just starts crying. I ask her, "Those Indians over there, what did they do? Did they have some kind of a sickness that they died over there?" My grandmother just cries. One long time later she tells me, she tells me White people kill lots of our tribe there.

White people sent a Mexican scout to the Yavapai. And some Yavapai understand Mexican. That scout tells the Yavapai to gather at Skull Valley. He tells them that the White people will make peace with the Indians, will make friends. "The White people will make friends with you, give you horses, blankets, cattle, houses, everything." And they believe it. The chiefs gather all the people and take them there. People from all around. And the soldiers are coming and line them up. Early in the morning. Three, four lines. And one Indian says, "Hey, looks like they are going to shoot us." But the chief said, "No, I don't think so. They are going to make friends. They are going to give something good to us. Let's go in. The first line gets the wagon first."

So they go in there. But they don't give them wagons. They don't give them horses. They don't give them blankets. They shoot them down. Kill them.

When the soldiers start shooting, my people run like deer, like rabbits. That's how many got out of there. My grandmother when she goes to that meeting she makes a dress of buckskin. But when she comes out her skirt and her leggings are full of holes from the shots. All torn. But she don't get hurt.

Mike Harrison's father, he got out of there, too. "*Wita*," he said to me, "I don't know how we get out. But we get out. There were bullets around us like when you throw gravel around. I don't know how we get out." Some other men came out. *Matamthi* and two brothers, *Watarammah* and *Purgashúe. Purgashúe*, that means "Blue Head."

He told me, "I was way in the line, but I get out. Lots of us lined up there. From *Tolkepaya* side, *Wipukpa*, and *Yavepe*, *Kewevkepaya*. The whole tribe lined up like that." Another man got out, but a bullet hit him in the armpit. But that time there were lots of good medicine men around. They prayed for that man and got some blackroot for him. So he heal up, heal up and heal up. And after that they call him *Selmakakayalva*, "Split Arm." When I was a boy I saw him. He is a small man, but he sure can run down a deer.

After that they left the dead ones laying there. We call this place *Bakwaeguó*. That means "Hair." That is, because a mountain there looks like a pile of hair. But the White people call the place Skull Valley. They named it after our heads.

Bakwaeguo (Skull Valley). 1977 photo by Sigrid Khera.

There used to be four tribes of Yavapai: *Kewevkepaya*, *Wipukpa*, *Yavepe* and *Tolkepaya*. This country here, Saddle Mountain, Four Peaks, Superstition Mountain, all the way down to Tucson, that's where the *Kewevkepaya* lived. Jerome, Clarkdale, Cottonwood, Camp Verde up to Ash Fork and Seligman, that's where the *Wipukpa* and *Yavepe* used to live. From there south it was *Tolkepaya* country, from Kirkland, Congress, all the way down to Yuma.

Lots of *Tolkepaya* got killed at different places. East from Prescott there is a place in the rocks. We call it *Kakauwa*. That means, "no one can get through here." That place is steep. Only one way to get in and out. The White people get *Tolkepaya* together there, and the scout tells them to drop their bows and arrows, all their things. So they do. They drop their bows and arrows. Some got long spears. We call these *pasatohe*. My people used to kill buffalo with that kind. They drop those spears. Some of them have a heavy wood for throwing. We call it *sotat*.

They drop that, too. Another scout takes brush and puts all that stuff in it and burn it.

Then the soldiers said to the *Tolkepaya*, "Come in, we'll talk." So the Indians believe it and go in that *Kakauwa*. They go in, go in, go in—the whole bunch of them. The place where you can go out is not very wide. Like a gate. In there it is like in a rock corral. And when all the Indians are in it, they shoot them down.

Lots of *Tolkepaya* got killed at Date Creek. At the mouth of Date Creek there is a canyon. Lots of *Tolkepaya* lived in there. There is water and the people made a ditch and planted corn and squash and everything. That time the *Tolkepaya* used to go down to Yuma and work with the Mexicans. That's why they understand the Mexican talk good. So a Mexican scout tells the *Tolkepaya* to get together there at one place at Date Creek. White people did to them, like to the people in Skull Valley. Tell them, they are going to give them things. Tell them they are going to make friends, going to give them houses, going to give them wagons. The *Tolkepaya* believe it. They get together there and the soldiers kill them. Some of them didn't believe the scout. "We go up in the hills and wait," they said. When they stayed over in the hills they heard shots go on. So they took off. But when the soldiers had left, they came down and pile the dead bodies and burned them.

When I was a little boy, my uncle *Pelhame* sometimes took me over there. My uncle was from over there. So I saw the place where they burned these people. You see the ashes. It is still there down at Date Creek.

Hakaonwa (Date Creek). 1978 photo by Sigrid Khera.

Sometimes I come down to Wickenburg with my grandmother and my uncle *Pelhame*. We come down to the Hassayampa River, and my grandmother sure cried when we come there. Lots of *Tolkepaya* used to live here because of the river. They live here and plant corn and squash. Then some White people come around and tell the Indians to go down to Yuma. Tell them, the White people down there are sure nice and will give them lots of clothes. Some *Tolkepaya* go down to Yuma and bring lots of clothes with them. Give it to the others. But then they all get the smallpox. Lots of them died from that. They call the smallpox *hamalutha*. They say, it is like you get burnt with water. And when it goes away it leaves marks all over. Some of the old people I saw used to have these marks. My grandmother said, that disease is hard to heal. She said, some people got all right, using some kind of medicine. But lots of them died. Some of them, she said, got killed right away by the *hamalutha*. If the disease stays inside the body, don't come out (in blisters), it kills the person right away.

There used to be *Tolkepaya* from Wickenburg to Yuma. There were lots of wild sheep in the mountains and they get these. And there were springs all over and the people plant. The *Tolkepaya* were a big tribe. Now there is no Indian left in the *Tolkepaya* country. The White people say, "Indians are not very many people." How can they be many people when they kill them all? Men, women, they kill them all. Nothing left to breed any more.

When one looks into that cave at Salt River Canyon, or Skull Valley, Bloody Basin, Date Creek, one finds no gun, no machine gun, no rifle that belongs to Yavapai. Yavapai had nothing to start war with the White people. But the White people talk about "Indian War." They come and kill all of us and call it "Indian War."

When the White people come around, they kill all of my people. They kill all of my relatives. I don't know why. I guess, they just like to kill. They must feel good when they kill.

The soldiers kill my people, kill them, kill them and kill them again. There is a bunch of my people left. They round them up and bring them to Fort Whipple at Prescott. From there they march them to Camp Verde. The people get tired and hungry on the way. They come to Cherry Creek Trail. When they get close to the springs, the soldiers tell the people, "Let's stop here overnight. We'll give you some rest." Then the soldiers give the people chunks of meat. Some of them are pretty hungry and they cut it, cook it on the fire, and eat it. They fell down and died. That meat was poisoned. So the soldiers gave them a rest all right!

My grandmother said, she didn't eat the meat because it smelled different. She dropped it. But before, she holds it like this in her hand and she got sick from it for a long time. She got shivers all over. My grandmother died of old age. Still that poison stayed with her all her life. She got these shivers all the time. When she gets that, I wrap her in blankets, but she still keeps shaking from that poison.

Many other people threw that meat away, also. The ones who ate the meat at Cherry Creek Trail, they died right there. Those who carried it and threw it away, that's the ones who got sick. Lots of them died later on the trail, when the soldiers marched them on.

From Cherry Creek Trail they take them to Camp Verde. Stop them there. Then they march them on to San Carlos. When they walk on the trail all around the mountains, that's a good way. But the soldiers make them go straight over the mountains. The people don't have a wagon or horses, nothing at that time. Just walk. My grandmother had babies, children to take along on that trail. The children were young when they took them from there. One old man, he carried his wife in the burden basket. That woman was too old to walk, real old. Her husband is old, too. They make it to San Carlos, but don't live very long there.

Many of them carried children in the burden basket. Some people were sick from that poison and they can't make it. Some of them were real sick. The soldiers just poke them with the gun to make them walk faster. But some of them just went down and died. They leave them there. Like dogs. Like killed flies they leave them there. Just like that, all the way down to San Carlos.

When they come to the (Mogollon) Rim, there is a lumber camp there. The soldiers know the people are hungry. They come to the camp and it looks like there is an eating place there. A big building, and one man looks like he is a cook. He has a white cap on his head. After a long time he comes out with a pan. It has handles on both sides. Puts it down on the ground. But the headman of the Yavapai says, "Don't eat it, don't eat it. Leave it." They call a dog and throw him a chunk of meat. The dog eats it. A little while and he twists around, falls down and dies. So they don't bother with that meat in the pan. And one man said, "I wonder why the White people hate us. Why they want to kill us. We don't do anything to them."

When they march them to San Carlos it is winter time. It is raining, so there is lots of water in the washes and rivers. But the soldiers make them cross the rivers. First time they cross, lots of my people go down the stream. So some men go and get long sticks. Make a rail with it. One man standing here holding it, another one over there, and another one over there. People hold on to it and go across. They use it at lots of places. Those men carry the sticks along. They cut green ones that stay pretty good all the way to San Carlos. Dry ones would break.

The soldiers make the people cross the rivers at winter time. On cold days. There is lots of water in the rivers and they make them walk through. And that poison, when they cross the cold water gets stronger and kills lot of people.

My grandmother was sick and they had to cross the river. Maybe she was slow. The scout hit her with a gun, right at the wrist. Her wrist was crooked all the time. "How you do that?" I asked her. "The scout hit me with a gun," she said. "Right here and he broke the bone." She could use her arm, though. Her cousin was a good medicine man and he prayed for her.

There was an old lady whom I knew when I was young. She had no ears. I asked my grandmother about it and she said, "Don't say that." Later my grandmother told me, up in the hills, the soldiers cut that woman's ears off. And she told me, another woman, they cut the fingers off with the bayonet. I don't know why the White people hate Indians so much.

On the way to San Carlos, when a baby was born, the soldiers don't let them rest. They just push them along, push them along. Sometimes they can get up and walk along. But sometimes they have to wait, maybe an hour or two hours. They have to wait and cannot do anything. But the soldiers push them right along. I don't know why they do that.

My grandmother said, when the soldiers take the people on the trail down to San Carlos, they had a chance to kill all the soldiers. There were not very many soldiers that take them there. If they wanted to, they could kill all the soldiers before they get to San Carlos and they can come back from there. But the chief had said, "Don't kill the White people." So they don't do it. The chief said, "They don't let us go if we kill these White people. Others will come after them." So they just walk on to San Carlos. Not many of them get there.

Some people, they sneaked out before the soldiers get them for the march to San Carlos. They hide out. My wife's cousin's mother's mother and her husband were hiding at a cave near Camp Verde. They were both old people and the man was sick. They were hiding in that cave for a long time. But a scout saw them. That scout comes into the cave and he pulls his white gloves off. Warms his hands on the fire. When he warms his hands, the old man tells the woman, "Make it look like you get water. Take your moccasins and go out. When you hear a shot, don't come back. Just keep on going." So the woman takes the olla. Make it look like she goes for some water. Stuffs her moccasins under her arm and takes off. Then she hears a shot.

There were other people hiding out and she joined them. But they never did go back to see the old man. I think the bones must be still there.

I want to talk about it all for a long, long time. But lots of people they don't like to listen to that. They don't care. They have been raised when everything was quiet and going like that. "Oh, these old people died anyways," they say. "They are gone already." Well, they are gone. But they are my people. My people around here, they kill them and kill them. My God, that is awful for me. I sure get mad sometime. I feel bad. I feel like I cry.

I used to work at a cattle ranch. One morning that ranch man and I were going to round up some cattle. I shoed my horse and he was shoeing a horse over there. "Hey, John," he said, "Hey, John, know what?"

"What?" I said.

"The Indians who stayed here, they tried to fight. But the White people killed them all and got the land here."

"What are you talking," I said. "I don't want to hear that. Look out! My relatives died in that cave. You don't say that again, or I kill you." And I took the heavy rasp and walked over there and he took off. Went in the car and went away.

17 The White People Meet the Yavapai

Two, three days after this I tell his brother Lean. "Hey, Lean," I say, "you better tell your brother he don't say that again. That place he talks about, where they killed my people, that wasn't funny. If you see a dead man lying with his guts shot out, you think that is funny? That is not funny! When he talked about that and laughed, I don't like that. He had laughed, 'hahahahaha.' You don't talk about a dead man and laugh!"

I had worked at that ranch for ten years. But then that man talked kind of funny. So I got mad and quit. Well, he was a good friend of mine, but he talked wrong. So I don't like that and quit. That's no good, the way he talked to me. That's awful.

The White people don't bother the Pima and the Mohave, the Chemehuevi, the Hualapai, the Quechan. They don't move them out. They all stay at their own places. But my old people, my grandmother and my uncle *Pelhame* told me why they think the White people start killing all the Yavapai.

There is one *Tolkepaya, Pakoteh*. That means "Big Man." He is the first man who goes over to Washington. The White people take him over there, and they give him a medal. He has that medal all the time. When he comes back the Mohave tell the White people the Yavapai kill White people all the time. They bring a little White girl to the Army camp. They had put blue marks all over her face and under her eyes, and they say the Yavapai have done that. They say, they fight to get the little girl back from the Yavapai. But they lie. We don't put blue marks under the eyes. The Mohave, the Quechan do that. Not us. Anyways, the White people think we took that little girl. They take the Yavapai to some scout camp down near Yuma somewhere and kill lots of us.

The Mohave did that to the little girl, and they said the Yavapai did that. That's why the White people are mad with us, my uncle said. [Editor's note: This refers to the Olive Oatman story, March 1851.]

The Yavapai didn't try to fight the White people. They just took off. When the White people first come here to our place, my grandmother's father is the chief. He told the people, "Don't kill the White people. Leave them alone. If we kill them, they go and put us in a bad place. They put us in a hog pen and the pigs are going to eat us. Don't kill the White people."

The chiefs of all the tribes, *Kewevkepaya*, *Wipukpa*, *Yavepe* and *Tolkepaya*, they tell the same thing, "Don't kill the White people." They go round and tell the people, "Lots of White people are going to come here, but don't kill them." There are lots of good men around at that time. They sure can run fast. They run to the next camp and tell them. They send other men around and tell the next ones. And the news goes around like a radio.

At that time, when we were still in our place, before they take us to San Carlos, we could kill White people easy. My people see a few of them at one place and they could kill them easy. But they don't do it. They just watch them. That's all.

But the Yavapai killed those Pima and Maricopa, those Mohave and Hualapai and Chemehuevi who are Army scouts. They fight against us for the White people.

Once the Yavapai watch the soldiers go over the Verde River. About there, where Beeline Highway is now. They lay behind the bushes watching them pretty close. The Yavapai never move. If we move and show up, the soldiers come back and kill us pretty quick. So my people lay down and don't move and the soldiers don't see them. The first bunch that crosses the river is White people. The next bunch is White people. Next bunch is White people. They let them go. The last bunch, it looks like they are Indians. They have long hair, the skin is dark. *Pakakaya* is the one who leads the Yavapai. "These are Indians," he says, "so we are going to get them. We are not going to get even with them. But anyways, we are going to do something to them. Let's get ready, up on the pass over there." So the Yavapai jump out and kill all those Indian scouts: Pima, Mohave, Chemehuevi, Hualapai. Kill the whole bunch of them. My grandmother and her cousins and everyone got in that fight with the scouts. Kill them fast. Make no noise. They can do the same to the White people, but they don't want to do it. The chief said, "No, don't bother them." So they didn't do it.

There is a cross on a little hill on Beeline Highway near Shea Boulevard. That's the place where the Yavapai killed those Indian scouts. There at that rock where the cross is, there used to be hair. Long, black hair. That's from the dead Indian scouts. They left them there. When Beeline Highway was built I went up there and I could still see the hair. It is gone now, I think.

When the Yavapai killed those Indian scouts, they didn't shoot them. They chop their heads off with some kind of a knife. They make this knife themselves. It is copper. They heat it on the fire, pound it, pound it, pound it. Then grind it to make it sharp.

Some of the scouts, the Yavapai just held them and choked to death. Others they hit with a club. That club is like a blackjack. We call it *baawe*. That means, "kill the people." It's a piece of ironwood. Sure heavy. We make it round at the end and put a hide over it. Make the hide wet and it gets dry and hard like rock. Solid. It has a strap through the handle and you put your hand through it. My grandmother carried one all the time. When I was a boy I asked my grandmother, "Why you carry that all the time?"

"Don't say anything. Just leave me alone," she said. That thing, it looked like there is some blood on it.

I asked her again, "What is this one here for?"

"Keep quiet, get out of here," she said. "Get your head down and I show you!"

We kill the Indian scouts all right, but we don't kill the White soldiers. White people bother us all the time, but we don't kill them.

I had a *napó*, kind of a grandpa from my father's side. His name was *Haló*. That means "Rabbit."

"No, you can't do that," he said, "You can't kill White people. But," he said, "I killed one. Just one! I'm waiting. Maybe they still come around and chop my head off for that."

That White man was Buckey O'Neill. That's the only White man the Yavapai killed. Around Prescott there, he used to chase my people all the time, all the time. When he sees Indians, he kills them right away. He had a long knife at the hip (sabre) and he chopped people's heads off with that. Five, six in a row when he got them.

[Editor's note: William O. "Buckey" O'Neill came to Tombstone, Arizona Territory, in 1880, and then to

Prescott in 1882. He joined the Rough Riders in 1898 and was killed later that year on San Juan Hill in Cuba. It was in 1875, five years before O'Neill came to the Arizona Territory, that the Yavapai had been rounded up and removed to San Carlos. John Williams and Mike Harrison said Buckey O'Neill was the only White man the Yavapai killed. Clearly, there may be confusion about the name. It is an unsolved mystery with an explanation known only to those who have passed.]

There was an Army camp below Prescott and another one below Humboldt. That's where Buckey O'Neill started out riding on that trail. And that morning some Yavapai men were going to hunt antelope around there. There used to be lots of antelopes in that valley. The Yavapai camped in a canyon below Jerome Mountain and the men come down from there to hunt. The men didn't see Buckey O'Neill coming. If they see him, they said, they took off. But they never did see him that day. There is a little ridge. And when they come over that ridge, Buckey O'Neill sees them right close. So they know they can't get away. Two men run this way and two men run the other way and *Haló* runs straight ahead to some brush. He jumps over that brush and gets to the ground. Gets ready. Buckey O'Neill comes with his big horse to jump over the brush. He comes over and *Haló* hits him with the arrow right below the throat. "Ahhhrrrr," hollered that White man and died. "He knows now it hurts," said *Haló*. "But he never cares if it hurts the Indians. Now he knows it all right!"

Buckey O'Neill fell from the horse and the men cut off the saddle. Burned the saddle and all the things. One man wanted to get the jacket. It is a buckskin jacket with lots of strings all around. But the others said, "No, don't do that. It don't looks right to take it." So they burned it all. They leave the dead man lying. Halo said, "I never go back there again. I don't know what they did with him. I guess the White people found him."

The horse, the men took along. Take it to the camp at *Churkakwoya*. That means, "Walnut Deep." They kill the horse and eat it. This horse sure could run fast. Chased people up the hill like nothing.

"If we let that man go," *Haló* said, "he do that over and over again to us, chop our heads off. So I killed him. Nobody else killed a White man. I'm the only one."

My uncle *Pelhame* told me about another man who killed the Indians all the time. That man lived in *Tolkepaya* country, at a place called *Mo'ulchacha*. That place is somewhere near New River, I think. My uncle is half *Tolkepaya*, and that's how he knows about it.

That man was half Indian, but they don't know what tribe. He come out here with the first White people, and he is the first man who has cattle around here. He had the cattle and a little place where he stayed. He killed the Indians all the time, and he did that for a long time. *Pelhame* said, he was a real bad one, worse than the White people. He had big dogs, and he used to trail the Indians with those dogs. When the Yavapai stopped some place, the dogs come around barking. Then that man goes over there and kills the people.

One time three Yavapai boys shoot the dogs with bow and arrow. After that he can't trail them with the dogs anymore. But he shoots the Indians wherever he sees them. Finally, the Indians killed him. They killed him just like Buckey O'Neill. They have only bow and arrow, and they cannot shoot far with that. So they want him coming close. He sees two, three boys, so he comes up to them with his big horse. They shoot the horse, and the horse falling on the man sitting on its back. So they killed him easy.

My grandpa *Haló* used to have a tobacco pouch. I see that bag and it has funny hair on it. I asked this grandpa, "What's that there?"

"Ah, ah, ah, no good," he said all the time. But one day he told me. "I peel a White man. Peel his beard off. Make a tobacco pouch with it. But I didn't kill him."

At Lynx Creek near Prescott, there is a place we call *Howakanuakagewa*. That means "Mosquito Crossing." That place *Haló* met a White soldier, kind of a headman. He had a blue jacket with lots of buttons and a yellow string all the way across it. He tried to shoot *Haló*, but *Haló* jumped to the side.

"Well, if he don't shoot me, it's all right," *Haló* told me. "But he shoot me. He don't get me the first time and he can't load again quick. So I jump up and hit him like this, with my hand on his neck. Put him a little to sleep. Lay him with the face down. Pull the string off his jacket and tie his arms and legs together."

That time White people had long beards. Whiskers all the way down. And *Haló* peeled that Army man's whiskers off. Chased the horse away and let the man lie there. Maybe the horse went back to Prescott. "He kill us all the time," *Haló* said to me, "and I like to kill him, too. But the chief told me not to kill White people. So I don't kill him. Just shave him a bit."

I had another *napó*. His name was *Koahlaka*. That means "Stumbles." He too lived up there around Jerome Mountain. One time when he went hunting he met two soldiers at the other side of Humboldt near Dewey.

The soldiers are riding on horseback. They see him and they stop right there. He knows what they are going to do. He stands there and says, "How d'you do?" He told me, "I don't know where I learned that, but that's what I said."

He has nothing with him. No knife, nothing. Just bow and arrow. He has the bow with the string around his back. Has the arrows in a bag over his shoulder. And he has a rope to pack a deer or something from the hunt. A rope made out of horsemane.

Pretty soon it goes 'pang.' The soldiers shoot at him, but he jumps aside. The guns are charged, so he knows they have to load up again. He jumps between the horses and pulls the men down on their long beards. Hits them in the back of their neck with his hand. Like karate. Then he ties them up. Pulls their arms down behind their backs. Pulls their legs up and ties them together. Then he pulled their boots off, put them on some dry weeds and burned them. "I don't kill them," he told me. "I just let them lay there. Right in the trail there. I know that the next one coming will find them. I pulled their shoes off and burned them, but these White men sure got stinky feet!"

Then *Koahlaka* got up on one horse and lead the other one. He went to Jerome Mountain. Lots of people were in that camp. They shot the horses with an arrow and ate them.

When I was a boy and I come to Fort McDowell, I see *Pakakaya* (? -1918). *Pakakaya* is my *nikó*, a grandpa from my mother's side. Cousin to my grandmother. And this *Pakakaya* told me many things. When I was a boy he lived up there around Four Peaks all alone. But he come down here to Fort McDowell often. He was a big man and could run real fast. Big feet! That man didn't wear pants. Just a strap. He wore a blue shirt and he put a vest over it. He had a button on a ribbon hanging. He said, "This button tells me things." He was a medicine man. He sure could sing and dance all night. He sings a song for war. He was the only one who knew this song.

In old days, before they send us to San Carlos, *Pakakaya* did many things. That time my people lived around Four Peaks and the White people had put up Fort McDowell. Soldiers kill the Indians all the time and we don't kill them. But *Pakakaya* takes the horses away from the soldiers and they never can get him.

The soldiers have an adobe corral at Fort McDowell. They have horses in there, and one night *Pakakaya* comes down here. He goes to the corral and looks around, looks around and there is a dump over there. He finds some scout clothes on that dump. Puts the jacket on, gets the scout hat on, and puts his strap in. There is a guard sitting right there and another one over there. Both asleep. He goes in that corral and takes two horses out. And just when he is ready to get out, the guards wake up. *Pakakaya* lets the horses go and runs back and jumps over the wall. And there is another one, an ocotillo fence on the other side. He just jumps over that and gets across to the other side of the river. Goes to a little hill over there. Two other boys are sitting there and they hear "tututu" from the trumpets and 'pang, pang, pang.' There are lots of lights in the corral. Looks like lots of soldiers down there. But they don't get *Pakakaya* and his boys.

I think it was in 1917. That time an old Pima man used to come to my father's store here at the Fort McDowell Reservation. That Pima man was selling vegetables and my father, he buys it from him. We called that Pima *Hatsalla*. That means "Horse Feet." I don't know why they name him like that. Maybe he has big feet or small feet. *Pakakaya* was there at the store and he sees that Pima man. *Pakakaya* said, "My God, this Pima here tried to be a soldier over here (at the old fort). I take two horses away from him and he don't see me."

That Pima man said, "He is just like a coyote, that man. We are watching and he leads two horses out. I sure like to kill him, but I'm sorry for him to die."

Pakakaya laughed. "Ah! You can't hit me, *Hatsalla*! I jump like that over the fence and you can't see me anymore. Do you?

"*Hatsalla*," he said, "he sleeps too much. Can't see nothing. Watch anything, but can't see nothing. I fool him. I play lots of times with him. He don't do nothing. Just sleeps."

Over there where Tom Mike lives now, there was lots of grass. At night *Pakakaya* was coming around and there was a tent with a White man and a lady laying in there. They were sure sound asleep. Hold a rope with a horse on it. *Pakakaya* cut the rope off and take the horse. Take it over to Four Peaks, kill it and eat it. The man and the lady are sleeping there, just holding the rope.

Another time he goes over there again. But there is no horse there now. The same tent and the man and the lady laying in there with a blanket on. *Pakakaya* takes the blanket off and runs away. He sure is a fast one. Like an automobile. The Indians then didn't wear much clothes. He said he cut the blanket, split it halfway. Use it as kind of a vest.

One time the soldiers from the fort chase *Pakakaya* with horses. He is a fast runner, but he knows they can catch up with him. At that time this here was just open country. Not very many mesquite trees around. Just a few. *Pakakaya* gets behind one tree with big roots, big stump. Goes behind it and stops there. The soldiers run by like this. They go across the river and search for him there. Lots of them get up on the high hill and shoot, 'pang, pang, pang.' He just sits and watches them.

Before the White soldiers come around and bother us, we see the Mexicans. It is different with the Mexicans. We have no trouble with them.

There lived Mexicans around Tucson. When my grandmother was a little girl the Yavapai went down there and helped the Mexicans build a church. The men make blocks and take them up high on the building. Then the Mexicans gave them some coffee. Green one. And they tell the Indians to cook it, make something. My grandmother said, some of the Mexicans put the beans in a basket and put some coals in there. Work it round, work it round, work it round. And when the beans get brown, they take the coals out and grind the beans. But the Yavapai thought that is something to eat like a gravy. So they put lots of it in a pot and boiled it. They eat it and it sure is bitter. They think it is a poison. So the Mexicans show them how to cook the coffee right.

First time my people see the Mexicans here around in the valley (Fort McDowell site), there were no other White people around. My people were around the Four Peaks. In the spring they see something green down here at the river. Looks like something is planted here. So the chief sent two men down here. "Look what's over there," he told them. They come down here closely and see. When they come back they tell, "These people down there look like Indians. Got black hair, dark skins, but they have lots of wool in the face." Next time the chief sent four men down. They watch these people with hair in the face closely. They are planting lots of things. Corn, squash, everything. They work all the time, work all the time. The four men tell the chief, and he says, "Next time you go down there, you go right to these people. Maybe they are going to kill you. So only two of you go up to them. The other two of you stay back and watch. If they don't kill you guys, the two more of you go in, too." They did. First time they go to these Mexicans, the Mexicans boil something for them. Corn mixed with tomatoes and onions. They give that food to the Indians in a pan. But the Indians dump the food in a hole and give the pan back to the Mexicans. The Yavapai plant corn and squash themselves. They know it's good. But they are afraid to eat that one. They were afraid it is poisoned.

Next time before they go down to the Mexicans the chief told them, "Only one of you eat it. Eat it and sit for a while. If he don't die, rest of you can eat it, too." So next time when they go down there and the Mexican woman cooks corn and squash, they eat it. It tastes good. And the Mexicans give them some more corn and some squash, and they take it with them.

After that the chief called them *haiko hanna*. That means "good White people." The Mexicans were the White people who didn't kill us.

Some of my people live down this way in Mexico. Some *Kewevkepaya* are over there. The White people don't get them. When my grandmother was a little girl, *Kewevkepaya* go down the other side of Tucson. The Mexicans have a little church there, Catholic church, and the Indians help them build it.

"I helped them build that church," my grandmother said. The women are packing the mud in the burden basket, and the men take the rope and pack things. Take it way up the building. The men are packing the blocks. And that preacher, he is the one that is working, too. Put the mud on, put the block on. We call the preacher *se'ulva*. That means "many beads." There are not very many Mexicans that help building that church. But lots of Indians. Lots of Indians from over there. Papago (now known as Tohono O'odham), I guess. And Indians from here. Lots of people from here go over there and help. *Kewevkepaya*, when they get there, they work just like ants. But my grandmother said, when they get through with that, they don't go to church. They just come home. And after that the White people come around and gather them and kill them. But some *Kewevkepaya*, they stay over there with the Mexicans, and the White people don't get them. But I don't know which place.

Oral History of the Yavapai

Chapter 18

♦

The Land the White People
Let Us Have

When the White people take us over to San Carlos, they give us some land there. They give us land on the right hand side of the river, on from where the slaughter house used to be.

And when Geronimo got out of San Carlos, the White Army headman told the Yavapai, "If you follow Geronimo and get him, you can go back to your country." So that's how they got started as Army scouts. All those Yavapai. My father was a scout, and Mike's father, my uncle *Pelhame* —everyone. All the old-timers became scouts. I think they never said "no" to the Army people because they thought they might get punished.

When they were scouts, they wore uniforms. Blue ones. *Pelhame*, my grandmother's old man, was a sergeant. My uncle, he has stripes on his sleeves. He said, they always had to walk stiff. When they march, they always holler at them. Put the gun up and down and holler at them.

Al Sieber, they were under him all the time. He is a White man, captain of the scouts.

My uncle, when they lived over there in Prescott, he still got his uniform. When the First World War is over they have a parade in town. One old man, way back there, looks like it's my uncle. That old man got in that parade. He was the real scout, coming in last. All alone. Carried his rifle. Big, long, Army rifle. He was the only scout around town at that time. The last one.

After that they give him a drink, and he passed out. So they take him up there in our camp. He lays like dead right there. That time my grandmother still walk around. She poked him with a little stick, "Looks like there is a dead soldier here," and she laughed.

Yuma Frank, the one who became chief at Fort McDowell, he was a big man among the scouts. He got lots of marks on the uniform. I think, he was a lieutenant. He takes care of all the scouts. Marshall Pete was another big scout. My father said Marshall Pete had a stripe on his pants. There were three headmen for the scouts. The third one was a Mission Indian from California. Don Juan. That Mission Indian was married to a Yavapai. He came over there to work for the government as a cowboy. So he is herding the beef cattle and butchers the cattle, too. After Geronimo got away he worked as a scout.

People got money paid when they were scouts. And when they got out from the Army, they got a pension every month. Not much. Just a little money. They get it when they come here from San Carlos.

18 The Land the White People Let Us Have

Before they gather us for San Carlos, there was an Apache scout, *Nantarri*. My grandmother told me that. *Nantarri* means "First." He got into the scouts first. When they take us to San Carlos he was kind of a headman with the Indian scouts. Kind of a boss over there. But he was a mean man. Like that Buckey O'Neill. Real mean. Kill anybody that guy. When they put the Yavapai to the scouts over in San Carlos, they work with him. But he never went around with the bunch. He is just coming around with the White men. Trying to tell the scouts what to do, and trying to tell them where to go.

This is how Geronimo got out and got bad. The big Army man got Geronimo's brother. The soldiers tied a wire across his thumbs and hung him up like this. They killed him that way. And that way Geronimo got mad.

When the Apache found the dead man, Geronimo called his people together. He told them, "Everybody get ready to go away." Then they went into the cabin of that Army man who had killed Geronimo's brother, shot him and took off.

You see, the White man did that first, but the Indian is bad, they say. If they do that to my brother or father, I do something, too!

My uncle *Pelhame* said that Geronimo can do anything. The Army never can get him. The Mexicans did. The scouts, when they go in an open valley behind Geronimo, it starts raining. It rains real hard and the scouts stop some place. Geronimo takes off. He had asked for that rain. And there was some time when the wind blows hard. The scouts wait, wait, wait. Maybe four hours until they can go on. One time, *Pelhame* said, there was a mountain. All open all around. They know Geronimo is coming across there.

137

Then the wind blows and the rain starts. So the scouts stop in a little canyon. Very early in the morning, maybe 3 o'clock, Geronimo is up on top of that mountain. He had a dance, and they heard him singing over there.

The scouts go around the mountain. But when it gets daylight, he is gone. The scouts get up the mountain, and nobody is there. The fire is gone and everything.

"The Army boss," *Pelhame* said, "he don't want us to go right there to the Apache. The Army bosses, they hold us back, hold us back. We know the Apache went right there, but the boss don't want us to go right up. So we just follow the Apache, follow them, follow them, follow them. That's all. And we are not the ones who got them," he said. "The Mexicans did. They meet him at one place one morning. There is fighting, and it looks like Geronimo kills lots of Mexicans. But these Mexican scouts were sure lots of people. So they got him. But we never see the Apache fight."

When the Yavapai were scouts and they followed Geronimo, they went way over to Texas. There were people from other tribes from Oklahoma who were scouts. One time when they had their camp over there in Texas, the people want to run a race. They ask the Yavapai, "You want to do that?" The Yavapai don't say anything first. Then my uncle *Pelhame* and *Pakakaya* and one *Tolkepaya* —I don't know his name—said, "You want to do that, all right, let's go." Next morning they start. They have a 150 miles race. *Pakakaya*, he is the one that leads the race. They go a long ways, and he slows down sometimes and looks back. He is the one who gets there first. My uncle and the *Tolkepaya* man coming right behind. The three of

National Anthropological Archives, Smithsonian Institution NAA INV 02048100   Photo by A. Frank Randall

Boy and *kathak* (burden basket). This excellent photo of an 1886 Yavapai camp is rich in detail. Two other water-carrying vessels, baskets made watertight with pitch, are at the boy's feet. Another *kathak* is seen on the roof of the middle wikiup, a Yavapai dwelling made of sticks and branches with some canvas cover. The boy is holding a bow and arrow, and a quail hangs. The other children wear no shoes. Cooking is done outside. Sitting on the ground, the women are wearing camp dresses, a style still worn in 2012 by older women and for special occasions. Walter J. Dickson (1900-1972), a Yavapai, was living in his wikiup at Fort McDowell in 1955. As late as 1981 some still lived there in brush shelters. The Yavapai were confined at the San Carlos Apache Reservation for 25 years, 1875-1900. This 1886 photo may have been taken at San Carlos. The famed Apache Geronimo, who kept escaping from San Carlos, was captured in 1886, the year of this photo.

them getting through first. All the other people, Apache, and Oklahoma Indians coming behind them.

Another time when they camped, a big colored man wanted to box. My people said, "No, we don't want to do that. You work for the government, and we are working for the government. We are not going to fight with you. We don't fight our own people. We are trying to fight with another people."

"Come on, come on," he said.

Pretty soon one Yavapai, Bill Waterman, got mad. "All right," he said, "get those things (gloves) off." Another colored man is getting gloves and trying to put them on Waterman. But he said, "I'm not going to use that." So the Black man said, "All right, I take it off." He came over and they started fighting. Waterman knocked him down. Bill Waterman is sure a good fighter.

When they chased Geronimo, the scouts were away for a long time, and their families stayed back over there in San Carlos. There is one man, his name is Willie Hunt. *Awila Quiva* is his Indian name. He is with the scouts chasing Geronimo. That time his old lady sometimes went over to the scout camp in San Carlos. When *Awila Quiva* came back from Texas, his wife had a baby, and she said to him, "Hey, that's your daughter. That's yours."

That baby was all dark and had short kinky hair like seeds on her head. From that they called her *Yachi*, that means "watermelon seeds." When you open a watermelon and you see the black seeds in there, that's how her hair looked like. The old man didn't say anything. "But anyways," she said, "I made a little mistake. When the baby comes out, I get a little *iqualla* (herb) and boil it and wash the baby. Next morning she is tanned like this. She is a real Yavapai, but I wash her with that *iqualla* and she changed color."

That *Yachi* is my relative, my *napi*, but she looks like a real Black lady. She has a voice like a Negro. When she laughs, it sound like a real Black people. And when there is music, she just like to dance around. She lived here in Fort McDowell. One time the superintendent—Wilson was his name—he told her that she has to get out of this place. He told her, she is a colored people, and colored people are not supposed to live with the Yavapai. She said, "All right, but these here are my relatives anyways."

So she left Fort McDowell and went up to Prescott. She stayed there for a while, and when she came back here, she got the prettiest boy in Fort McDowell. She got him, and they stayed together until he died. And after that she got another man, real good looking, too. But she never had any kids.

When my aunt Viola had her first baby over there in Prescott, my mother said to her, "Let's go and wash the baby with *iqualla*, and let's see what is going to be."

Viola said, "All right, go and get it." My mother gets lots of the weed and boil it, boil it. Put it in a can and wash the baby with it. They laugh and laugh and laugh when they do that.

They wash the head and everything, and roll the baby in a blanket and lay it over there. Pretty soon they come back and take the blanket off, and the baby never changed. My mother laughed and laughed, and Viola said, "She hasn't changed, yet."

And my grandmother asked my mother, "Why you do that?"

"Oh, I don't know. But anyways, that lady who has *Yachi*, she said the weed turn the baby in a different people. So I want to see if the baby turned into that. That's why we wash it."

The Yavapai stayed at San Carlos for more than 25 years. Then the government let them go out and go home. When they are ready to go home, the White people give the Yavapai some paper. They said, "When you go back to your own country, don't bother anything. Don't be bad. If you be good for three years, you can stay over there."

That time Marshall Pete was chief. He told the people, "25 years are up. Let's go home. We are prisoners for 25 years, and tomorrow it's going to be up. So we're going to get out. If we don't go back, they send us to Oklahoma or some place across the ocean. We should be going home." That's what he said, my father says. "You people follow me right now. I hitch my wagon already, grease it and everything. I'm going to go early in the morning. When you hear the wagon, follow me."

So, that's what they did. Left everything over there in San Carlos. Horses, chicken, turkey, cattle, leave it there and go home. My father left lots of cattle over there. And Yuma Frank, he is a chief, so he had lots of cattle, too. The White people had given five heads of cattle to each chief. To the other people maybe one or two heads of cattle. So the people had lots of cattle in the San Carlos mountains. But they just leave it there and come back. I asked my father, "Why you doing that for?"

"Oh," my father said, "Chief Pete, he said, if we stay here, they move us away, maybe across the ocean some place. Move us over that way. We don't want to go over there, that's why we come back. We don't want to lose our land." The White people sent Geronimo over there some place, so we are afraid they send us there, too.

People wanted to go home to their own country. My father said, "I left cattle over there (in San Carlos). But that cattle ain't worth my land. The land isn't going to wear out. I keep it all my life."

And my grandmother said, "I had a few head of cattle and a few head of sheep. And turkey and chicken. But when they want us to come back, that chicken hit me nothing. When they want us to come back, I feel like to fly." My grandmother said, when she was back over there in San Carlos, she sure was thinking of home always. "*Wigidjassa* (Four Peaks) and *Wigidjisawa* (Superstition Mountains), that is in my heart all the time. But anyways," she said, "when they let us loose from San Carlos, it hit me different. My father and my mother and my grandmother died in that cave over there. That's why I don't want to see that place *Wigidjassa* and *Wigidjisawa* any more. But I want to come back to my land. That's why I come back."

That land over there in San Carlos, the Mineral Strip, Marshall Pete leased it to the White people. White people find gold and all kinds of things on that Mineral Strip. And they pasture their cattle there. Marshall Pete leased that land, and two witnesses were with him. I don't know who the witnesses were. Marshall Pete was the one who got the paper. On that paper it said that this land belongs to the Yavapai. The Apache want to get that land all the time, and we don't know where that paper is. When the Yavapai moved back to their own country here, the Apache followed Marshall Pete and they killed him at *Chokasiva*, Rim Rock, near Camp Verde. We think they did it because they wanted that land over in San Carlos.

Marshall Pete was chief in San Carlos. His Indian name is *Pita*, "Short, Stumpy." White people call him "Pete."

Ohwalla Siutawa was another chief. They call him Mohave C-5 when he is scout. Mohave C-5 was grandpa from my father's side. And when Pete got killed he took over. He is chief of the *Wipukpa*. But he stayed not too long around. He got sick and died. After him there was another chief, but I don't know him.

Only a few Yavapai stayed back in San Carlos. Robert Roy, *Marikoka* we call him, he stayed in San Carlos. He is my relative, *kinya*. He got a big store, and he is a blacksmith. He fixed the wagons for the White people, wheels and everything. Some of the cattle which the Yavapai left behind, *Marikoka* got it.

When I was a young boy, I went over there to San Carlos with Sam Jimulla and Viola. We stayed over there for two weeks, and our relative *Marikoka* said, "When are you people coming to get the money from the lease and the cattle? That's your land, your cattle. You leased it out and took off. When are you coming for it?" But we never get the land back. The Apache have it already.

That time I like it over there. I was a cowboy, and they have lots of cattle there, and we work on it. That time I find I have lots of relatives over there, and I want to stay with them. "No, there is lots of Apache. Apache going to kill you," Viola said. "You going home." I want to stay with my relatives and Viola said, "We ask your grandmother, and if your grandmother says all right, we send you up here."

We go home and I ask my grandmother. "No, you can't stay over there. They are mean ones over there. They're going to kill you." I have lots of relatives over there, and I want to go. But she said, "No!"

When the Yavapai come back from San Carlos, those who come from around Camp Verde, they go over there. And some of them from around Clarkdale (*Savokalhulva*), they go back there. *Kewevkepaya* turn off and come down here to Fort McDowell. My grandmother is supposed to come down here. But she goes over to Prescott country (*Wahagsigiita*). Her old man is from over there. Many of the *Tolkepaya* went back to their country. They went over there, but they all died. When they come back from San Carlos and go back to their own country they all died of TB.

My father went to Camp Verde. Across the old bridge, right up on top of that little hill there, he stays maybe one week, maybe two weeks. But there is not very much to raise cattle or raise horses. So he talks to his wife, "What do you think, want to go to Fort McDowell?"

The lady said, "If you want to go there, it's all right. It's all right with me."

He comes down here on horseback. He used to have good horses. He came down along the river. I think he made it in one day from Camp Verde to here. He stays here about two, three days with Mike Nelson, his relative from his mother's side. And soon lots of these people here come together and they say, "Hey, you want to come down here? That's all right." They go around and tell everybody they have meeting. And in that meeting they vote to let my father stay here.

But that time when *Kewevkepaya* come back from San Carlos, they don't move in here to Fort McDowell right away. They had to live at the hills around here. Mexicans and White people lived in here. They lived here and planted things. My people then worked for these Mexicans and Whites. My mother said, the people came down from the hills and cut wheat for the Mexicans. My mama cut wheat for them, too. Work all day. But they don't pay them much. Maybe ten cents, maybe twenty cents. They give them some beans. And that's all we live on then: beans.

That time Yuma Frank is in Fort McDowell. Yuma Frank (*Kapalwa*) is *Tolkepaya*, but he is married to a *Kewevkepaya* lady. That's why he moved down to Fort McDowell. Yuma Frank knows how to talk well, so they know he makes a good chief.

One time the people were working for the Mexican and White farmers in the ditches at Fort McDowell. About noon they are ready to eat and get all together. Then Frank said, "Let's get three men and vote on them. The one who is going to have more votes, he is going to be chief. What do you think?" All the people said, "All right, that's good. Let's do that. We get three of them now."

Ovea Johnson got my father. George Dickens got Ovea Johnson. And my father got Yuma Frank. "All right, let's vote on them now."

They mark three lines on the ground, and each of the three men stands on one line. When they vote, two men go and stand with Ovea Johnson. Four men stand with my father. And the whole bunch of people stand with Yuma Frank. So Yuma Frank is going to be leader.

"OK," he said, "I don't know anything much. But you guys want me for leader. I'm going to say something two weeks from now."

Two weeks are coming. When they sit together again and eat, he said, "You people got me to lead you. You want me to do something for you. So I'm going to go to Washington. When we live here, we are going to own this land. This is what I'm going to ask them over there in Washington."

"All right," said the people.

Then he said, "Get everybody together this night, and tell me what you think. Tell all our people, the chief wants to go to Washington." That night they get together, and they all want him to go.

Yavapai Chief Yuma Frank (*Kapalwa*). National Anthropological Archives, Smithsonian Institution. NAA INV06431000 Photo by DeLancey W. Gill, June 1911.

Yuma Frank's wife (Mary Mischa), she wrote letters to Washington all the time. Asks for that land here. They get a letter that the government wants someone to go over to Washington about that land.

So Yuma Frank went to Washington.

That first time the chief goes over to Washington all alone. I don't know how he got there. His wife knew how to write. Maybe she gives a little note to her old man and the people show him the office in Washington. She didn't come along. Costs too much money.

He gets to that office in Washington and in that place it says, "No Smoking." He doesn't know that and he rolls himself a cigarette and starts smoking. A policeman is coming around and touch him, "Hey, you read that over there? There is nobody to smoke in here!" There was a Mexican behind him and he talks Mexican to Frank. Frank is a *Tolkepaya*, so he understands Mexican.

"You are not supposed to smoke here. But it's all right. What are you doing over here?"

The chief says, "I don't read nothing. I don't know anything. But I want to see the Indian office."

That Mexican said, "All right, I bring you over there. I'm working in there. Let's go." He takes him to that office, goes in and the Mexican tells the people in there. They tell Frank to sit over there. He keeps sitting and after a while the Mexican comes back. He gives him a meal ticket, gives him a room. Gives him a little money if he wants to go around and buy something.

"But," Frank says, "he takes me to the room, so I just stay there. I'm afraid somebody might kill me." So he is staying in that room. The Mexican had told him, about three more days, then they are going to have meeting. He stays three days in the room. He had a shower in there. So he goes and has a shower, then he lays in the bed and sleeps all day. And the next day and the next day. Every morning some man comes and gets him food.

Some morning somebody knocks the door. He opens it and the Mexican is there. He says, "They are going to start the meeting. So let's go." So Frank put on his good clothes and goes with him to the office. The Mexican said to Frank, "You get the land. Don't be afraid. I help you get it."

When they get to the office, the Mexican leads him over to the chair, right close to the White man. And the Mexican gets Frank's arm and he says, "That guy is coming a long way. He wants to say something. He is a Yavapai and he is a long ways from home." So they say, "All right, go up."

And the Mexican asks him, "What do you come here for? What do you want to do?"

Yuma Frank said, "We people have been Army scouts and we want to have that land." His wife wrote it down on the paper, I guess. So he said, "I got the paper here."

The Mexican said, "Give it to me." So he gives it to him and the Mexican takes it over to the White man, I think. But the government people say, Frank is only one. They think that's not right. "You come again. Get three, four others with you. Then it's all right. If you bring other men from your tribe, we'll see what we are going to do. We can't do anything now."

So he goes back home. The same day when he comes back from Washington the wife goes to the railroad depot with the horse. She knew when he comes back. The

Mexican wrote a letter to her. He sent it to the wife about two days before Frank comes back. So she goes over to Mesa to the depot. The train comes in, and there he is with the good clothes on him. They got those for him in the Indian Office in Washington.

She don't bring a wagon. Just a horse. That time the horses ate loco weed. They ate that kind and Frank's wagon horse died. So they got only one horse, and the lady saddled that up and got to the depot and met the man. They ride home double. The man in the front and lady in the back.

So he comes back here to Fort McDowell. He tells my father to call all the people together. So my father saddles his horse and tells all the people to get together. That time all the people used to come when they have meeting. They don't miss it like now. They all go to the meeting place and the chief talks, "I went to the office all right, but they want to see more people. So I want to get somebody with me. We want to go back to the Washington office."

Then he tells my father, "I want you to go with me."

My father said, "All right, I'll go."

"But anyways," the chief said to my father, "get another one." So he got George Dickens.

And the chief said, "Tom, you get another one. There is going to be four of us. Get another one!"

So my father got Silver Harney. That's his nephew. He is a good education man. He can read and write and talk English good. "I want to take him with me."

"All right."

And they had another meeting. They said, "It costs money if we go over there!"

So the people said, "We can get the money."

The chief said, "We are going to cut some wood and the ladies will make baskets. We will sell that. Lay that money away for us until we have the tickets. Then it's all right."

All the people said, "All right, we can do that." Then they said, "Let's vote who wants to do that, selling those things and get the money for the people who go over there." Everybody raise his hand up. Only one man don't raise his hand up, Sam Axe (*Palkahavo*). Sam Axe, he is the only one in there who don't raise his hand.

When the lady goes over to the depot in Mesa and asks for the tickets, how much is it going to be. They tell her and she comes back and tells everybody here.

Lots of them were cutting wood. Some cut cord wood and some cut post wood. They bring it to town in their wagon. That time you don't get much for wood. Three dollars for a cord, five cents for a post. Some of them plant things, squash and corn, raise turkey. They take it down to the city and sell it. The ladies make baskets. Take it to town and sell it. Put the money away, put the money away. And they get the money together.

I don't know how long, maybe over a month and they make the money. So the lady goes over to the depot again and the money is enough for the tickets. But the people, some of them say, "Let us get some more money for the people to use on the way. Maybe they want to buy something when they stop somewhere on the way. Eat at an eating place. Maybe they get a room to sleep over there in Washington. We get some more money." So they did. Over $250.00.

Then the chief tells everybody, "That's enough. We are going to go. You people don't tell the stockman we are going. Don't say anything to that man."

That stockman was the superintendent from the Indian Office. He told them, "Don't go over there to the Washington again! I'll put you in jail!" The chief don't say anything. Just shakes his shoulder. He always did like this with the superintendent.

They were ready to go. But before they go, Silver Harney died. Died just like that. My father told me, two ladies from here shake hands with him. And after that he died. My father told me, "Don't shake hands with these ladies." They witch Silver Harney and he died. So they got Charlie Dickens to go to Washington with them.

They get together in the morning. "I think we going to go this evening late," the chief told them. They take the wagon. The lady takes them over to the depot. But not all at one time. Some walk on for a little while and she picks them up on the way. They don't want that the superintendent sees them going there together. That's why they hide and walk one by one some way.

When the chief and the others are gone, the superintendent asks my father's wife, "Where is Tom gone?"

"I don't know. Maybe he make wood. Maybe he work in the ditch some place." So the big man goes up to the ditch, looks around and don't find nobody there. He sure gets mad. He comes down here and asks my father's wife again, "Where did he go?" She don't tell him. And pretty soon he goes to Yuma's wife and asks her.

She says, "I don't know where Frank is. They want to go to San Carlos. They were going to go to San Carlos. Maybe they are over there now."

"Ah," he says, "we'll see!" So he goes back.

When they go to Washington, that train is not very fast, they said. "I don't know how many nights we go through to get there," my father said. Sometimes they stop, sometimes they change car. They go on, go on, go on.

At Washington, that Mexican is still there, and he helps us. They go to that Mexican and Frank says, "I'm back. I bring a bunch of men here now."

"All right, we are going to have meeting tomorrow."

My father used to work pretty hard in the ditches and with the plow. So next day, when they have meeting and the White man sees his hands, he says, "This man here works pretty hard. If they want that place, we have to do something about that. We do something now, today." And then they tell them, "Wait for tomorrow." So next day they have meeting again. They look at the men's hands and all four of them have tough hands. "So you think you can do something on that land? All right, it's yours now."

Theodore Roosevelt (1858-1919) give that land. Theodore says, "I give you the military boundary line. Nobody going to bother you. You just keep that boundary line. It's yours now." They don't say how wide and how long it is. They say, they give us the military boundary line. They give my father the map and say, "This is the line." They mark it with a pencil. So my father knows the boundary line of our reservation is way out in the mountains. There are cement posts out in the mountains and on top of the posts it says, "Camp McDowell." My father looks for the posts and he finds the places. So he knows where the boundary line is. Later my father told me about it. He took me out, trying to show me all the way round the boundary line. It was way out in the mountains, in the McDowell Range. But that time I was young and I don't care much. I go back to Prescott. That military boundary line was there before we get the land as reservation. But nobody has that old map now.

That day, when they come back from Washington, Yuma Frank's wife takes the wagon over to Mesa and waits for them. She gets in there first in the morning. After a little while the train comes in, brings them back. On the way home, at Lehi, at the little Chinaman's grocery store, they stop and get some groceries: potatoes, beans, everything. My father always eats meat, so they get lots of meat. They come home about evening.

Then the chief tells my father, "Go around and tell all the people to come on over here tonight. There is a meeting here." So he did. He saddle his horse and start way down and back. They have the meeting.

That time we have no chair, no box to sit on. Just laying on the ground or sitting on the ground when there is meeting. And the chief told the people, "We come back from Washington, so we can tell you guys, we got the land now. That is our land now." And they get the paper and they make Leonard Hayes read it. They told him, "You read that for the people." He never did that before, but he did it that day.

He read it, "We got the land, this is our land now."

And my father said, Theodore Roosevelt told him, "Don't sell that land. Don't lease it. Don't give it away.

That's your land now. The military boundary line, that one is yours. Nobody going to bother you again."

Then the superintendent comes in that meeting and he asks them, "Why did you guys go over there to Washington?"

And the chief said, "We've been in Washington. We got that letter here. We got that land here now. This is our land now."

That superintendent, he talks pretty bad. So Mike Nelson told him to sit down. Mike Nelson was the first policeman. The government paid him. He don't talk English right, but he is a good policeman. He told the superintendent to sit down. And the chief said, "This here is an Indian meeting. You White man has nothing to say here."

So the superintendent sits down and keeps quiet.

In 1911 they try to move us out again. They try moving us down to the Salt River Reservation. The White people from the Indian Office say they want us to live close to town, so we can make money. They said, "If you plant something, you can sell it quick in town. There is lots of water right there. You can plant lots of corn and everything. Take it to town and bring it to the store and sell lots of that stuff." From here to Phoenix it takes all day in the wagon, and people can come back only the next day. So the government man said, "This is too much work for you guys. You drive in the wagon too much, that's why you get sick all the time."

When they tell that to Frank he is laughing. "Don't get fooled. If I'm around and the leader of you, you follow me. I'm going to tell you something right. They say you are going to make money down there at Salt River Reservation. But what are you going to sell to make money? How are you going to make money? Nothing down there to make money with."

He also said to the people, "What are you using for firewood down there? Over here we can get firewood anywhere. Nothing but *tahsilga* (a small, gray plant) down there. Here we can get firewood and sell it anytime we need money. Down there, where do we get wood to sell it? You live here, right in the middle of money. Nothing for us down there."

Then the people vote on it who wants to move down to the Salt River Reservation. Only eight want to go. All the others want to stay.

Before they get that land here, the people live in the hills. When they get the land, they all move in. It is our land now. But the White people always want to take it away from us. Keep on trying, keep on trying, keep on trying.

In 1912, I was here at Fort McDowell and we camped at Yuma Frank's place. I was just a boy then. That time a stockman was superintendent. That stockman wanted the people to fence a place here for cattle. He gathered the people for a meeting there where my father's house used to be. He asked them, "I want you to fence this place here up. Just a little. I'm going to put cattle in here. And when the cattle has calves in the spring and fall we give it to you guys. To you people, all of you. You say, 'all right,' and it's all right."

But Yuma Frank said, "No! I don't want no fence around my house. If you want to fence my land, fence the

156

whole country. Fence it all around the ocean. This is my home. But you are not going to fence my house."

Next time we come down here it was in 1913. That was when my mother died. Yuma Frank was pretty sick then. At the meeting he was laying on kind of a bed. Two little chairs had been put together with a board and a rope was put several times across. He was lying there and he told the people, "When that White man says, 'fence that place up,' don't let him do it. You are not going to get anything. You just lose the land if you do that. You are not going to have cattle, you are not going to have anything. So don't let them fence this up round your house. When I said 'no,' to him, don't say 'yes.' Every time when that man asks you, don't say 'yes.' Don't talk to him. Let him go home.

"That White man, when he talks, he talks like a snake. Puts his tongue out all the time, like a snake. Do you know the little hummingbird? When he wants to eat something, his mouth goes open all the time. That man's mouth is just like a hummingbird's mouth. Opens all the time when he wants something. Don't let him put that fence up. Get my word. You will get nothing. Only lose your land."

Then he said, "If you want a good man, a headman that tries to lead you guys, get Surrama." Surrama, that was my father. "Get him, nobody else."

After Yuma Frank died (about 1913 or 1914), my father went round and tell everybody to come down here. Gathered the meeting here. When everybody gets together, George Dickens said, "I'm going to be chief. I went to Washington anyways with Frank. He died and so I'm going to take his place. I've been in Washington, and that's why I'm going to take that job. I'm going to be the chief."

He called himself chief right there and nobody said anything that day. My father didn't say anything either. When George Dickens went away, he said to the people, "They want us to vote about that fencing of the land. When that stockman wants you to raise the hand up for the cattle, don't raise your hand up. I know they are not going to give us that cattle. I know it is not going to be true. I know how the White men are. That one just wants to get our land. He just wants to fence it up and say, 'this is your land.' That's what he is trying to do."

I come back again in 1914. George Dickens talked again to the people. He said, "We are going to be the richest people. We are going to have lots of cattle. I know, cattle breeds every fall and spring. He gives us maybe four, five heifers and we have five calves. In the fall five more. That is ten. In one year we have ten calves. Raise your hand and don't say 'no.' Say 'yes.'"

They have a meeting here again and that White man Cato Sells comes in there. "What are you going to say, George?" he says. "Like I told you, we want to put that fence up. I know your land is farther out there, but I'm going to fence this place around here and give you cattle in here. Give cattle to everyone of your people. This is going to be just a cattle fence."

And George said, "All right, all right! Everybody raise the hand up. We are going to have lots of cattle in a little while." So they raised their hands up. The rest of them said, "All right."

That cattle fence was made in 1915. They got through with it in 1916 and brought the cattle in all right. Lots of cattle. It has the government brand ID. No Indian brand.

Mike Harrison with early 1900s Dodge. Carolina Butler collection.

All the kids used to play with that cattle, trying to rope it. One time a bull got real mad and hooked Peter Harry's (*Romsa's*) horse. The guts are coming out. There is one old man, Sam Jack, *Homutalva*, he saw it. He pulled some hair out from the horse's tail. Punch a hole, punch a hole in the skin and sew the wound together with the hair. Maybe one week and that horse heals up all right. But the skin is kind of rough on that place. And *Romsa's* father, he said, "What's the matter with my horse? Right here the skin is kind of rough." I guess, Romsa don't tell his father. I don't think so.

I come back from Prescott in 1917. I ask my cousin Quinna Harris (Queena Harry), "Let's go over there and practice cattle roping again."

"There is no more cattle now, John."

"Where is it all gone?" I ask.

"The government took it away."

That same year the government took the cattle out again. Took the whole herd away and we got nothing. We get no cattle and we get no money either. We don't know where they take that cattle. At that time, when they take the cattle out again, Cato Sells left, too. Maybe that's the way he quit. Took the cattle and went off with it.

We got nothing but that fence here. And the government called it our "boundary line." And that is how again we lost our land.

When Yuma Frank died (about 1913 or 1914), they do everything like that. All bad things came up after Yuma Frank died. In 1916 they moved that cattle out and left us the fence. Call it our boundary line.

In 1920 they tried to move us out from that land altogether. There was one Yavapai man, Gilbert Davis. He was not chief, but he spoke English better than the others. So the government people talked to him to move the Yavapai out of the Fort McDowell reservation. Maybe the White people gave him a little money, too. The White people want to do something with our land here. So they want us to move out. They told that man, they would get a place for the people somewhere below Red Rock (Mount McDowell). They built irrigation ditches and headgates there and then told that man, "All right, we are ready now. Move all the people down here. Everything is ready."

So that man went around and told the others, "They want us to move down there."

The people asked him, "Who told the White people to fix that place down there for us? We don't want to move.

We are going to stay here. If you want to, you can move down there. We don't."

The White people hadn't asked the tribe. This one man spoke for the people and the people didn't know about it. So the people didn't go. Then the government people talked to the people here. But they said, "No, we can't go down there. We don't do it."

These White people had built ditches and the headgate down below Red Rock (Mount McDowell). They lost money on it, because the people here, they didn't want to move. So the government put that Yavapai man in jail. Montezuma (Carlos Montezuma, *Wassaja*) come up here to the trial. The Yavapai man didn't know what to say and nobody of the Indians knows what to say. So Montezuma helped them. But the government people want that Yavapai man to pay for the ditches and all the work. So that man sent a letter around to all the Yavapai asking for money. Sends it to Prescott, Mayer, Clarkdale, Cottonwood, Camp Verde, all over. He says, he goes over to Washington now and gets us some good stuff. "I'm going to get something good for you guys. You put up money, so I talk there in Washington." We believe it and put the money in. After 15 days or so, he wants money again. So we again collect money. I was a young man and working, so I put money in, too. I was then over in Prescott with my grandmother. Well, we put money in first, but it didn't cover the bills down there in Washington. So we get some more money together and that pays up all the bills.

That man came back, but he never said what he did for us over there in Washington. He died around 1938, but he never said anything what he did there.

It was in 1939 or 1940 that we lost that land where Fountain Hills is now. That time we have a meeting going on. We start early in the morning all the time. That time, when we have meeting, one White man comes down the road with his car. "Are you the president?" he asks me.

I said, "No."

"Who is the headman here?"

So I said, "Here is the man coming right over there."

This White man carried a paper in his hand and he called over to the headman. Talked to him. "Hm?" said the headman. Then he said, "All right, all right."

The White man brings the headman up to the car, to the hood, and puts the paper down there. "We want you to sign this paper," said the White man. "I'm going to build a shack over there. Not in here, inside the reservation, just outside. When I go hunting and get late, I want a place where I can stay. I don't want to bump into those chollas all the time when it's dark."

The headman only said, "Aha, aha." He didn't say anything else and put his name on that paper. And then the White man called me and asked me, "You want to put your name on it as witness?"

I said, "No, I can't do that."

Quinna Harris said, "No, can't do that. You are supposed to straighten it with the meeting, with the council. We can't do it outside of it." Quinna Harris talked English better than I do. He said, "I don't want to do that. I don't want to be witness for something I don't know." So nobody signed that paper for witness. Just him, the headman.

When the headman had signed, the White man patted him on the shoulder and said, "Oh, boy, this man knows everything. He sure is a smart headman!" Then he told him, "You know something? I give you the key to this shack I'm going to build. You can stay in that shack. You can stay in there any time." Then that White man went to his car and drove off.

Later we have a sweat bath and I go over there. Then the headman said to me, "You know what that White man said? He will build a house over there, so we can stop in any time. He is going to give me the key. I can't wait getting the key."

Well, we're still waiting for that key. When I look over there, I don't see much of a shack. There is a big city now. It doesn't look like they let me have it, and it doesn't look like they let me go in there either.

White people are crooked like a dog's hind leg. They sure can fool you any time. When they want to steal something, they get it the easy way. They talk crooked and get it.

This little strip of land which is left to us, it is too small for a fly to turn. But White people never leave us in peace. They are out all the time to take that little bit of land away from us.

But our land goes way out beyond that fence. Lots of kids are coming up. My relatives are coming up born. We need the land outside the fence. That's what I want, my land outside the fence.

Some Indians down in Oklahoma, they fight for the land and that's how they got it. Same down at Supai (Havasupai Indians). You don't fight, you don't get anything. I want my boundary line back. Maybe it is too late to bring that out. But I don't stop talking about the land.

My mother's sister's old man, he got the reservation over in Prescott. Sam Jimulla, I learned from him to be a cowboy. He is a good man. *Jimulla*, that means "Red Ant."

I was with him when he got that reservation. In 1930. We were going to get wood, and a car comes over there and stops. So I put the motor off and the man from that car says, "Hey, Sam." He sets a little table up, and he has papers in there. Kind of a roll.

"You see this," the man says, "this line from here, this way around to Mexico and Gallup, this is Indian land. If you want to sign your name, we will give you land there."

Sam said, "Wait a little. Maybe you come back next week or next month. Then I can tell you something."

The White man said, "All right Sam," and he took off. That man works for the government.

Sam told him, "I let you know when I'm ready."

About one month, I guess, that man come back again. Sam, he don't go to school and he talks just a little bit. The man said, "Sam, are you ready now?"

"Yes," he said, "I am ready. I am ready to say something."

"All right, say it."

Sam said, "You see this land here? Indians live here all the time. You send us from here to San Carlos. When they turn us loose from San Carlos, the people went back to where they used to be. So," Sam said, "I can't go no place. I can't leave. Right here in Prescott is my home.

My father's home, my father's grandfather's home. That's why I stay right here."

"All right," the government man said, "I take you down to the big man's office."

They go to that office and the man who takes care of that big man said, "You can't bring that big man out." There was a little funnel in the wall and he talked in that. Kind like a telephone. He talked through that thing with the big man. Then the big man come out. He is a big man! He got lots of buttons all over. Look like danger for me. Then that big man and the other government man said, "All right, that land you own, we talk about that."

Then he put out a map on a little table. He said, "We are going to fence that land up for you. Don't say you got no money. Tell your people to fence it up. So we are going to give you that land. Just go ahead and tell them to build that fence." So Sam did.

I was supposed to live there with them in Prescott. But I come down here in 1930 and so I lost my place over there. I was laid off by the city of Prescott. Lost my job. I moved right the next day. I come down here to Fort McDowell, to my father, and I stay here.

The government man had tried to move Sam to another place. But Sam, he said "no" to the man. He said, "I can't do it, I can't leave." If Sam don't say anything, they move him out. But he says, "This is my land." So he stays in there and he got the land.

Oral History of the Yavapai

Chapter 19

◆

When Everything Began

I don't know about the White people. I don't know who they are, where they come from. We people don't come from nowhere across the ocean. We were raised right here in this country. We come out at Sedona, the middle of the world. This is our home.

My people used to teach the kids every day about these things. Teach them about everything. In that cave where they kill my people, when they get together there, they used to teach the kids. Tell them how to live, how to do everything, how to get round. My grandmother used to tell me these things every day, every night. She told me how we got raised in Sedona. We call Sedona *Wipuk*. *Puk*, that's a kind of a stone. *Wipuk*, that means "below that kind of mountain." Some of my people, they call themselves *Wipukpa*. That's the ones who live up there around Sedona. My father was a *Wipukpa*. My grandmother and my mother, they live around here. Four Peaks and

Superstition. They were *Kewevkepaya*. All Yavapai come from Sedona first. But in time they spread around.

Across the river at Camp Verde, maybe four, five miles north from there is Montezuma Well. We call it *Ahagaskiaywa*. This lake has no bottom and underneath the water spreads out wide. That's where people come out first.

Navajos and Hopis and those people up that way, they come back and get water from Montezuma Well. Just get that and pray. But my people, when a baby comes out, they get that water. Get that water and give him the first bath. Only those of my people who live around there. Sure nobody bathed me, when I come out. Me, they threw in the trash. But that's how I live a long time, I guess.

Ahagaskiaywa (Montezuma Well), 2011. Photo by Elias Butler.

Long time ago, there was no water in that lake. People were living down there. And one chief, the one who is around the world first is down there. He has a daughter, and when the daughter is asleep the leg was showing. He was standing over there and feeling on her. The daughter was laying asleep, but she open the eyes a little bit. She sees that he is touching her and she don't like it. He did something wrong to the own daughter. He did that four times. So the daughter got mad. She said, "You are not supposed to do anything dirty like that. So I'm going down the river there."

There was a river running and there was a log across it. He goes there every morning. Goes there every morning. Goes there every morning. Goes there for the toilet.

There is a real big frog down the river. He is sitting there. And the frog said to the girl, "What are you thinking? You are thinking pretty bad. You want to do bad to your father. I help you. In the morning the father goes over there to the water. Then you turn in me. And when he goes to the toilet, you eat that. Then he dies."

And she did. The daughter turned into a frog and goes under the water. She was sitting there under the log and he go to the toilet and the daughter swallow that every time. Four times. The old man got sick. He got sick and nobody can do anything. The old man got bloat. Bloat all over.

And one medicine man sing a blackroot song. He told the old man, "I can't do anything. Too late now. You going to blow out and bust. And that's going to be it. That's the end." The medicine man can't do anything. The old man is going down, going down, going down. He knows he is going to die and he knows a flood is coming. The daughter got mad and make the father sick and she wants to kill all the people. She is going to make a flood. The old man wants the people to get out. When he was sick and laying there and he know he can't make it, he said to the people, "When I go, burn me right away. But put my head that way where the morning come. Put me that way. Put a little damp dirt right there at the heart. And watch it pretty close. When it looks like something is going to come out, get some more damp dirt. All around, all around, all around. When something comes up, put some more water around. Don't put too much! I don't know how it is going to go, but I know the coyote is coming on. Go and send the coyote some place."

So when the old man died, the people asked the cat, "You want to go to the other people over there? We want them to come over here."

The dog (coyote) said, "The cat can't run. I can go."

They want him to do just that, but he doesn't know. And they said, "All right."

"I'll go, I'll go," he said, running off.

The coyote runs over three, four ridges. At the last one he looks, and he sees smoke go up. "I wonder why they do that for?"

The people stand around because they know the coyote wants to get the heart. That's why they block it. The fire burn the body up. Just a little piece is left in there. The coyote comes and he runs around behind the people, "Let me stand in there and cry! Let me stand in there and cry!"

There is only one short man standing there, the turtle. We call him *kàbít*. That was the person a little too short.

The coyote runs around, runs around, runs around and pretty soon he sees that little, short man and jumps over him. The heart is almost burned up. Just a little piece left. The coyote grabs it, runs away and jumps back over the same place. Eat it, right away, too. That's how the coyote eat dead people now. It's a bad one, that coyote!

After a while when everything is gone, the people say, "The chief said, 'If I go, you burn me up. And when everything is gone, you put a little dirt right there at my heart.' Well, that's what he wanted us to do. So we are going to do it and we will wait and see." They put some dirt in there where the heart should be and pile it.

Corn come up. Come up, come up, come up, up to the top. Real big corn. It grows up to this side of the well. Finally one man go up that corn and check it. He see this is a good world up there. "There is another world up there, so we can go up there."

One medicine man know there is lots of water coming already. And that sick old man had told them, "You go up there when I go." So the people go up on that corn. Go round, go round, and where the ears of the corn come out, between there, they sleep in there. The turtle almost got caught in there. He is short, can't go fast. But he made it up. I don't know how many nights they come up. Everybody come up on top there. Lots of people come from there, quail, rabbits, jackrabbits. And at that time when they come up, they all speak Yavapai. They get up on top. They look back and the water is coming. That lady make the water come up. The frog and the lady made the water come up.

The flood is in the Well. But the water don't come out. Just stays level in there.

That corn that came out from Montezuma Well, we get the seeds from there first, I think. Blue and white and red and black. And the people, when they got out from there, they made some corn gravy. Give it to everybody. Only the fly, the *thamburgka*, they didn't give it to him. The fly was sitting there and they didn't give him any gravy. They get more, they get more and they give him nothing. So there is no more gravy now. The fly get mad and get in some rock crack there. "I don't know why they don't give me the gravy. I'll go and burn the world." And he start fire. Rub the hands, rub the hands and rub the hands, and pretty soon he start fire and burn the whole world.

Can't do anything. Start fire already. Fly away. Fly away up there someplace.

That fire kill all the people. There is a little weed, dry leaves on top. The rabbit asked him, "When the fire hit you, it goes right over the top?"

That weed said, "Yes."

The rabbit said, "Can I go under you?"

The weed said, "Yes, sure."

So the rabbit went under. But there is a little place on the rabbit. You can see that. That's where the fire hit him.

And another one, the bobcat, he goes to the cattail, the water weed. The bobcat said, "Can I go under you?"

The cattail said, "All right, go under me. Go ahead."

So he goes under that. Where the fire hit the bobcat, that's where he has those marks on the fur.

The wolf go in the rock crack. Go in the hole there. The smoke hit him and make the wolf kind of brown.

The snake asked everything, everything, looked for a place. He went under a big hole. The snake rolls in the dirt. But some dirt got hot and made those black marks on the snake—the diamond marks.

One old lady got out. That lady is a beaver. That's the one who stay under water and that's the one who live. And when she came out, she found coal and she make earrings with that. After that they call her *Ochikasmalga*, "burnt coal earrings." After the fire we come out from this beaver lady. But that lady don't know much.

After some time there come another flood. The second time when the world gets flooded, it is just rain water. People do something wrong, and the rain comes. There is only two of them that come out from the flood. A girl and the woodpecker.

When the flood starts, people put that girl in a hollow cottonwood log. They put food into that log for her. Put a small hole in it. The woodpecker made that hole in the log. They made room enough to put lots of food stuff in there. Some kinds of seeds, jerky meat. But she can't make fire in there. She has to eat that food raw. The people who put her in there, they said, "Don't use the food right away. Wait when you feel it that there is a lake." They told her, "The flood will raise you. You will hit the sky. You will hear the noise when the log hits the sky. But just lay still. If you lay still, you will get out in the end."

People glued that log together with pitch. *Ahpihl*, they used. My grandmother thinks, the girl lay in there 40 days and 40 nights. Swim in the water 40 days and 40 nights.

So she lay still in there all the time. After some time the water went down. The girl had a dove with her, and she sent that dove out. She sent her out and the dove come down with a little weed. So the water was gone. There at Sedona, there is a high place. When the water went dry, the log hit the high place. This is the highest place all around. That's why the log stopped right there.

There the girl came out from the log. We call her *Kamalapukwia*. That means "Old Lady White Stone." She had a white stone. And that white stone is the one which protects the women. Her name means she got that kind of stone. She is the first woman on earth, and she got that stone. She is the first woman, and we come from her. She came out at Sedona, and that's where all the Indians come from.

And the other one, the woodpecker, he got out from the flood. We call him *cùkoó*. When the water comes up, he sticks his beak in the sky. Hangs there until the water goes down all the way. And when he hangs there, the water bubbles, and wear out the end of the tail. His tail looks kind of worn now. And now he is the one who always makes holes in trees and sleeps in there. But after they get out from the flood, they don't stay together, the woodpecker and the girl. He goes different places.

Kamalapukwia lived in a cave in Sedona. *Kamalapukwia* was all alone. One morning she ran over there to Mingus Mountain. Lay down there before the sun came up. The sun comes up and hits her inside. After that she went to that cave where the water drips down all the time. She lay down there and the water came down and hit her. Made her a baby. A little girl.

When that girl came to age, *Kamalapukwia* said to her, "Daughter, they did that and you come up. You go over there and do like I did. So we have another people." They were only two people. So they were lonely and wanted another human. The girl said, "All right." She went up Mingus Mountain and lay down there. That's the highest mountain around there, and that's where the sun comes first in the morning. But the sun did not hit her. Then her mother said, "Run down over there where the water drips, at the cave in Sedona. Lay under there, same way you did up there on the mountain." So the girl did. Went over to the cave where the water drips down. The water came, but he saw it is his own daughter. So he stopped the water halfways. The girl told that to her mother. But the old lady said, "All right, we'll fix it. I know how. Next morning you go up on the mountain again and do the same thing and I help you."

Wipuk (Sedona) cave. Late 1970s photo by Sigrid Khera.

Before the sun comes up the girl lay there, and the old woman on top of her. When the sun comes out, the old woman quickly move to the side, and he hits the girl. Then they go over there where the water drips down. The old lady made her daughter lay there, and she was laying on top. When the water came down, she pulled over and it went into the girl. She got pregnant, and when she got the little baby, it was a boy: *Sakarakaamche*.

When that boy was still a baby, a bad eagle killed his mother. An eagle lived up there on a mountain and eat anybody under him. *Sakarakaamche's* mother gathered wild spinach down there below the mountain. The eagle saw the lady down there, came down and get her. Take her up on top of the mountain where the two eaglets are and eat her all. Now there were only two of them. The old lady *Kamalapukwia*, and the little boy *Sakarakaamche*. The old lady raised the little boy.

In those days all kinds of animals eat people. Bear, owl, bull, eagle. They were bad ones at that time. When *Sakarakaamche* got a little older he wanted some bamboo to make arrows. That bamboo grew at some place where a big bear lives. The grandmother told *Sakarakaamche,* "Don't go over there, that bear is a mean one. He'll eat you."

But *Sakarakaamche* goes to that place and the bear comes out. *Sakarakaamche* said, "Wait, wait, I have a grandma over there. I want you to go over there and stay with her, marry her." Then he goes to that place and cut a lot of bamboo. Good, straight ones. Takes them over to the camp, to the cave where his grandmother lives. The old lady lays in there. *Sakarakaamche* takes the bear with him and goes into the cave.

Wipuk (Sedona) cave. Late 1970s photo by Sigrid Khera.

"Hey, grandmother, go and get my bamboo out there."

She goes out and looks and the bear is laying there in front of the cave. She goes in the cave again and says to *Sakarakaamche*, "Hey, that's what I told you. The bear has come after you. He is right here."

"No," said *Sakarakaamche*, "I bring him for you."

The old lady said, "All right, all right."

They got the bear into the cave and he stays with them. Sleeps all the time. When he is asleep the old lady tries to tickle him. All over, all over, all over, and he says nothing. Then she tickles him in the armpit. "Ahhh," he laughed. The heart is right there. They know it now.

Then they go and call the old man bear. Holler that there is something over there. So he jumps up and runs this way, and *Sakarakaamche* stands behind the corner. When the bear gets round the corner, *Sakarakaamche* stabs the bear in his heart with a long knife. Kills the bear.

Then *Sakarakaamche* cuts him into many pieces. Throws the pieces away, throws them away, scattered all around the mountains. And now the bears don't stay in one place anymore. The bear doesn't grow just in one place anymore. Grows all around the mountains now. There used to be one bear and it stayed at one place all the time. But *Sakarakaamche* killed that one, cut the body up and threw the pieces all around. And now bear grows all around. Way out in the mountains, in the pine.

After that Sakarakaamche asked the old lady where he could get a *mawal*. A *mawal* is that little stick they put at the end of the bamboo arrow.

"Where is that kind around here, grandmother?" asked *Sakarakaamche*.

The old woman said, "It's down in there. But there is an owl in there. Sure a mean one. He will kill you right away."

"No," he said, "I'll try it grandmother. I'll try it."

"No, no," she said, "don't go. That owl down there is pretty mean."

But *Sakarakaamche* said, "I'm going over there anyways."

And *Sakarakaamche* goes over there to the owl's place, and the owl is sitting there sleeping. *Sakarakaamche* stands there and watches. Then he goes in, and tries to cut some of these things for a *mawal*. The owl wakes up and comes down and sure is going to kill him. Tries to grab him, tries to claw him.

"Hey," said *Sakarakaamche*, "wait a minute *nikó*. I have a grandma down there. I want you to go down there and stay with her, marry her."

"All right," said the owl. "All right, cut the good ones for your *mawal*. Here in the middle is a straight one for the boy. Pack it!"

And *Sakarakaamche* takes it and goes back to the camp. Goes into the cave. "Grandmother, I got it over there. Peel it, and cut it for me!"

"All right."

She goes out to get the things and the owl is sitting there outside. The grandmother runs back. "Grandson, come in, the owl is sitting right there."

"No, no," said *Sakarakaamche*, "that owl is for you. I bring him over here, he is going to stay and help us."

"All right, all right."

And the old lady goes and gets the thing for the *mawal*, and the owl comes in. The grandmother peels the wood, peels it, peels it. Straightens it, straightens it, straightens it. But the owl sleeps all the time. The grandmother tickles him all over. Like she did to the bear. Tickles him all over, all over, all over. Pretty soon she scratches his feet a little bit. The owl laughs, "*hehehehe.*" That's the heart down there. Now they know it.

Then the old lady told the owl, "Go to sleep. We sleep, too." So the owl went to sleep again real fast. Then *Sakarakaamche* takes stickers, iron stickers. I don't know where he got them from. They make these stickers real hot at the fire and put them into the ground. And pretty soon the old woman hollers, "Hey, something is over there, it's going to kill us. Get up!"

The owl jumps up and tries to run out. "Ayayayaa!" he made, and went down.

Sakarakaamche chopped his head off and cut him all to little pieces. Like he did with the bear. He threw the pieces away, into the mountains. Now the owl doesn't stay at one place anymore. There are owls all over. That big owl used to kill and eat people. It had big, stout claws. When owls grow again from the cut-up pieces of the big owl, they grow much smaller. The way they are now.

There was a wild mulberry tree, *bomo'a*, we call it. *Sakarakaamche* wanted that wood for a bow. He wanted to go and get it. The grandmother said, "No, you can't do it. It grows in the middle between two rocks. These rocks go back and forth all the time. When you go in there, they will smash you. They go back and forth like a pump."

But he goes over there. The scorpion, *ishtequalka*, saw him walking there. That scorpion lives in the rock cracks.

"Where are you going?" he asked *Sakarakaamche*.

Sakarakaamche goes over there and looks, looks, looks. Can't see anything. Then he looks down into that little rock hole and sees the scorpion.

"Where are you going? What are you going to do?" the scorpion asked again.

Sakarakaamche said, "I want to make bow and arrow. I want to go over there, to those rocks and get the wood for my bow. My grandmother said the wood for the bow is growing over there."

"It grows in there all right," the scorpion said, "but the rocks go back and forth. It is going to smash you if you go in. But anyways, I'm going to tell you. I want to help you to that wood. That rock doesn't stand still. You can't go over there and get it like that. But you know the deer's horn? The deers lose them. You take a two-pointed buckhorn and put it across between those rocks."

He gave a deer horn to *Sakarakaamche*, and *Sakarakaamche* put it between these two rocks, and the rocks cannot move anymore. They just stay. So he goes and gets the wood for his bow.

Sakarakaamche kills everything that is mean, and cuts it up. *Sakarakaamche* cleans up everything around.

Sakarakaamche had the arrow. His grandmother said, "You can't straighten it when you hold it like this. You need a rock, *ataniwoyi*."

That's a blue rock and it has a groove. You put that rock in the fire and then straighten the arrow in that. The grandmother said, "No, you can't get that *ataniwoyi*. The snake, the red racer is there where that stone is. Nobody can get there."

Sakarakaamche goes over there for the *ataniwoyi*. The snake comes out. *Sakarakaamche* says, "Wait a minute, I want you to stay with my grandmother."

The snake said, "All right, what do you want?"

"I want the *ataniwoyi*."

"All right," said the snake.

They go home. *Sakarakaamche* leaves the snake right there where they live. The grandmother goes and gets that rock, and *Sakarakaamche* wants her to fix the arrow for him. The snake leaps all the time. But the next morning the snake feels like he is going to go to sleep. The snake crawls around and then goes to sleep. *Sakarakaamche* looks at them, takes a knife and cut his head off. Cut the snake all to pieces and throws them all around. Now that snake is not only at one place, it is scattered around. That way now there are snakes all over.

One day *Sakarakaamche* asked the grandmother, "You call me grandson all the time. I like to know why." Then he says, "You know, when my mother is your daughter, you call me 'grandson.' But I don't have a mother."

But the old lady, she didn't tell him. She just walked away.

Now *Sakarakaamche* had bow and arrow. He was going to shoot quail. *Sakarakaamche* goes around and around until he sees some quails. He goes in front of them, but they move away. So he goes around, but they move away. Finally he sees one in the open, and shoots her.

"What do you do that for, grandson?" said the quail. "You hurt me. You hit me badly."

"Well," said *Sakarakaamche*, "I'll fix it for you."

And he took blackroot and sang the blackroot song over the quail and that way made the quail's leg all right. That's why the quail's legs are black. *Sakarakaamche* got that blackroot song from when he got born. He got it from his father. His father is the Cloud, the Rain, the Lightning.

And that quail then said to him, "All right, let's sit over there and I want to tell you something."

They get up on a rock and sit there. "You want to know why you have no mother? I go and tell you now. You have a mother! Your grandmother's daughter is your mother. But there is a bad one around, an eagle up there, and he killed your mother. You see that high mountain up there? That's where that eagle lives. That's the one who killed your mother. When you were just a little, little boy, that eagle killed your mother. Your grandmother told you about that?"

"No."

Sakarakaamche sure got mad and went back to the old lady. Lay there and don't eat nothing for four days. The grandmother asked, "Did someone tell you something?"

And *Sakarakaamche* said, "Somebody told me I have a mother. But the eagle killed her. But you don't tell me! Why you don't tell me? I'm going to kill that eagle."

The grandmother starts crying. "I know it. That's what he did."

The old lady did not tell him about the eagle. She was afraid, and she did not want the boy get killed. But lots of people tell *Sakarakaamche*, "That eagle over there eat your mother."

One day *Sakarakaamche* saw a dove and she was flying away all the time. He shoots her, and she falls down. The dove made, "Ayayayay! What you do that for, grandson?"

"All right," said *Sakarakaamche*, "I'm going to fix the leg for you, and you are going to walk around again."

"If you get me up, I'm going to tell you something," said the dove.

"All right."

Sakarakaamche took some blackroot and put it over the legs and the legs got all right. That's why the legs of the dove are kind of red. Then they sit over there on a rock.

The dove said, "That eagle killed your mother. He lives right up there. But you cannot go up there. I'm telling you what to do. There is a bull laying over there. You kill that bull. But you can't just go over there and kill him. I tell you something: break those weeds, *okaja*. Break four of them. Shoot one up. And another one over there, another

183

one over there, another one over there —you shoot at four places. When the bull gets up, go there where he lays, and you'll get him. When you get him, take these wild grape leaves, put the bull's blood in and hang them all over you. Make a vest out of the bull's hide. Make the rope hold it together tight. Make a handle on that vest. Turn over to your back. The eagle won't get you three times. But when he is coming the fourth time turn over the other way where the place of the handle is."

The name of this bull was *aquakata kiega*. That means "cow that lay down all the time." It is a great, big bull. Kills anything and eats it. There is a place between Cottonwood and Sedona where that bull used to lay. *Matselehedad*, that's what we call that place. It is a sandy place with just one tiny tree there. The bull used to lie there and whenever he saw smoke somewhere, he ran over there and ate the people at that fire.

Sakarakaamche went to the river and got four of those weeds, *okadya*. Use them as arrows, and shoot them into four different places in the mountains. First one hit a pine tree and it burned. When the bull saw the fire, he thought people were over there and he ran to that pine tree. Then another pine tree was burning and the bull ran over there.

Then another one, and another one. Four times.

While he was away, the animals were digging a tunnel to the place where he lay. All of the diggers helped. The squirrels, the badgers, the rat, the gopher, the mouse. First came the little animals digging, then the bigger ones. The badger is the last, and he makes the tunnel bigger.

When that bull came back, the mouse went into that tunnel and started to take the hair off from the bull. Cut the hair off where the bull's heart is.

The bull asked the mouse, "What are you doing that for?"

The mouse said, "My kids are going to be cold. I want to make a bed for them with that wool."

"All right, take it off."

And the bull rolled over so that the mouse could get the hair. So the mouse takes it, takes, and takes it. Makes it plain where the bull's heart is.

The fourth time the bull comes back, that little bit of a bird, the hummingbird, we call it *minamina*, was sitting over there. The bull didn't see him because he was too small. He was sitting, and then came down here. He was telling *Sakarakaamche* that the bull was back. The people heat an iron. Make it red hot. I don't know where they get that iron from, but anyways they had it. *Sakarakaamche* gets in there into that tunnel. Rest of the people runs away pretty quick. The bull sits there and *Sakarakaamche* comes through the tunnel with the hot iron. He hit him right down under the shoulder, there where the heart is. And then *Sakarakaamche* goes back, back through the tunnel, and the bull almost get him. That bull had long horns, and he tried to get *Sakarakaamche* with his horns. Push them into the tunnel. Then that bull stopped there and died.

Then *Sakarakaamche* cut that bull up, and got all the blood. He made a vest out of the hide. Put it all over him. Put a handle on the vest. Then he took wild grape leaves. We call them *etcheéka*. He put the blood into these grape leaves, and tied them all over the vest. Then *Sakarakaamche* threw around the pieces of the bull. And now there is just cattle around. Bulls are no longer that mean. Don't eat people now.

Then *Sakarakaamche* lay down with his back up and shhhhht, the big eagle come. But *Sakarakaamche* had cut that vest tight, so the eagle missed him. There was nothing to hold on. Three times the eagle missed him. The fourth time *Sakarakaamche* lay on his back, and put a handle on his vest. Made a hole in it, so the eagle could grab him and take him up to his nest. He did want him try three times for nothing, so that he gives out. Get that eagle weak. That's why he let him get up the fourth time only.

There were two little eagles up there. "All right," the eagle said to them, "I killed something. I bring you meat. Eat it."

The kids said, "All right."

And pretty soon the eagle goes to get another meat. The eaglets were going to eat *Sakarakaamche*, but he turns round and makes "Shhht." So they never touch him.

Two times the eagle comes back, and the eaglets haven't eaten *Sakarakaamche*. The old eagle asks them, "Why don't you eat the meat I brought for you?"

"We try to go up to it and it always makes 'shhh.' So we don't know what is wrong."

"Oh, that's because it is rotten. Lots of air in the stomach."

The eagle takes *Sakarakaamche* and shakes him around. Throws him on a rock, throws him down. There is lots of blood all around again.

"I leave you for a little while," says the eagle, "you can eat that meat now."

Eagle Rock where *Sakarakaamche* killed the eagles who had killed his mother. And he also pushed the mountain down. Now called Courthouse Butte. Photo by Elias Butler, 2011.

Pretty soon the eagle went off again. *Sakarakaamche* went up and asked the eagle kids, "Where does your father stop, when he comes back?"

"There, where he sat. He sits there all the time. He sits there and looks round, looks round, looks round. Then straightens his feathers. This side, then this side. Puts his head way under the wings. He always does that."

"All right," said *Sakarakaamche*, "when he comes back, don't say anything or I chop your heads off."

Then the big eagle comes back and he asks the kids, "Why don't you eat that meat?"

"Oh," they said, "we are going to start now."

"All right," he said, and sat down on the rim. He sat there and looked round, looked round, looked round, looked round, just as the kids had said. Then he straightened his feathers. This side, then this side. Put his head under the wing. Then *Sakarakaamche* chopped his head off and threw it down the bluff.

Sakarakaamche asks the kids again, "Where does your mother sit when she comes back from the hunting?"

"Right here, where that cedar tree is. That little cedar here. She sits on it long, long time. Looks round, looks round, looks round, looks round, looks round, looks round. Straightens her feathers, puts her head underneath her wings."

"All right, don't tell your mother I talk with you, or I throw you down the hole."

Just then the old woman eagle comes up and says to the kids, "I thought you guys fell off the bluff."

"No," they said, "we are just sitting here. We are just playing here. We go no place. We are going to eat this here pretty soon. We are not hungry, but we will eat it pretty soon."

"All right," she said.

Then the woman eagle was sitting at the rim and looked around, looked around, looked around, looked around. Straightened her feathers this side, that side, put her head underneath her wings. *Sakarakaamche* comes up and chops her head off. Throws it down where the first eagle's is. Then he gets the kids. Chops their heads off and throws them down, down. All four eagles are gone now.

Now he was sitting there on that big mountain. Singing the blackroot song and trying to push the mountain down. He keeps his eyes shut, and the mountain go down. But pretty slow. It don't go down all the way because he opens his eyes. Just leave the mountain like that.

He is looking around, and there is only one people down there. The bat. There is lots of green leaves, spinach down there. She is getting that all the time. That eagle used to kill anyone there. But not that bat, the *kanpanka*. The eagle never take her. No good. That old woman stinks too much. Too much water running out of her. That's why the eagle don't get that woman.

Sakarakaamche sees the bat. The old lady is down there with her burden basket, with her *kathak*, and he hollers at her, "Hey, grandma, come up and get me!"

Pretty soon she looks around and she sees him up there on the mountain. He is waving down to her and she says, "What are you doing up there where that man, that mean one is?"

But he said, "Just come up *kollah*, grandma, and get me."

Now this old lady came up to *Sakarakaamche* with her *kathak*, her burden basket. Tsk, tsk, tsk, goes up, goes up—all to the top. There is a crack in that mountain from the bottom up to the top. The old lady bat comes up in that crack. The mountain is too steep to come up straight, so she jumps from one side to the other in that crack. Finally she gets up there.

"What are you doing up there?" she asks. "This one here is a bad place."

"I'm just staying here," said *Sakarakaamche*.

"All these eagles, where are they?" the old lady asked.

"I killed all those eagles, and I threw them down here," said *Sakarakaamche*. "You take me down there and I show you."

189

Then he said, "All right, bring me down in your *kathak*."

But the string of the basket was sure a thin one. Real skinny. "I wonder how I will sit in there," he said. *Sakarakaamche* thinks it is not very good to go down in such a thing. It will not hold.

"Oh," she says, "this one is pretty stout." Then she says, "I'm going to make it stouter." She pulls one hair out from her chest to make the string tighter. But he still doesn't believe it yet that it will hold.

"You think you take me down?" he asks her.

"Yeah, sure. I'm going to show you."

There is a big, blue stone up there on the mountain, a *wi havasue*. When the eagles brought people up there, they swing them on that rock. Kill them. That's why they got that big rock up there. She rolls that rock in the basket. Roll it in, and carry it. Rolls it around in the *kathak*, and dances around, dances around and it doesn't break.

"All right," he says. "I'm going to get in there now."

And when he is ready to come into that *kathak*, the old lady tells him, "Close your eyes and don't open them. Just close them, close them till I get down there. Just when I tell you to open the eyes, when we stop, then you open your eyes. Don't open them before we get down."

"All right."

He is sitting there and closes his eyes, closes his eyes. They go down—deng, deng, deng—a long way, long way.

"I wonder where my grandmother goes?" he said to himself. He opens his eyes a little bit and that string bust. Hit the old lady on the leg, threw her down so she broke all to pieces. Broke the legs, broke the wings, broke her all over. She lays there like this and cries.

"That's what I told you," she says, "don't open your eyes. I know you open your eyes."

"I opened my eyes," he said. "But I go and fix you. Don't cry, grandmother."

He sings the blackroot song over the old lady. Rolls some blackroot on his chest, get the grease from his chest. He takes that grease, because his body helps healing the people. And where the bones broke he rolls it on, and puts everything right. When he fixes that bat, he pushes the bones together again. These bones were kind of old, because the bat was an old lady. But he prays, sings, and blows on her. And that lady comes up again. You can tell where the broken pieces were. You see a lot of joints. That's the way *Sakarakaamche* fixed it.

"All right, grandmother. I want to show you where I throw that eagle down there." The eagle is laying there and she says, "Pull these feathers off for me."

"All right."

He pulls the feathers off, puts the fine ones around the *kathak*. And she dances around it. Sings and jumps. She sings like this, "*Neta e, neta e, neta e!*" *Neta* means "going down like this."

Round, round, round she dances. "Glad to see this one killed," she sings, "he eats all the people."

And pretty soon *Sakarakaamche* asks the old lady bat, "Did that eagle kill my mother?"

"Yes, yes, he killed your mother. I saw that eagle get your mother down in here. But you got him. That's all right."

Then *Sakarakaamche* takes the long feathers of the eagle and takes them home. He doesn't say anything to his grandmother, yet.

The grandmother asks, "Where you get these feathers?"

"Oh, I found them down below there."

"Is that the eagle's feathers?"

"Yeah," he said.

"How you pull them out?"

"Oh," he said, "I got up there and pulled them out. I killed all the four eagles on top of that mountain."

But the grandmother said, "I don't know you can do that! I want to tell you long time what that eagle did. But I was afraid he will kill you. Kill both of us."

Long time ago, when the people first come out, everything talks. Trees and everything. And one cedar tree, he says "Shhh" all the time. His roots come up like this. It turns into a man. Grows from the rock. There, right at the trail. They call that man *wi masmawe. Masmawe*, that means "roots."

When the people go on that trail he kicks them down into a hole. He has lots of family down there. Lots of wives. He is an early Mormon, I guess. And when he kicked somebody down into that hole, the bunch down there cut him up into pieces and ate him. That man with roots lay there all the time. He has roots like a tree and cannot move. He lays there still. Just kicks his legs when someone comes along.

Sakarakaamche was going along on that trail. His grandmother had told him, "Don't go on that bluff. On top of that, there is a man that grows on the rock. He is a bad one. Kicks people off."

But *Sakarakaamche* didn't believe her. He goes over there. The old man tries to kick him off. But he missed him. Then *Sakarakaamche* had a fox with him. He let that fox go over the man with roots, and the man tried to kick the fox down the hole. The fox is pretty lively. He jumped and that man missed him. *Sakarakaamche* called the fox back, and the man tried again to kick that fox down the hole. When the fox had come back, *Sakarakaamche* asked the man with roots, "Why do you do that for?"

"Well," the man said, "I'm laying there all the time, so my leg gets kind of stiff and hurts. So I kick my leg."

"If you want to kick, kick this one here!" and *Sakarakaamche* put a big, yellow snake where the man was laying.

That man tried to get up and jump away, but he could not move away. *Sakarakaamche* chopped the man's head off, and rolled it down into the hole. Cut him all to pieces, threw the pieces down, too. He just kept the stomach. He took the stomach and went down into that hole.

These people down in that hole, they kill people with their eyes. They look at you all the time, and pretty soon you fall down and die. *Sakarakaamche* went down there and made a cross out of blackroot. Put it on his leg. When they look real bad, he puts his foot up and makes a spark. Then they closed their eyes, and he got all right.

Four times he did like that. Then he threw that stomach into the fire. "Hey, look at that thing. Don't look at me. Look at that thing." And everybody looks at that thing. "Come in close, come in close," says *Sakarakaamche*, and everybody comes close. And the kids say, "It's going to bust, it's going to bust, it's going to bust." They all look at it. But one little boy, he had a tanned buckskin. He went behind it and he looked through that little hole where they shot that buck.

Pop! That stomach bust, blew all the hot ashes and hot coals over these people's faces, into their eyes. They fell down, and *Sakarakaamche* chopped their heads off, and threw them away. But that little boy, the ashes did not get him behind the buckskin. *Sakarakaamche* got that boy and wanted to take him home. On the way the little boy said, he had to go to the toilet.

Sakarakaamche said, "Sit right here. Don't go no place."

But that boy slipped away where there is a crack in the rock. The boy crawled up into that crack. *Sakarakaamche* ran after him and tried to get hold of the boy's leg. Just pulled the shoe off, and the kid went in there.

And the boy hollered to *Sakarakaamche*, "Waterboy! *Ahathawa!* I'm going to go south. I'm going to eat you up. When I come back, I'm going to eat you up."

He called *Sakarakaamche* "Waterboy" because *Sakarakaamche* came out from the dripping water.

There is pine pitch, lots of it there. *Sakarakaamche* makes a fire in that cave with the pine pitch to sweep that little boy out. But the boy doesn't go. Stays there, stays there. *Sakarakaamche* got late. Before he went away, he put that yellow snake in the cave where the crack with the little boy in it was. Told her to watch out for the boy.

"Hey, when that boy comes around here, you bite him," he told her.

Sakarakaamche went a little away from the cave. He lay down and slept. At that place one can still see the pillow of clay where he laid his head on.

But you know how a snake is! He just coiled up and slept. And that boy stepped over the snake and went away.

194

On a July 16, 1975, field trip, John Williams exiting cave where *Sakarakaamche* tried to smoke the boy out. Photo by Sigrid Khera.

There is that white rock. When you put it into the fire it pops. That boy who ran away from *Sakarakaamche*, he did that. Threw the white rock into the fire and "pop," a man came out. Then another one. Four times he threw rocks into the fire, and every time a man came out. There was lots of oakbrush around that place. If you throw that oakbrush into the fire, it pops all the time, just like firecrackers. The four men who had come out from the white rock threw oakbrush into the fire and "popopopopopop," lots of other men came out.

That's the Pima who come out from that rock. That's how the Pima grew. That's why we call them *Yùbaginétha*, "Killer with eyes." The Pima, they look at you, look at you, look at you. They can look at you until you fall down and die. They are grown from rock. They come from that man with roots. Yavapai grew different.

Then that boy took some clay and tried to make a horse. But just burro came out. My grandmother thinks that must have been around Black Canyon. Lots of wild burros used to live there.

At that time everything used to talk. And something told *Sakarakaamche*, "Your father is the Sun." The grandmother had told nothing to *Sakarakaamche*.

"How do I go over there and meet him?" he asked people.

"Don't go right over there. It is dangerous. His eyes are like fire. You go in there and you get burned up," he was told. But anyways, he just kept on going. He met lots of things on the way, and told them, "I'm going away to my father."

But all these people told him, "No, don't go."

He kept on going, kept on going, kept on going.

When he goes there, the spider sits in a little rock crack. He has the string, the net set up. We call that string *nyul*. *Sakarakaamche* walks, falls down, comes back again. *Sakarakaamche* kicks it and falls down again. Falls down again. He is looking around and the spider is sitting over there and laughing.

"Come in here, grandchild, I talk to you."

"All right," says *Sakarakaamche* and goes to the spider's house. And the spider tells him, "When you go up that way to your father, your father is going to say, 'Let's run a race, all around the world.' You don't say 'no' to him."

"All right."

"You will beat him all right. I'm going to help you. You know that string? I'm going to put my string under his leg, and he is not going to be too fast. When you are going, you are going to be first."

Sakarakaamche comes up to the Sun's house. That place there is sure dangerous. Heat! All red, like you heat the iron, and it is coming up red, red. And when he gets there, the Sun doesn't leave him alone.

The Sun said, "Let's make a race."

So *Sakarakaamche* and the Sun go 'round the world. Run around the world. And the spider puts up that string, and the Sun gets his legs entangled in that string. He stays way back, and *Sakarakaamche* goes 'round first. Makes the race all right, beats the Sun. He goes up to his place first, and sits there for a long time until the Sun comes up.

"All right," said the Sun then, "I guess you are my son."

Wipuk (Sedona) cave. Late 1970s photo by Sigrid Khera.

Below Fossil Creek there is a pit. That is the place where they run the race with hair. Nothing grows there, from the hillside down to the river. They want to see who has the longer hair. It is the Sun who said, he has the longer hair.

The old man Sun said to *Sakarakaamche*, "You do it first."

But *Sakarakaamche* said, "No, you want the race, so you do it first."

Vialnyucha (Fossil Creek). Photo by Elias Butler, 2001.

So the Sun is laying there and his hair is big. A big pile of black hair, like Indians' hair. It is a great, big roll, and it is tied tight with a string. The Sun turns the hair loose, and lets it roll down, down, down to the water, to the river. But it doesn't go across. Just hits the river, and that's the end.

Sakarakaamche says, "All right, I'm going to do it."

Sakarakaamche has a little roll of hair. He is laying there and opens it up, roll it, roll it, roll it across the river, over a little ridge, over another little ridge, and he beats the Sun.

Now the Sun wanted them to take a sweat bath. It was a place where he burned the people that they died. There came a certain kind of a fly along. It is yellow striped and kind of wooly looking, and it flies to where something has gone bad. We call that kind *thamburgka*. That fly didn't want *Sakarakaamche* get burned. So he helped him. Everybody helped *Sakarakaamche*. That fly asked *Sakarakaamche*, "Where are you going?"

"I'm going to visit my father," he said.

The fly told him, "When you are going there, I'm not going to leave you alone. He is going to have a sweat bath. That's what he is going to tell you. But don't go in first. Tell him to go in first. I'm going to stay right behind you. I'm going to blow that heat away from you, so you are not going to get hot. Go on in there all right."

They go to the sweat bath.

The Sun says, "Let's go in there. If you are my boy, we'll see."

The boy says, "All right," and starts open the door. And the Sun says, "You go in first."

But *Sakarakaamche* said, "No, you go in first."

So the Sun goes in first. He puts rocks in there, makes them hot, puts a little water on it, and makes them steam. It gets all red hot in there. The Sun sits over there and his eyes are red hot. He looks at *Sakarakaamche,* and he was going to burn him. The *thamburgka* sits behind *Sakarakaamche's* ear and blows the heat away. So *Sakarakaamche* doesn't get hot. He just sits there all right. Closes the door, and stays there a long time. Sings four songs. But the Sun gets real hot. He gets so hot that the steam comes out from his eyes.

But *Sakarakaamche* said to him, "Hey, why don't you build the fire? I'm freezing!"

The old man Sun falls down, goes to sleep in there, and they drag him out. They drag him over there to his old lady. His old lady puts something on him, and pretty soon he gets up again. That was the Sun's wife. But not *Kamalapukwia*.

And the Sun said to *Sakarakaamche*, "All right, I know you are my son."

But when that fly, that *thamburgka*, blows the fire away from *Sakarakaamche*, it burns up everything. Burns up the world.

The rabbit saw some weeds. They are just burned on top a little. Just white there. The rabbit asked them, "How you doing that?" The weeds said, "We burnt up just on top like this."

"All right," said the rabbit and got under those weeds. Got in there and the fire goes over. That rabbit got burned at one little place only. It has a little yellow mark at his neck. That's where he got burnt.

The bobcat asked the water about the fire. And the water said, "The fire just goes on top over me." So the bobcat said, "All right, I go in there." And he goes into the water. But then the fire came and it hit the bobcat on the back. That's how it got that little stripe on the back, black one.

The other animals died. Burned up. But *Sakara-kaamche* brought them back to life again. He sings and prays, and they come back.

The Sun said again, "Let's run a horse race."

There comes a little hummingbird to *Sakarakaamche*, the *minimina*. He said to *Sakarakaamche*, "Your father is going to tell you, 'Let's race a horse.' He has four different color horses. Four of them. The gray one, that's his horse. The one, that's the Cloud, the Lightning. Get this one!"

Wipuk (Sedona) cave. Late 1970s photo by Sigrid Khera.

"All right," said *Sakarakaamche*.

The Sun came and said to *Sakarakaamche*, "Go in there, get the horse. We are going to run the horse race now."

There are four horses. Three of them are nice looking horses. The fourth one, it is gray and skinny.

The Sun said to *Sakarakaamche*, "There are lots of good horses over there. Get one."

But *Sakarakaamche* said, "I'm going to get this gray one over there."

The Sun made "haaa"—he was so shocked. Pretty soon they run the race. That gray horse was the Cloud, the Lightning, and it goes fast like the lightning strikes. It goes first all the time. And that's the way *Sakarakaamche* beat the Sun, beat the old man.

The Sun said, "It's all right, you are my boy."

After that the Sun said, "All right, you are my son. Let's do something now. Over there, there are medicine men. We go over there and listen."

The boy said, "All right."

When they go to the place, the Sun said, "Go in first."

But the boy said, "No, you go in first. You wanted to go."

And he makes the Sun go in first. They go in there, and there are the medicine men. That was not in a cave. It was under a tall cottonwood tree, with sky, at the Sun's place. The boy goes in, and the medicine men kill him. Cut his throat. Butcher him and cut him across into four pieces. Make four piles with his arms and legs and everything.

Sixteen medicine men were in there. Four and four and four and four. They try to get him up again. They sing over him, sing over him, sing over him—nothing. They are trying to sing and get him up. All of them sing and try to get him up. But he won't move. Just stays like that. Then the Sun sings over the boy and makes him almost move. Move just a little bit. That's all.

The Cloud is over there. "What's you guys doing over there? What you do to my son? That man whom you cut all to pieces, how do you think he gets up again? But anyways," he said, "I'll try it. This is my son."

So the Cloud starts singing. He sings four songs and the lightning hit under the boy. He got up. Full body like this and stands there. The lightning had gone under him and raised him up. And the Cloud said, "You see, this is *my* boy."

Wipuk (Sedona). The cloud is *Sakarakaamche's* father. Photo by Elias Butler, 2011.

Sakarakaamche is the Cloud's boy. It is not really the Sun who is his father.

And when *Sakarakaamche* gets up and stands there, the Cloud says to him, "Go down to your grandmother. Your grandmother is getting pretty old now. I want you to go back over there. Sing again and do what I did to you and the lightning will strike into the old woman's home inside. I want to help your grandmother. I want to help her to be well again. Like I did to you, you do the same thing to her."

Sakarakaamche sings and the lightning strikes him and he goes down to the old woman's cave.

"Grandmother, I missed you for a long time. How have you been?"

The old woman looks very old. She is almost gone. "Grandmother, what you crying for?"

"You are away a long, long time, so I'm crying all this time. I'm too old now. I can't walk anymore."

"Well," he says, "I'll bring you back."

Then he starts singing. And he sings on four mornings. Four songs. Then he gets the ashes, white ones, puts it in the hand and marks the old woman. Prays and prays and gets her up.

The first time she moves a little, little bit. Next time she moves a little more. Next time she moves even more. The last time she gets up and is like a little girl again. *Kamalapukwia.*

That's the end. I don't know where they are gone. I don't know where *Sakarakaamche* goes, and I don't know where his grandmother goes.

But just before *Sakarakaamche* was about ready to go away, he makes something out of mud. Looks like a man. He makes a mouth in there. Then *Sakarakaamche* got up and sings a blackroot song. Blow it in the mouth, blow it again. Blow it four times. The fourth time that mud man comes up as a human. Gets up and kicks the legs. There are now two boys: *Sakarakaamche* and the mud man. That's not too good. *Sakarakaamche* is thinking what to do. Puts this to sleep. Gets one rib out of him. Makes a woman out of that rib.

That was over there in Sedona. And that's the way we breed from there. This here is our home. From there all the way 'round this country. *Sakarakaamche*, the one who made the people, he came out from that old lady *Kamalupukwia*, the one who was inside the log. He made the people out from mud, out from the ground, up there in Sedona. He is the one who can do anything. He is the same like Jesus. It was the same one. They said the same things. When we pray, we call that boy all the time. He is the one we ask for help, and everything. He just went away. He is alive over there. That's why we pray to him above the sky some place.

Sakarakaamche had no wife. He is alone. *Sakarakaamche*, that means "One Man alone goes around." We call Jesus the same. When he gets through with everything, he went away. They don't say where he went. But my grandmother said, she thinks he went to his father, to the Cloud. *Sakarakaamche* said, "I learn everything from my father. When he made me, he made me like him." *Sakarakaamche* said the same thing like Jesus, "I come back again, but not right away. When I come back again, you'll see something. Something comes up wrong, something comes up which has never been around here. You know then it is closer for me to come back. Watch close. Keep clean in your body, clean in your way, so you go on the same way I go."

Sakarakaamche goes up, but that man he made stays down there. That man and his lady stay at a place around Sedona, down below Oak Creek Canyon. Lots of farming there. Pears, apricots, everything in there.

The God told the man, "Anything here you can take. Take anything! The one tree in the middle, don't touch that. I plant that tree here, but not for you. Don't touch it."

So the man goes out and looks for deer. Goes around and comes back about evening. And the lady meanwhile looks for food and sees that bush in the middle and thinks it looks pretty good. Looks like lots of berries on it. She stands there and looks at it, and there was a snake hanging in there.

"Hey," he says, "where you going, lady? I want to tell you something. Did God tell you not to eat from that tree? You know why He do that? He said, if you eat these, you know everything like Him. That's why He don't wants you to eat these. Eat it! It's good. Then you can see everything."

That snake sure fooled the lady. She breaks some of that fruit off and eats it. That's the way she sees everything now. When her old man comes back, she saves a little bit for him and gives him some. They eat it. And he looks at himself, and he has no clothes. So he takes some kind of a leaf and put it all around him. Now they know they have no clothes. So they go into a hole and hide. That's the way they do. So the lady do something bad first when the people come first.

And God is supposed to come around here in the evening. He checks on them all the time. He comes around and he doesn't see them at the camp there.

"Where are you?" He hollers four times.

They holler from down there, "We hide here!"

"Why?"

"We don't have no clothes. That's why we put something over us. That's why we hide here."

"All right," God said, "you go away."

From there all the people spread out.

Wipuk (Sedona) cave. Late 1970s photo by Sigrid Khera.

Chapter 20

◆

Other Tribes

akarakaamche, his grandmother, she told him everything. She made him know things like a medicine man. That's how he learned everything: from the grandmother. And *Sakarakaamche* is the one who is teaching the men who come up. He made them medicine men.

There is this cave in Sedona with lots of marks on the wall. *Sakarakaamche* made those marks. *Sakarakaamche* took the people in there and gave them the right song. Teach each one the right things. *Sakarakaamche* gave lots of feathers to some of them. These were the Oklahoma Indians. He taught dances to others. These were the Hopi Indians. Some people listened well to what *Sakarakaamche* said. Some didn't. He tried to teach the Yavapai something. But we didn't get it. We didn't listen. So he gave us a stick with a string on it. That's the bow and arrow. And he gave us the four sacred things: the blackroot, the yellow powder, the blue stone, and the white stone. We Yavapai were like the dove. *Sakarakaamche* told the birds how to make their nests. The dove didn't listen. Now the dove makes the nest with five sticks only. The dove didn't learn things, just like us.

When people come up, they were one tribe: Yavapai. We come out the same men. They all were Yavapai. All of them spoke the same language, but from that cave they all went different places. Get different names. And pretty soon they all talked different. The blood is the same, but the talk is different. Only the Pima came out of that rock.

My grandmother said, only two people were left in the cave. They don't know what to do, where to go. They don't like to leave. They keep sitting on a ridge there and think. Then they turn into rocks. Just a man and wife and their baby. These rocks are there in Sedona.

Havasupai and Hualapai, they used to be Yavapai for a long time. They stayed together. The kids were playing together all the time. They take little sticks, put a little mud on it and throw it at one another. But one boy hit another in the eyes. The stick slipped out of his hand and hit the other right in the eye. The children start fighting, and pretty soon the old people start fighting, too. Then the Yavapai run that bunch off. Run them off, run them off, run them down the canyon (Grand Canyon). Let them go there.

After that, they chase another bunch off. That were the Hualapais. There is a gambling game with rocks. We call that *nòhówe*. You take a rock, make four bumps with sand. Hide the rock in one and let people guess. People play that all the time. Pretty soon they quarrel. They chase that bunch off and leave them down at Kingman, some place over there.

The Yavapai used to meet other tribes. They used to trade with them. We used to go over there to the Navajo and trade all the time. The Yavapai who are real good runners went over there. Like *Pakakaya*. We traded silver and blankets from the Navajo. Give them buckskin and mescal and mesquite powder for it. Make a lump out of mesquite powder and bring it over there. Long time, when there were no White people around, the Navajo used the silver. We didn't know about silver. But the Navajo knew it. I don't know where they get that silver. We get rings from the Navajo and bracelets. Thick bracelets which you put on the arm when you shoot bow and arrow. We call that kind of bracelet *sal'ami*, "protect the arm." It protects the arm from the bow string. A wide silver bracelet on leather. We have no sheep, nothing. So we trade blankets from the Navajo. Trade a blanket for two or three buckskins. We used to plant corn. But sometimes we got blue corn from the Navajo.

My people used to trade with the Navajo for a long time. Trade with them and make friends. One time when they go up there, they see some Navajo go off the trail. See them go around the other side of the mountain. So the Yavapai wait, "Let us see what they are going to do." The Navajo come out to the trail and they start shooting with bow and arrow. Then the Navajo took off. But my people used to be pretty fast runners, too. They get two of these Navajo. Tie them together. Tie them to a cedar tree and leave them there. They know, some Navajo, when they come back, they will find them there. "We don't kill them," my people said, "we just tie them up and make them learn." From then on we never went back to the Navajo and the Navajo never came here.

When my grandmother was just a kid, she went over there. They go together, cousins, uncles and nieces. They go over there, a whole bunch of them. But not very many go over there all the time.

Sometimes they also go down the canyon (Grand Canyon) to the Supai (Havasupai). But they don't have very many things down there. Dried peaches and corn. Blue corn and red corn, and they trade it for something.

One time the Yavapai went down to make friends with the Supai. The Supai have a rifle. When the Yavapai go back, the Supai shoot one man. They hit him and try to scalp him. The Yavapai start fighting just with bow and arrow. That was way early in the morning. The Yavapai have a medicine man and he prays for that man who got hit with the bullet. Drag him in the shade, pray for him and suck the blood out. Get the bullet out. In the evening, when the sun goes down, the man that got shot gets up.

"All right, we start fighting now. Come on!" He just stands there and talks. And these Supai said, "I don't think this is a real people, a human. Maybe they are devil or something. You can't kill them. Let's go home." They leave the Yavapai and walk away. But the Yavapai never went back after that.

Before the White people were around, the *Wipukpa*, they get acorn and piñon down there below Seligman. Lots of them went over there to get the seeds. But the Hualapai sometimes used to take things away from them. When the Yavapai were over there and leave something in their camp, and some of them were out to get some more food, the Hualapai came in and get what they have in the Yavapai camp. Take it away. And some of the Hualapai are real mean, too. Kill my people.

There is a Hualapai chief. His name is *Wadjemodema*. He is a bad one. He sure kills lots of us Yavapai all the time. Not just one time. But after some time the *Wipukpa* get mad. They send a man around to tell all the other Yavapai. Like a newspaper. He called lots of our people together, up to Seligman. We get all together. *Wipukpa, Tolkepaya, Yavepe* and *Kewevkepaya*. We go over there and camp there maybe four, five days.

At Seligman, there is a mountain there. Kind of a clean looking mountain. The Hualapai went round this mountain this side, the Yavapai the other side. The Yavapai said, "Let's see and let him try now. If he wants to fight, that's all right. Don't pull back. All of us come one behind the other." *Wadjemodema* was coming over the hill and he said, "All right, come on boys. Come on and have fun." And the Yavapai chief said, "All right, come up here, boy! We want to see how strong, how tough you are!" And one Yavapai jumps out from the side, hits *Wadjemodema*, and gets his scalp off. The old people said, if you scalp the people, you cut all around the head and pull the hair up. The hair don't grow in the head. There is only a little string that holds the scalp up on top and you cut it. That's what they did to *Wadjemodema*. They took the scalp to the camp. Put it on a stick. His wife was there, and the Yavapai made that lady hold the stick and dance with it. Dance around, dance, dance, dance all night. Then they made a pit. Put rocks in there. Put hot coals on top. When the morning came, they threw the hair down in that pit. Throw the lady down there, too and roast her. Eat her.

Wadjemodema's brother is there on a little hill. They talk to him, "You see that? Your brother's wife carry your brother's hair around. How you like that? If you think, you are going to do something, just come on and do something, and you are going to be like this lady here."

He is on that little hill and the Yavapai surround him and hold him there. Don't let him go back. And when they are through with that, they ask him, "What do you want to do? You want to fight again or what you want to do?"

"Well," he said, "that's all. I give up. I'm not going to do anything."

"If you are meaning to do this, it's all right. Let's shake hands. You go home and we are going to go home. And we come back and get what we want: piñon, acorn, anything."

"All right," he said.

"We are not the one," the Yavapai said. "You people kill us all the time when we come around. That's why we do that. We know, we can do that for a long time, but we don't do it. But when we want to start it, we can start it, and nobody is going to stop us. We are the meanest people in the world."

My uncle *Pelhame* was there. But he didn't tell me what was the name of *Wadjemodema's* brother. All those old people were there and saw it. *Haló* and *Koalakha, Matamthi, Pulkarzhuha.* They were there and saw it.

The Hualapai made a monument over there where it happened. Two rock piles. One for the Hualapai and one for the Yavapai. One Hualapai showed me that monument. I used to work over there with a Hualapai for a long time. We were breaking rocks for the smelter. So that Hualapai said, "That's where they killed *Wadjemodema*. I want to take you over there and show you." He showed me those rock piles. "*Wadjemodema,* he killed lots of people. He is the same way with Mohave. With Hualapai, too," he said.

Well, he was a pretty strong man. But they got him. My people, when they get mad, they sure get bad. But they never killed White people. They knew, if they do that, White people will come all over the place.

Long time ago the Pima did the same thing. When my people came together and gathered something, saguaro fruit and mesquite, the Pima came around and killed them all the time, all the time. Us Yavapai, we lived around here and up in the mountains. But we went down to get the mesquite beans and the saguaro fruit. And after some time the Yavapai get tired of the Pima. And mad, too. *Pakakaya* and some boys, they went over to the Pima place, Buckeye, somewhere there, and they got their horses. One Pima boy herds the horses and watch them, watch them, watch them. Pretty soon the boy is trying to go home. That time the Yavapai get in there and get the horses and bring them over here. Just fool them. Get the horses to get the Pima up here. They know the Pima follow them. So they run the horses across the desert all the way up to Black Canyon.

Over there, where the big bridge is now, there is another valley. They brought the horses in there. Killed the horses and eat them. The Pima were coming in. A big bunch of them. The Yavapai let them come in, let them come in, let them come in. When they were in the canyon, the Yavapai come down from the rocks and killed them all. Then another bunch of Pima was coming and another and another. They killed all those Pima.

When Yavapai get bad, they get bad! They were tough. They had no rifle. They used their muscles. When they get those Pimas up there at Black Canyon where that big rock is standing up, they make no noise. Pull the Pima down the horse and choke them. *Melokhewinneh,* that's what we call choking. *Melok,* that's the neck, *winneh,* "choke." Some of my people get them down and they carry a rock. They hit them on the head with that rock. No rifle, nothing, just a rock.

The Yavapai also put some poison on the arrow. You get scratched with it and you die right away. You walk a little, then you swell up and you die. It is like burnt all the way down. That's how my people killed many of those Pima. I don't know what they use for the poison. The man who made that poison is my grandmother's brother. Only *Kewevkepaya* use it.

The Yavapai saved only one Pima boy. They take him over there to the camp. They cook the horse meat and give it to the boy. Make him eat it. "All right," they said, "we take you home pretty soon. We are going to fix your shoes."

They put patches all the way round his shoes. Make them good. Those saguaros have a dried place, like pottery inside. They get that kind and tie it around the boy. Put some water in there. We call that kind of cup from the saguaro *amuqualla.* Then they sent him home to his people.

They said to him, "Go over there and tell your people to come over here. We stay right here, yet. You go and fetch your people. We are waiting for them."

Lots of Yavapai come down and stay right there about New River. All of them wait. One guy sits up on top of a peak and watches if they come round. They don't come round. But he sees smoke over there. The Pima are

Fort McDowell. Yavapai Minnie Williams picks mesquite beans to grind. 1976 photo by Sigrid Khera.

burning lots of stuff from the dead. And *Pakakaya* was going right close. He heard lots of people crying there. Four, five nights.

The Pima don't come back. So the Yavapai turned around and spread out again.

But two Yavapai—*Pakakaya* is one of those—they went over there to the Pima place and listened. They know how to talk Pima. They understand Maricopa. They understand Yuma. *Pakakaya* went in there in that Pima house where they smoke pipe. They let the pipe go round. They give it to him, too. He is sitting there and listens what they are going to say. "Nobody goes over there and bother the Yavapai. They are like a bear. Don't bother them no more." When the morning came, and everybody went out, he went out, too. Then they knew who he is. Maybe they wanted to kill him. But he took off.

Pakakaya, he used to go over there all the time. When the Pima had meeting, he just went. The Pima had a house buried with the dirt. They have the meeting in there. Lots of chiefs. And *Pakakaya* went over there and stayed with them. The Pima didn't know it. They thought he is a Pima. They talk, and he stays there, stays there and listens to them. Smokes, too. He listens to them, and then he knows what they are going to do. The next day and the other days. When the morning came, he got up and walked off. He heard it in how many days they are going to have the next meeting. So he goes down there to the next meeting. He is scared of nothing, that boy. But he don't goes there in the daylight. He goes there in the dark.

One day *Pakakaya*, he went over there to Gila Bend. Somewhere around there where the Pima planted corn. He got there early in the morning. He got up there and was trying to break some corn. Took a rope and put it around the corn. He was going to pack it and take it home. Pretty soon an old woman sees him breaking the corn and she hollers. Hollers and people come. One over there, one over there, one over there, and another one over there. A lot of people come all around him. He just runs down the river. Dives in the water there. A little ways down he sees a cottonwood tree. The water runs around the stump. There is a hole in there. He goes in there and stays there. Lots of Pima come around. Look in the water, look for tracks, find nothing. He hears them talking, "Looks like that is the devil. Nothing around here." And pretty soon they all go back. When they are gone, he comes out, takes his rope and breaks corn again. Takes it home. He runs like a horse. He is fast that boy!

One day *Pakakaya* was over there around Casa Grande where the Pima live. In old days people used to eat pack rats, *málka* we call it. They have their nests in the chollas, and *Pakakaya* was looking for these. He looked for the rat nests and then he saw Pimas were all around him. They are on the horses and he can't go no place. He sees a hill and he walks fast to it. There is a hole in the side. He crawls in and that hole goes right up to the top of that little hill. He crawls all the way up to the top. Pulls a tumble weed and plugs the hole. All these people look for him round and round and round. And he is right there in that hole and watches them. Then they stop and line up and he hears them talking, "I think that is the devil. Let's go." So they go back down that way. When they are gone a little ways, *Pakakaya* comes out from that hole. Puts fire on the chollas. They burn pretty fast! Then he runs back and forth yelling, and the Pima think there are lots of Yavapai around. They don't come back. *Pakakaya* takes his rats and goes home.

These Pimas weren't living around here then. They lived way down in Ajo, Gila Bend. They were staying over there. But when the government built a place here, they get the Pima here. So they are coming up, coming up, coming up, and they are growing here right now. This is Yavapai country! From here all the way to Tucson.

When the White people meet the Yavapai first, they ask them, "What are you? What's your name?" Pretty soon one of our men said, *"A'baja."* That means "people." The White man said, "Hey, that's Apache! Apache!" But *A'baja* means different than Apache. Sounds different. Now the White people call us "Mohave-Apache" and "Yuma-Apache." But we are not Apache, we are not Mohave, and we are not Yuma. We are Yavapai! Long before the White people come and take us to San Carlos, there was no Apache around there. Nothing but Yavapai lived around here. There was no Apache here. Snowflake all the way down there, that's where the Apache lived. Only when they take us to San Carlos, the Yavapai girls get Apache boys, and the Yavapai boys get Apache girls. Before, they don't marry Apache. Only Yavapai marry together. But from then on, when the Yavapais married Apache, some of the Yavapai stayed over there in San Carlos, and the kids were raised as Apache. These kids are Apache now. Some of them come over here and there are Apaches now in Clarkdale, Cottonwood, Camp Verde. They don't live there before. We call the Apache *Akhwakaya*. That means "Red Eyes."

Now my people marry with different tribes. That's why they get bad. I guess. They don't help one another now. They don't stay together. They don't listen together. Kids don't speak their language any more. Long time ago, they don't let them marry other tribes. Just Yavapai stay together.

Wipuk (Sedona). On a September 1975 field trip, Fort McDowell Yavapai Minnie Williams and Emma Shenah step over a large, ancient mescal cooking heap. Peter J. Pilles, Jr., Coconino National Forest archaeologist, accompanies. Photo by Sigrid Khera.

Oral History of the Yavapai

Chapter 21

◆

Pray, Sing, Dance, Heal

Sakarakaamche, he is the one who teach us everything. He knew how to sing. He knew how to make people well again. He knew everything. He learned from his father, the Cloud. *Sakarakaamche* knew about all the weeds which cure all the sicknesses. He learned about the weeds from the old lady, his grandmother. The old lady planted weeds for everything. This one for some kind of sickness, that one for another one. We don't know where she learned it from. But *Sakarakaamche* learned it from her. And he is the one who is teaching the humans who come up.

Sakarakaamche gave us four things to help us. He gave us the blackroot, the yellow powder and the blue stone and the white stone.

Blackroot is the best medicine. We call it *isamaganyach*. Blackroot, it is good against pains and sores. It is a very great medicine. When you broke something, hit something, you put it on you and you get all right. *Sakarakaamche* had a blackroot right there on top of his cave. Blackroot grows in the mountains among the pine and cedar trees. That's where the blackroot grows. The flowers are yellow and the leaves are not very big. You pull it out and the juice marks like red ink. The mark stays for a long time. The roots are not too thick. Smaller than a finger. Sometimes it has two roots. They go down a long way. When you go down to the end of the root it has lots of medicine.

The yellow powder, we call that *etchitawa*. It comes from that water weed, the cattail. When that powder comes out, it doesn't last too long. Maybe one day. The wind blows and it is all gone. When it is ready, you go there and knock that plant and lots of that powder comes out. My grandmother said to me, "My grandchild, this here yellow powder looks like nothing but powder. But it is like the sun coming out and shining over the world. That's why they give it to us and we use it all the time."

When he heals somebody, the medicine man puts it on that person. The yellow powder, when people use it, he puts a little on you. Put some in your mouth, turn you round and mark you with it. We learn that from *Sakarakaamche*. That's why we do that.

The blue stone and the white stone, that's what protects us from bad things. The blue stone is for the men, the white one for the women. If something bad tries to hit you and you have that stone, that stone will crack. But the bad won't hit you. Sometimes a witch tries to hit a person. But that stone will protect him. The man never gets sick with that stone. The blue stone which people wear on a ring, that's not the one that protects people. That's just like a toy. But when it is blessed by a medicine man, then it will help people.

The first time when the people pray, when they sing, they have that blue and that white stone, and the yellow powder and the blackroot. That's what protects them. And when they wander around, they carry these with them.

My people, they asked for things, prayed, and things came right. They used to ask for things that were true and right. They knew how to pray from the beginning. From way back the people knew it. They don't read or write, they have no song books, but they used the old songs. *Sakarakaamche* teach them how to do it. And they pray for the sick people, for the ones who have trouble. I know that my people know what God is to them. They don't read the Bible. But they talk just like Bible sometimes.

White people say that Indians don't know nothing. But before the White people come around, the Indians, before they do something, they always pray. They used to sing every morning. They sing what they are going to do. When they get up in the morning, they pray, they sing. When they eat, they pray, they sing. When they go someplace, they pray, they sing. When they come back from somewhere, they pray, they sing. That's, what they say, help. They say, that way they never get tired, never get hurt, nothing. When they want to do some heavy work, they never get tired.

My grandmother used to pray every morning. All morning she used to pray. Asked for help. Asked that the kids don't get into trouble. I can hear it. I wish I was learning what she was talking about. I don't like to listen at that time when I was a little boy. Kids don't like to listen. My grandmother, she prays, prays, prays. She told me, "If you go and ask the Little People to help you, they will help you and you will be lucky all the time." I did not believe my grandmother. But when she is gone, I sure believe her. I have never been in school, but I have been working all the time. They help me pretty good. I think, my grandmother sure tells me right. She tells me, if they help you, you have a good way.

When we go out and go someplace, my grandmother, she stop and ask, pray. Stop at two, three places. I was a little boy and I didn't like that. I pulled her skirts, "Let's go, grandmother, let's go."

My people, they pray for the fruit, like mesquite beans, cactus fruit. They pray for that and the fruit comes out just good. The mesquite beans come out thick. But now, when the mesquite beans come out, they are thin. Like a paper. This is because people don't pray any more. Same with saguaro fruit or prickly pear or all the others. When *Sakarakaamche* was up on the mountain, he started to sing and that mountain got smaller. When you go to Sedona, you see that big, red mountain that sits there. It was the highest mountain around and *Sakarakaamche* made it smaller by singing. When we pray, when we sing, things come right.

In old days people were sometimes singing all night. Talk and sing and talk and sing. The different songs, too. All night they were singing. Lots of people got together. They sing all together. One is the singer and he starts it, and then they all get started and sing all night. Women were singing also. *Suare*, that means "singing."

Saguaro blossoms hold promise of fruit, food for the Yavapai. 2011. Photo by Elias Butler.

In 1918 there was a big flu. People in Clarkdale pray to push it away. They sing and that's how they pray to push it away. That time an old man told us, "Lots of people are going to die. Mexicans and Whites and everybody. But there is going to be only one Yavapai with it. Only one Yavapai lady is going to be with it." And it is true. At Clarkdale and Cottonwood lots of Mexicans and Whites died. But only one Yavapai died there. This lady's name was Lara. At Fort McDowell many Yavapai died. But at Clarkdale only one.

That old man, John Urki, he knew how to sing and he pushed the disease away from us. His Indian name is *Ichiquama*. He sings to the people all the time.

Ima, that means "dancing." Sometimes we dance for fun, but sometimes people dance for something. They ask something, pray for something. They make a dance and it is kind of praying. To ask things from God. We pray from the dance.

For anything that comes out, we dance for that. For the rain, for the crop, for deer. Food comes up good when we dance. *Aqua paya*, that means "something comes up." That's how we call the dance to make food grow good. Cactus fruit will come up big when we dance. Mesquite beans will be thick. Now there is nothing. People don't know how to ask for it.

Aquaka ima, that's what we call the deer dance. They used to hold two sticks in the front and use them like legs. Jump like deer. They have a good song for that, too. *Pakakaya*, he still knew how to dance that. I think he was the last one who do that.

They also had a dance for the buffaloes. Before the White people came around, there were lots of big buffaloes down in the desert. Not up in the mountains, but down there. People hunted the buffaloes with a spear. They had their own dance for that.

Sometimes my people made the Crown Dance. *Kakaka ima*, we call that. The crown dance, the first time, the *Kakaka* teach the people. The *Kakaka* are just like Indians. But little, tiny Indians. They live in the mountains. Four Peaks, Superstition Mountain, Granite Mountain up there in Prescott. They can get in and out the mountain. They are just like the wind, like air. You can't see them all the time. But it can happen sometimes that you see them. But quick like that and you can see them no more. They talk Yavapai. But they don't talk to everybody. Just to the teacher, the leader. Like medicine men. The *Kakaka* never die. They are 2000 or 3000 years old. They were around before us. The *Kakaka* were first. They were first in this country here. I think the *Kakaka* are here before *Sakarakaamche*. They are around all the time. All the tribes know about the Little People. The Kachina of the Hopi, that's the same ones.

My grandmother said, the people have a dance over there at Four Peaks and the *Kakaka* come in. The real ones. My people learn the Crown Dance from them.

The *Kakaka* have a head just round. And when my people dance the Crown Dance, they put buckskin all over the head. Tie it and make the head round. The *Kakaka* head has no nose. Just holes in there. So people put wool or something around the nose, so the nose doesn't stick out. Make the face real round. Make a little open for the mouth. Make holes for the eyes.

When the people make the crown, they use horsehide. Cut it round. Take a little stick and bend it. Sew the hide on that little round stick. Then it stands up around the head. Before they use horsehide, they use the buckskin, my grandmother said. Put it in the water and wet it. Let it lay in the sun and dry it. Make it stiff. Then it stands up good.

They put marks on that crown. The Cloud, the Sun, Moon and the Star. And the Lightning on the side. The Lightning—us Indians are just like this. That's why we put it on. Us Indians, we come out from the Cloud. *Sakarakaamche* come out from the Cloud and the Lightning, and we come from *Sakarakaamche*.

The Sun they make round. Moon they make a half circle. Star, they make five ends. They make the Sun and the Moon and the Star yellow. They use the yellow powder for that. They take *manat* (Spanish Bayonet) yucca and squeeze it, squeeze it, squeeze it. Take the juice out. Mix it with the yellow powder and use it for paint. It never come off. The Cloud is kind of dark. They use black dirt for that. *Matkanyata*, we call that (graphite). Mix it with the *manat* juice and use it. The Lightning on the side, we make that with the blackroot's juice. It is red like ink. All the people do that. *Kewevkepaya, Wipukpa, Yavepe, Tolkepaya.*

When a person dances the *Kakaka ima*, the *Kakaka* Dance, he can see anything. He can see things way off. It is the older men who dance the Crown Dance. And always two ladies with them. But good ones, young ones that don't go around with men. Girls. When people dance, they holler four times. The real *Kakaka* do that. People make a cross on the ground, and then sometimes the real *Kakaka* come in. People know when the real *Kakaka* come in the dance. They can smell it. The Little People have cedar leaves wrapped around them. My grandmother said, that cedar sure smells good when they come in.

When I was a little boy up there in Mayer, I dance for the Crown Dance. We kids know how to dance it. We go out on the other side of the town in a little canyon. We dance every Sunday, all day. Sunday morning we could be over there and dance and dance and dance all day. I don't know, I never get tired of that. Eight or nine of us are in there all day. Just the relatives in the whole bunch.

One boy showed us. He is the one who is the leader. *Kowara* is his Indian name. And my uncle Tom Jones' boy. His name is *Wasyumje*. My cousin Mabel's (Mabel Hood Thomas, 1904-1982) eldest sister was coming in the lead. She had a necklace all around her with little mirrors on each side. It is shining all over. Before my people have the mirror, they use shell. File it, file it, file it until it is sure nice and shiny looking. *Halkurava* we call that kind.

I don't wear a crown. I was the funny one. They call that *chita uya*. That's like a clown. They make my head all round and I put lots of white ashes all over me. When they dance, I was coming way behind. When they go some place, I just go out this way. When they look back and go this way, I holler and they come back. They build fire on four places, and I jump over. Jump this way and this way and this way and this way. I holler, "uhu, uhu, uhu." I was quite a little fellow that time.

I have a little stick in each hand. They make them like knives. We call those sticks *ah'qua*, "knife." And when we dance, we use it like a knife, do like filing it. Before the White people come around, we use a hard stick and chip it like a knife. Make it shiny with some sort of a powder. Over at Superior there is a little hill with this kind of ground. We call this shining powder *ihchinikha*. When you wet it, it sticks like paint. That way we put it on the sticks and make them look like knives.

We sing, too. The *Kakaka* song. It is sure a good one. But I forgot. One woman, Nellie Quail, she was going to get some wood. And then, she said, she heard something singing down that little canyon. And she look down there and this was me and the whole bunch in there. Dancing away. "I heard you singing good songs. And I feel like hollering for you. But I didn't." That's what she told me later.

Just us kids dance in there. My uncle's boys John Jones and Terry Jones, my cousin Mabel's two brothers *Taktika* and *Taksabe*, Mabel and her older sister, and that boy who is the leader and his brother. Eight or nine of us dance there all day. The old people know we do that, but they don't say anything. They want us to sing Indian. So they let us do it.

Over there in San Carlos, the old people used to dance the Crown Dance, too. But not in Mayer. They all quit when they move over there. They don't do that any more. But just us kids. I don't know why they quit. I guess the church don't want them do that.

I would like to go back to that little canyon and look where we put the cloths. We put those crown dance things off and put them in the brush there. Maybe they are still there.

The *Kakaka* live in the mountains and they are still around. They are around where the people are supposed to be. Around Prescott, around Jerome Mountain, Fossil Creek, *Kathatkullo* (mountain at Bloody Basin), Red

Mountain (Fort McDowell), Superstition, Four Peaks. One time I saw them myself. Above Horseshoe Dam, there is a little white mountain. Chalk Mountain they call it. I was on top there one time to get the cattle. I see two Little People coming right down. I see them walking and then they are gone all of a sudden.

The *Kakaka* also have houses. Like over at Tihuan Ranch near Prescott. There is a rock ledge there and they have a house with little rooms. Same over there near Horseshoe Ranch. There is a *Kakaka* house up on the cliff and a ladder hanging down all the time. I was a cowboy over there. That Horseshoe Ranch boss has a brother, Wallace Colby, and he always said, "I want to take that step ladder."

We had a Mexican cowboy and that Mexican told him all the time, "Now, don't bother that. The Indian ways are different. That's Indian stuff over there, you don't bother that."

But one day—we were working way up on the river —the Mexican boy came along and he said, "That loco gringo is going to get that ladder over there. If he did it, it is going to be too bad for him and his brother." I knew it.

"Well," I said, "if he got it, he shall bring it back over there. But I can't go and help him. He shall leave it where he got it."

So about two days later they went where the step ladder was. And that man Wallace Colby pack it on horseback and take it home. And a short while after he got crazy and died. His brother the same thing. Both of them died.

There are many *Kakaka* houses here at Fort McDowell. One is over there at the highway near John Smith. From there goes a tunnel right up to the Four Peaks. That tunnel goes under the river, way under and then up, up, up to the Four Peaks.

Long time before the White people come around, my people used to camp here. And one young fellow, the *Kakaka* take him in that tunnel. He goes in there and take a walk down in the tunnel and the *Kakaka* take him all the way up to Four Peaks. He said, it takes two days to get up over there. But the people missed him for a long time. I think over 40 years or 30 years. When he comes out he goes down to Fish Creek where the people have a camp.

He come to the camp and he said, "I don't know, I've been away and it is like 3 days ago."

Lot of the people said, "No, long time!"

He tell his name and his father's name and his mother's name.

"Yeah, we know you now. We missed you a long time."

So he tells, the Little People live under the mountain. He said, it is just like day in there. They can see pretty good. They have lots of room in there, too. And there are some of the Little People in there making something like gravy. They eat it some time and they sleep some time. Pretty soon they get up and they come out at Four Peaks.

That boy who comes out from the mountain, he is a medicine man. He said, he knows there is something going to be wrong. "You know," he said, "something going to be. Something going to kill you guys."

He said, the *Kakaka* had told him, these people are not going to live too long. "If you want to go with me, come with me. I'm not going to pull you. I'm not going to drag you. But if you want to come, you can come."

So he goes back up there to the Four Peaks. But nobody follow him. He is gone all alone. Pretty soon they see his tracks. There were lots of trails and his tracks go in there. Then it looks like he stop and stand there. His both feet are printed like this. That's all. They don't go no further. They go up in the air, I guess. And after maybe four, five days the White people come and kill the people in the cave. He told us ahead already.

The *Kakaka* are never mean. But the people are scared of them some time. They think sometimes they take people away. But my father said, no, they don't do that. If you want to go with them, you can go. They don't drag you in there. And when you go out with them, you can go back. They let you go.

And they tell people what's going to happen, what's going to be. When a good man is singing, people hear them holler up in the air some place. They like the sing, I guess, and they holler. Four times, that's all. They have very good voices. And sometimes a medicine man knows what that holler means. He can tell the people what it means.

Sakarakaamche, he was the first medicine man. Up in Sedona where he taught the people to be medicine men, they painted many things on the wall and they learned from there. The red markings on the wall, these ones are from the blackroot. If you put on blackroot, it is just like red ink. Stays red for a long time. That's what they make in the caves. Make it like a church. *Sakarakaamche*, he marked four medicine men in this cave. He drew up four medicine men on the wall of that cave. And whoever wants to become a medicine man, he is to go up there and lay in that cave. You lay there all night by yourself, and one of those medicine men on the wall is going to sing. And that's the song you are going to take, the prayer, whatever he says, you going to get into you. You learn to sing and you learn to pray for the people, the sick people. You stay there four nights. Use the yellow powder. Put it on you. You can eat all right. But don't talk bad, get mad or something like that. That's no good.

That cave in Sedona, that's where Mike Harrison's father became medicine man. They used to live in Sedona and they live right close to that cave. He stay in that cave overnight. He said, "You want to do something, you mark it on the wall. You want to learn that and you want to learn singing, you lay down there and you dream what you want to do and about what kind of song you want to learn. You learn it! If you want to learn, if you want to learn a song, it might come around. Don't tell anybody. Just leave it alone. And you will learn more."

When my people stay over there in San Carlos, the medicine men learn over there. There is a big, long mountain over there. We call it *Wikilqua*, "Long Mountain." Lots of old houses on that mountain. And the people learn over there. They stay there, and the *Kakaka* teach them. That's how my uncle Tom Jones learned, and Mike Nelson, and Tom Ralphson and John Urki. They stay there and they learn in there. They want to learn to sing. They dance, dance, dance and pretty soon the Little People come in. You can't see them, they say. Just like wind. Just shhhh...they talk. We call that wind *matequirra*. Sort of a whirlwind. Pretty soon it turn into a body. The wind, the one that blows hard, it is *mat'haya*. The little one, that twists around is *matequirra*. That's the one you get and learn something.

Wigidjassa (Four Peaks). Elev. 7,657 feet. Photo by Elias Butler, 2010.

Up at Four Peaks it is the same way. You go over there and stay there and you learn something. The *Kakaka* are in there.

When the people learn at that mountain at San Carlos, they stay there all the time. Maybe a month, maybe two. They don't come down to camp. They stay together, stay together. In the night they drum and try to sing. They can't get it straight. Next night they try again, next night try again. Then the first song, it just comes. Then another one, after that another one. They just get it.

Tom Jones, my uncle, he stayed with the other boys at that mountain at San Carlos. They dance. My uncle stayed alone. And then, when they were dancing, he just get up and sing. He said, "I don't know how, but anyways, I just get up and start singing. And something told me, 'go down there. There are people down there who need help.'"

So he did. And after that, he is a good medicine man, my uncle.

Mike Nelson (1880-1955), he became medicine man when the lightning strike him. Before that, he used to be quite a rough boy. Roped any cattle, kill it and take the best parts. Leave the rest laying. He do anything, cared for nothing. People told him, "When rain falls, lightning strikes like that. Don't run around when lightning is like that."

He don't care. He just runs around when the lightning is starting. The *barave*, the lightning, knocked him down. Knocked him down and he was laying there for I don't know how long. He heard talking, it said, "You never believe anything, you never care nothing. So I'm the one who take you down. But I'm going to get you up again. And you help the people. Sick people, or when something is wrong with the people, you help them. I send you back." Mike Nelson told me, "I was listening like that and look up and I see the sky and the stars and moon."

The other boys took off when Mike got hit by the lightning. They got scared and took off. Mike got up. There was that camp over there and they had a fire there. So he goes over there and sits on a rock. That time he was going to sing the song. He said, he was sitting there and singing. "From there," he said, "I learn singing every song, every song, every song. Nobody tells me to do it. But anyways, something makes me do it."

Mike said, "Lots of people want to buy the medicine man. They want to be medicine man. So they go to the real medicine man and give him money or give him anything and want to learn. So that medicine man teach them to sing. Teach them doctoring people. I don't do that. I learn myself." Several of them do that over there. Pay and learn singing. Mike said, "That wasn't right. They don't last long. Maybe one day, maybe one time. That's all. But mine lasts all through my life."

A real medicine man doesn't go around and tells everybody, "I am big, I can do that, I can do everything." They don't say anything like that. But they are the ones who can do things, help people.

My uncle Tom Jones, he knows everything, but he don't say much. He said, "I learned when I was over there at the San Carlos mountain. Something from the air wanted to teach me. I didn't get it from the man. I got it from the spirit."

He had six or seven songs. "This is all they give me," he said.

And I asked him, "Can't you teach me to do that?"

"No, I can't. If you learn something for yourself, you learn it. I can't teach you."

Me, and my cousin John Jones, we always went on asking him for that. "Ah, you two is crazy," he said, "I can't tell you anything. But when you dream, maybe you learn. When you sleep and dream, maybe you get that song. They give it from up there." But I learn nothing. I want it, but they don't give it to me.

When the world burned and all the animals burned up and died, *Sakarakaamche* brought them back to life again. He sing and pray all the time. That's what my people do. When someone is sick, they help. A white doctor goes and gives people a shot and they are all right again. But we don't do that. We press and pray and use weeds and sick people get all right. When someone is sick, the one who knows how to sing, he sing over him. Mike Nelson, he knew the blackroot song. I helped him singing. But he said, "Don't miss. If you miss, you are going to ruin the song I'm singing here. Don't make a mistake." You sing the song four, five, six times and more sometimes. When the pain doesn't stop, the singer gets going, gets going. Sings 'til the pain stops. When the pain goes down, the singer stops.

The blackroot song, *Sakarakaamche* sings that first. His grandmother sings it for him and he got it. The boy was growing up and the old woman was singing it for him. He learned it from her. I don't know where she got it from. But the people learned it from *Sakarakaamche*. Everybody learned it from him.

A good doctor, when he sings and helps people, his power is going up. Makes more power. Mike Nelson told me that, too. "If I help no people, my power goes down. That's why I go around and help anybody. Then my power is going up. If it's a different tribe, it's better," he said. "The power gets more stronger. That's why I doctor anybody. Colored, White, Mexican. I heal somebody and my power is going up stronger." Mike went anywhere to heal people. Apache, Pima, Cocopah, anywhere.

My uncle Tom Jones helped Whites, Mexicans, anybody. And John Urki, he said, "They have the same body we have. The only difference is the color. But the blood, the vein, everything is like ours, like Yavapai. I see the blood is the same, the heart is the same, the liver is the same, the kidney is the same."

But there is only one thing bad this way: witch. There were certain things you had to watch out for. Old timers knew that. Pima, Yavapai, all of them had that. But we got medicine men to cure it. Those people then, they knew how to make a witched person healthy again. They knew if a person was sick from a witch, a *dabuye*, or from something else. They sing and find out. They sing over the sick man and find out how he got sick and who did it. They pray and sing and they see it. Like in a newspaper they see who it was. *Sakarakaamche*, he never did any witching. But he cured this kind. He knew what medicine is good for that.

When people witch you, you may be far away. But they say something and put it on you. My uncle Tom Jones said, they put something into you inside. They don't touch you, they just put it into you.

When I was young, I used to play cards, gambling. After quitting time I go and play cards with the other Indians. I win a little money, four, five times. Then that woman, a relative of mine, witched me. I get some money and she feels bad about it. I play, and something hit me right in the arm. The pain hit me, and my arm starts swelling. I am holding my arm and I run up to John Urki's place. John Urki is a medicine man, and he told me already, "If they do that to you, come to me pretty quick. Don't hold it too long. You can die right away. But if you come quick, I can fix it for you."

So when I come, he said, "I know you are coming. I help you." He starts singing and sucks my arm. He sucks, and the pain goes away. He takes something out of my arm, and it is a little piece, all red. It moves like life is in it. "That's no good, but anyways, I got it," he said. "I didn't get it all," he said. "But that little piece left don't bother you any more. I got the live one out."

That little piece left in my arm, I still can feel it. It is a little nudge, but it never bothers me.

That girl who witched me, she was my *nohd*, my cousin. She was young, maybe 18, 19 years old, and I was 15 or 16.

I didn't know my relative is going to do that. But anyways, she did it. Her grandmother was a bad witch. My grandmother always said that. The girl's father and mother were like that. So the kids were witches, too. The whole family like that.

Witches hurt people and their power gets stronger. Something tells them, "Go ahead and do it. Go ahead and kill that man." When they kill people, they raise up their power. Raise it up, raise it up. When they kill three, four people, they get more and more power. But if a witch don't kill people any more, he is the one who is going to die. That's why witches have to go on killing people. They are afraid.

When you have the blue stone and the white stone, a witch cannot hit you. It protects your body all around. One time I feel bad. Real bad. I look at my stone, and my stone is broken. Then I know somebody tried to witch me. But they can't hit me, just crack the stone.

The blue stone and the white stone carry life. If a man has a good body, the stone is showing life all the time. But when a man is weak, the stone goes down a little, too.

Sometimes the blue stone can tell you things. My uncle Tom Jones, when he was young, he don't listen much. He is wild and don't care for nothing. So they punch two, three holes in his ears and put blue stones in it. That way he learned to sing. He learned it from the blue stones.

When I was little, my uncle Tom Jones gives me blue stones in the ears and ties them around my neck. He told me, "That stone protects your body. Don't throw it away, don't give it away. That's why I made it for you." There is life in these stones and he prayed over them to protect me. But later when I was a cowboy I lose it somewhere.

The witches hurt people and their power is getting stronger. But Mike Nelson said, "They can't do anything to me. My power is more stronger. Nobody can do anything to me."

Mike Nelson was good in making people well when a witch hit them. The Pima often called him, and he went there lots of times. Then I go with him and help him sing. But one day he was going over there to Salt River, Lehi, and he said to me, "I don't want you to go over there. There is a bad one over there."

A Pima man's wife is paralyzed. Won't walk and do anything. So they get everybody to work on her. They can't do anything. So they come and get Mike Nelson. He says, "All right, I'll see." Then he said to me, "I'm going over there, but I don't want you to go with me. I'm just going alone. If we both go over there, it might not work right for you. Maybe you get sick. I'm going to go alone."

The next day we have a sweat bath and I say, "Hey, Mike, what you did over there?"

And he said, "I did it. I went over there last night and I found put things on the trail."

That Pima man had put something in. He came behind Mike and Mike said, "Hey, what are you looking for? You lost something?"

That man said, "No, no, I just look around here."

Mike reached down, and he pulled up feathers and a wooden doll and things like that. Four things. "Hey, you are looking for these?" he said. Mike got it all, this witch stuff. He could see it. If somebody touches it, he gets sick right away. But Mike, he know how to do things. *Sakarakaamche*, I guess, told him how to do it.

They went to the house. Then, Indians used to have a fire in the middle of the house. Mike broke all that witch stuff to pieces. The Pima didn't say anything.

Mike did some singing and then he said to that Pima, "You tell me, who planted that?" Mike threw the stuff in the fire and then he said, "Nobody did anything. You yourself, you are the one who made your wife bad. You gave her the sickness yourself. Nobody else." He said, "You know why she is sick for a long time, ha? She didn't go nowhere. You try to witch her. But you make it slow, slow, slow. Long time and your wife is going to die. But I got that thing in the fire there now. Maybe that lady is still alive for a long time. But she'll stay like this, paralyzed."

And that man's son, a big boy, he sits over there. He gets hold of that Pima man, take him by the head and hit him with a stick all over. "What do you do that to my Mama for?" he shouted. And the old man made, "auw, auw." Mike then went out, goes on his horse and comes back. That was down at Salt River, Lehi.

Sometimes a man goes around with a girl and that girl don't want to marry this man. And this man might try to make the girl crazy. One woman from here, she got bad one day. Poured water out, pulled her hair off, and her head goes round like this. She got real crazy. There was a Hopi boy where she went to school. He was trying to get her to be his wife. The girl went the other way. So he got mad and made her crazy. He got a butterfly. Pulled a hair off her and tied it to the butterfly and send it away. And that woman get crazy. She pulled her hair out, throw out water from the ollas, scratch herself. They had to tie rags over her hands and hold her because she didn't know what she did and scratched herself. One man who used to sing with Mike Nelson had to hold her. She sure scratched him.

Mike Nelson, he pray for that girl. He said he found out what is wrong, and he said, "That thing is going to come back to me." Little after the sun is up, the butterfly come in here. The hair was still on it. Mike take the hair off and burn it.

The girl knew which boy it was. Mike sing over her and that boy is going to come around. He wants to see the girl, what she is going to do. Mike tells the mother to take the girl away. Take her to the river some place. Pretty soon that Hopi boy comes around with an old car. He comes over here, sits here and stays here. Mike was watching him all the time. The Hopi looks round and round. He wants to see the woman, how she is. He wants to do it over again when he sees her going around. He is going to do it worse now. After some time he leave. We don't see the man no more. The woman got all right. And that man who held her when she was crazy married her. "I hold her and she feels soft, feels good," he said to me.

One time a colored lady came to Mike. She lived over there in Chandler, and she thought her husband is sick. Mike said, "All right, let's go," and he went over to Chandler. Her man is lying in the shade, and the woman said, "This is my husband. He never does anything, never works, always feels something hurts. I want to know what is wrong with him."

We stayed at those people's for one night. Then Mike rubbed his hands and he said to the lady, "You know what? Your husband, there is nothing wrong with him. He is not sick. He is just lazy. That's why he wants to play sick all the time. That's all."

So we went back the next day. Four, five days later that lady let the man go, run him off.

There was a Mexican, Joe Chavez. When he was a little boy, his people lived across the river, on the other side. And when my people used to sing over sick people, he sometimes saw it. When he was a man he lived near the Salt River Reservation.

One time we were down at the sweat bath, and Joe Chavez came there. "Hey, Mike, can you help me?" he said. Mike Nelson said, "Well, if something I can do for you, I give you help. It's all right."

"Sing over my wife, can you do that?"

"Oh, sure, you Mexican are like Indians, I help you."

So in the evening we go down to Joe Chavez' place on horseback. Mike Nelson and me and Bootha Brown and Quinna Harris (*Queena Harry*). Joe's wife go blind. They take her to the doctor, but he can't do anything.

We go over there and Mike sings. He said, he'll see what is wrong with the woman when he starts singing. He sings three songs. Used the yellow powder on that lady. Joe was sitting there and Mike asked him, "Two days ago, did you go down to Guadalupe?"

Joe said, "Yeah, our friend is down there."

His wife had said, "Take me down there, I want to see my lady friend."

Mike said, "Hey, Joe, you visited the wrong friend. That lady, when she came out of the house, did she touch your wife's face?"

The lady said, "Yeah, that's what she did to me. I don't know what's in her hand. But when we come back from over there, I can't see. It looked like kind of dark, like a shadow. Next day I can't see nothing."

Mike said, "All right, that's what you want to ask me. I can't do anything with your wife's eyes. That Yaqui woman is a witch. That's all I know. That's all I'm going to tell you. I stop now."

Joe said, "All right. Thank you, Mike."

Next morning Joe went down to Guadalupe and shot that woman. She was not too old that woman. She had witched lots of people down there, too. After he had killed that Yaqui woman, they put Joe Chavez in jail. He got five years, but after three years he came back.

My grandmother, she always got sick. That was from that poison the White people gave her on the way to San Carlos. When that sickness comes out, she shivers all over and kicks around. Like when a dog passes out. We hold her down and put blankets over her. Sometimes little bubbles come out of her mouth like spit.

When that sickness got her, my uncle Tom Jones pressed her and prayed. But he said, "She is not going to get well. She is going to stay like this to the end of her life. I can't do anything for her. That poison she got on her head is a bad one. It will stay with her all her life." One time Mike Nelson was in Prescott and that sickness came out on her. Mike came over, but he said the same thing. "No, I can't do anything. I don't think anyone can help her."

Sometimes she passed out. When she passed out, she said, she see lots of things.

Before she got sick with that poison, something tell her to help people. "You are not going to be a real medicine man, but you are going to help people." She did. When people have baby, she helped them get the baby out.

When the ladies have a hard time to get the baby, she just comes around and they have it right away. One day I was working at the road camp near Lynx Creek. An Apache lady was there and she was going to have a baby. She had a hard time for four days. Four days the baby didn't come. Four nights she cried. I never go to sleep. Hollering and crying that lady.

My aunt Viola (Viola Pelhame Jimulla, 1878-1966) told that woman, "I go over and get my mother. She is pretty good for that kind."

"All right," said the woman's mother and cried, "Looks like we lose that girl."

My grandmother was not very far then. Camped at that rocky point opposite Fort Whipple. Viola went over there with the horse and got another one saddled up. She told my grandmother to get up on the horse. But she said, "No, I'm just going to walk."

While she walks over to the Lynx Creek she rubs her hands and blows them. When she comes to the tent where the Apache lady is laying, the lady hollers out, "It is all right now. We have the baby."

That baby had been laying across. That's how it couldn't come out. But when my grandmother was coming, it twist round and got straight. Came out all right. I guess, that was when my grandmother rubbed her hands. She didn't touch the lady. Just rubbed her hands all the time when she was coming. And she didn't sing either. But the baby came out all right.

I ask her, "How do you do that, grandmother?"

"I don't know," she said. "It's my hand, my body, I guess."

"You see something or dream something?"

"I don't know," she said, "I've been like this all the time."

My uncle Tom Jones, he is just like that, too. He didn't touch anything. Just goes and looks and helps the ladies when they have a baby.

And my mother's sister, Viola, she don't have no problem. She had babies just anywhere. She had no help. When she goes to get seeds or those wild bananas, she come back and have a baby on top of her *kathak* (burden basket). She had four girls. Maybe my grandmother pray for her. That's why Viola never has any trouble with the baby.

I don't know if Mike Nelson helped people to have babies. But I know he helped people who were sick. He got them OK.

There was one woman who used to sing when people were sick. Sing just like a man's song, too. She was a real medicine woman. She was sucking people and made them all right. Her name was *Sheshaya*. That means, "Young, fat girl." *Sheshaya*, she was my *nohd*, my cousin. That woman never got married. I don't know why. She used to stay up there in Prescott. Later she came down here to Fort McDowell and she died here. That's the only woman singing when people were sick, that I know. But my grandmother said, before they were killing all our people, there were many ladies around who do that.

Jim Mukhat was a great medicine man. In San Carlos he got shot three times, but they don't kill him. He said, in the night he dreams that already they are going to shoot him. Something told him, "In the morning you are going to get shot. But anyways, I got your spirit out of your body already. Just your body is going to get hit. I put your life back in you again. You are not going to die."

In the morning one crazy man shot him three times. Two he gets in the hip, one in the throat. Two of the bullets he pressed out, but one stayed in him. Stayed in him all his life.

They bring him to the Army doctor. The doctor looked him over and then Jim Mukhat said, "I want to go home." The doctor said, "No, you can't go home. You are pretty bad hurt."

But Jim said, "I want to go home."

So the doctor said, "All right."

There was a policeman around, and the doctor told him to bring Jim home in the buggy. "That man is going to die," he told the policeman, "but anyways, bring him home."

Next morning the doctor went over to Jim's place. Called him from outside, "Jim Mukhat, you're around?"

Jim said, "Yes."

He is still there. The doctor goes in the house, and Jim is eating.

The White doctor asked him, "I thought you are going to die last night."

"Doctors never die! I'm a doctor. You doctor me, but I don't think you are a doctor!"

That day Jim went in the sweat bath. He asked his old woman, "Put the saddle on my horse, I want to go down to the sweat bath."

The lady said, "No, you are hurt pretty bad."

"I'm not hurt. Well, looks like I'm hurt, but it don't bother me. I want to go. Put the saddle on my horse." So the lady did and he went down to the sweat bath.

A medicine man can sit here and know what is going on far away. Nobody is here to tell you what is over there, but the man sits here and sings, and sees what is way over there at the other side of the mountain. Just like TV. A long way from where he is sitting something goes wrong, and he knows. Medicine men can understand the language of everything.

My grandmother said, when *Sakarakaamche* give us the eagle feathers, these feathers are talking. Like a radio. Eagle feathers, people pull it out from the bird and don't cut the stem end. They leave it full at the end. They hang it on something, and that feather talks. When it tells things, they hear it. I don't hear it. Mike Nelson used to hear it. And if you know how to talk to it, it will protect you. You carry it and never get sick. Like flu, measles, they never hit you.

If you kill an eagle, don't go and pull the feathers out. That is dangerous. But if you mark a cross on the ground, put him in there, use some kind of a medicine on him, at that time you can pull his feathers out. But don't just go over and pull it! The eagle is a great thing. We don't play with the eagle feathers, big feathers, small feathers. You pray for them, and then you can use them. You can store them where you want them.

Sakarakaamche, when he put the eagle feathers around the basket of the old lady, the Bat, he said, "Don't play with it." He told us, "When the ends are not cut, it is alive. Don't play with that."

Sakarakaamche put the fine, the little feathers round the basket of the old lady. That's what my people use, the fine feathers. *Sakarakaamche* was the first one, and he showed everybody how to do it. So, don't play with the eagle feathers when they are full. If people want to use it for something, like bow and arrow, they cut the stem end off first. We call that end *badak*. Then they let the feather lie for a few days and it is all right. If you don't do that, you get sick. Get crazy.

Sakarakaamche, he made the first *igugwawa*. That means "stick talker." We also call it *eheteletileti*. That's another name for it. It is like a board, not very big. People don't cut it out of a piece of wood. But when lightning hits a pine tree and splits a piece of wood out, that's what people use for the *igugwawa*. You peel it, peel it, and make it flat like a small board. Make marks like lightning and triangles on both sides. Make a hole on the side and put a string through. Swing it and it makes brrrr. It talks. The men who use it, they can understand what it says. They ask what's going to happen. When they sing over people who are sick, they use it. They swing it, and it is telling them if the person is all right or going to die or something.

My grandpa, old man *Haikotó*, said, "If you don't know how to use it, don't use it. Nobody tell you how to do it, how to use it, don't use it. But if you know, if you dream, or you see something that tells you to do it, you do it. Then you know. That way you get help. Nobody tell you nothing, you don't do it. You get sick, too," he said.

When we want rain, we ask the *igugwawa*. When it don't rain for a long time, you use it in four directions. Mark a cross on the ground. From there go in all four directions. Swing the *igugwawa*. That's how we ask the

Cloud. Ask for rain. That's when people want the food come up good. But you don't play with the *igugwawa*. If you play with it, the string will break right away.

The rattle can talk also. Tells a man what's going on and what's going to happen. The man who knows how to listen to it, he just knows what's going on, what's going to happen. Mike Harrison's father had a rattle hanging on the wall. Sometimes when he was laying there, it talked to him, "Someone is going to get you." Then he got up and got ready. Sure enough somebody would come and get him to help a sick person.

My uncle Tom Jones said, when you pray for people, you sing a little bit and shake the rattle. It is something like when you turn the radio on. Shake it, shake it, shake it. And from there the voices start in.

The rattle tells the medicine man what song to use when they sing over the sick people. Drum the same thing.

Some medicine men used the drum. My uncle Tom Jones, he used the drum when he helped the people. Hit it and hit it and hit it and pretty soon the words come from some place. Come in the drum. Tell the singing. *Sakarakaamche*, he was the first one who gave us the drum. And he makes the medicine men use it.

Long ago, they used cottonwood for the drum. Make it hollow. Put a little water in it. They put a buckskin on top and fasten it with a buckskin string. Make it tight. Then they put a little water on the buckskin and rubbed some ashes on it. They also made some pottery for the drum. They made the edges round. And when they put a string around there, they could make it tight, tight. Now they use some cooking pot or an old barrel for drum. Put little water in it and put a cloth on top. Sometimes, when people had a dance, they used a Levi jumper for the top. They dance all night, and at day they take it off again and wear it. You could see the mark on the back then. That's where they rubbed flour or ashes on the cloth and put water on it. That way they made it real tight. Closed all the little holes in the cloth. Then it sounded good. And when they hit the drum right, the water comes out from the bottom.

Sakarakaamche gave us everything: the drum, the gourd rattle, the buzzing stick and the flute.

The flute, people use it when it is not raining for a long time. The man who knows how to do it, he do it.

The flute, the boys also play it for the girls. One time *Sakarakaamche* played it way out in the mountains. Pretty music! The girls were looking for him, but he was hiding out.

There is that kind of shell that looks like a rock. It is solid. They get it from up in Sedona. That is from the time of the flood. My grandmother said, they sometimes use that for medicine. The medicine men use that and some of it is like feathers. It talks. Many people used to have that shell on a string round their neck. Old timers used to have that. My grandmother has it all the time. It sure helps her. "That's why I live a long time," she told me. When the White people gave her that poison, that little thing helped her. "Maybe if I don't have this, I die right away," she said. "But that shell helped me, so I live a long time. Lot of people died on the trail from that poison." We call that shell *adjilta*. That means, "little round thing."

That shell which we have in the ditches, we play with that. But it can help, too. Some men know how to make it work, so it helps us. If you know how to talk to it, it can be used to help people. Everything can help people, if you know how to talk to it.

Sometimes the medicine man smokes the pipe when he sings over sick people. Just the medicine man smokes it. That pipe is like a cigar. When they make that pipe out of clay, they put a little stick in the middle. When they burn it, that stick inside gets all burned up. They take a little stick and clean it out, fill it with tobacco, and put some hot coal in it, too. They let it lay until it gets red hot.

My grandpa, old man *Haikotó*, he sucks it when it is hot. I sit one time with him when I was a little boy. I said, I want to try it.

"All right," he said. I sure got burned.

"Want another pump?" he asked me.

"No, I don't like it no more!"

The medicine man swallows that smoke from the pipe, the *maluh*. When he sees what is wrong with the people, the smoke comes out from his body. Then he sees what is wrong with the people when they are sick.

Sometimes, when we hear something bad, he uses the pipe. When they hear the owl, he smokes it. He finds out what is going to be. The owl talks too big sometime. When they hear the *yuh*, the owl, the medicine man takes the tobacco and smokes. Then he knows what is going to be. When it is going to rain, or no rain next summer, or something like that.

Same way with the eagle. Eagle, when they come around some place, the medicine man sings and prays and finds out what the eagle came around for.

Long ago, over there at Cottonwood we hunt jackrabbit one day. We put them up on a rack and eagle comes and wants to eat them. The people knew the eagle wanted to say us something. And there is a medicine man, his name is William Neil. He tells us, "The big bird wants to tell us something. There will be a sickness all over. Lots of people going to die." It was true. That was when the flu came.

I don't know why, but not too long ago one eagle came to my house here and sits on the mesquite tree, he sits there for four days. That eagle wanted to say something to me. But I don't understand. That's why he stays there for four days. I don't know his language, so do not say anything and just went away. If I could talk with him, he would have told me something. But I don't talk and so he waited and then he went away.

Over there, at the *Tolkepaya*, there was an old man, *Haikotó*. That means, "White man fool." He could tell people what is going to be. The people asked him, they want to know how the *Tolkepaya* is going to be. And that old man said, "All right, we will see."

Tolkepaya country. Hills west of Mayer, August 1975. Photo by Sigrid Khera.

That medicine man had a little tipi with cottonwood all around. It was open on top a little. That medicine man *Haikotó* was singing in there four songs. He sends for the people gone long time ago. He sends for the spirits, the *mìéh*.

"I stay here, but I just go up like that," *Haikotó* said, "You see me here, but I go up like that."

He said, he travels like wind. He went over there and send for four *mìéh*. Three go away, say nothing. Then one *mìéh* came to *Haikotó*. That *mìéh* comes like air, like wind. *Haikotó* said, he couldn't see him. He was just like glass.

He came over there and he said to *Haikotó*, "I've been gone for a long time. My name is *Kulasmalgagava*." That means, "Jackrabbit Split Ear."

"That's what my name is. You want me to tell you something, so I tell you. But I'm not going to tell you, 'you die tomorrow or next day'. No, I don't know that. But I tell you, our country is just like smoke. Lots of smoke. Nothing but smoke. Maybe there is no *Tolkepaya* around not too long. That's all I'm going to say." Then he left. That *mìéh* was a *Tolkepaya*, too, when he was alive.

He said the truth. There used to be lots of *Tolkepaya* from Skull Valley down to Hillside, Kirkland, Congress, Wickenburg, and from Date Creek down to Yuma. They are all gone now. No *Tolkepaya* over there.

People used to sing to get rain and rain comes down. There was a medicine man, Jim Mukhat. That man was a *Wipukpa*. That time we were in Cleator, the other side of Bumble Bee. I think it was in 1916 or 1917. It was after my mother died. Over there, there was a cable with a basket on and with that they haul ore to Mayer. I used to work there. There was a store owner and he asked Jim Mukhat, "Jim, when is it going to rain?"

Jim talks English pretty well. "What do you mean?" he said. "You are the one who knows everything! You got a machine for everything, knowing when the wind is going to blow, knowing when it is going to rain, knowing when it is going to be cloudy. You do that! Mine is different. If I want it, I can pray, and it rains. But I know, you don't believe me. You got it on the machine. I don't. I'm talking to God. I pray for it."

"If it rains after a little while, I want to pay you," said the store owner.

"Why you want to pay me for?" said Jim. "You said you are the one who want to see the rain. So I'm going to do it. You don't have to pay me. You think you know everything. But I think, you don't know not very much."

Cleator, Arizona. Photo by Elias Butler, 2011.

He said that, and four, five hours later it starts sprinkling. That White man said, "I believe you now, Jim."

"What do you mean, you believe me? Me, I don't believe you! You don't know nothing. I'm talking to God. You don't."

One time Jim Mukhat got mad. Over there in Cleator, one White man asks him, "You're medicine man, Jim?"

"Yes," he said, "I am medicine man. I can sing, and I can talk. *Sakarakaamche* teach me from long time ago."

The White man said, "All right, you say that, and we'll see." The White man [Editor's note: E.W. Gifford?] put a machine there, and Jim Mukhat talks and sings. He sings the blackroot song, and he sings other songs. After some time the White man gives him some water to drink and says, "Maybe you rest a little bit, Jim. Just sit there and listen."

"All right."

And he put that machine on and Jim is singing in it. Jim got sure mad. The White man didn't tell him he was going to use the machine. After that the White man gave some money to the lady. He tries to give it to Jim first, but he didn't take it. I think it was $2.00 for a song. Jim was so mad, and he lay down over there. The old woman said to him, "You did, now don't say anything. You know the White people."

"But I am a medicine man," he said.

Mike Harrison's father, in the summertime, when it is getting hot, he make a cross. On the ground he marked a cross. And he got a blue horse. He brings it and stand it right there in the middle. Sing four songs. Cloud songs. Go around to each side of the cross. And after that it starts to get cloudy, sprinkling and raining a little. He knew everything, that old man.

A cross marked on the ground has four corners. That's for four people. Four different colored people. The Yellow Cloud, the Red Cloud, and the White Cloud, the Blue Cloud. Each one is at an end of the cross. That's the ones he sing for. He talk to them, sing to them and tell to them, "Don't move, just stay in the house. We are coming. We are coming to help you."

So the clouds spread out and start raining.

One time boys from here worked at a quicksilver mine over there around Saddle Mountain. Something happened. Fire started in those mountains around Four Peaks. A lightning strike a pine. Burned that country over there, burned it pretty fast. The pines, the thick oak, they burned. Many people try to stop the fire, cut down the trees. But they can't stop it. Can't do anything. Soon one boy from here, he said, "Hey, let's get together and pray. Make rain. But not the different tribes. Just us Yavapai."

They sent the Apache to sit over there. And another bunch, the White people, they send them to sit over there. Just the Yavapai were going to try. This boy said, "We'll see what's going to happen. You people don't believe nothing. Don't believe Indians. We're going try it. I'm going to sing. All the Yavapai come and help me."

They sing four songs. Then they see a cloud. Over there, a little spot like that. Just a little bit of a cloud. It gets big, it rains hard and it gets the fire off. This is Yavapai work. They were singing, praying. The people used to sing like this. When they need help, they sing. Over there, they sing for the rain, and it comes. That boy, he talked to the cloud, to the lightning, and it starts raining right away. Water comes all over.

And the White man, the ranger headman said, "I heard, Yavapai can do anything. I don't believe it. I see it now, and I'm going to believe you people."

When the fire stopped, he said to those Yavapai boys, "Meet me down there at the store at Sunflower on Sunday."

They said, "All right."

Next Sunday they went over there. And that ranger headman, he is also a policeman, he got beer for them. One case. Then the quicksilver mine boss came over there and he said, "What's these Indians doing over there?"

The headman ranger told him, "We almost got burned, but the Indians here stopped the fire. So we give them a little drink."

"Well," said the quicksilver mine boss, "You didn't give them enough. Give them more."

So they got another case of beer. That boss's wife comes around, and she puts another case of beer up for them. And then the store owner, he gets them one case. They get four cases of beer all together. One White old man, he is a miner, he lives down there. He told them, "Just take the stuff over there into my house. Nobody around here to bother you and put you in jail."

So they take the beer over there and they have a good time. There is lots of food in that house, too. That White man told them to cook it. They make meat, cook bread, eat all day, all night. Drink coffee, beer, everything.

That boy who prayed for the rain, his name is Frank Choka. He is the father of Richie Choka. Mike Harrison, he was with them singing.

There is one thing, I think about that all the time. One evening I was riding a horse the other side of Warren Nelson's place, and Mike Nelson was riding from the other side. He called, "Hey, come on John."

I thought, all right, I go over there.

"Oh," he said, "I thought it is John Smith. All right then, you tell him, I'm going to go. I got everything ready. Shined my shoes, ironed my suit, my shirt. Everything cleaned up already. I don't know how long it is going to be I'm around. Maybe I go right now, maybe when I go back to my house. You tell John," he said.

"All right," I said.

I went up there to John Smith. When I come back from over there, my wife Minnie comes out and says, "Hey, Mike Nelson, he passed out and they take him to the hospital."

And about one hour, one-and-a-half hour, his son Warren Nelson came down and he told us Mike passed out before he got to the hospital. He died that evening. He didn't look like something is wrong with him. But he knew, he is going to go. They said, when he came home, he took the saddle off his horse, brought the horse in the corral, come back into his room, laid down and was gone. I don't know how he knew he is going to go.

Mike Nelson, he wanted to teach me how to help people. He asked me if I want to learn how to help people. A bunch of Cocopah people came here and asked Mike to help, to pray for them. I was always helping Mike singing. So he got me and went down where the Cocopah stayed in that mesquite brush at the other side of the highway. The Cocopah had one lady with them, and she had cancer. Mike prayed for her. Singing maybe four, five songs and I helped him. Then he said, "I can't do anything. Inside her it's all eaten up. The lung is only a little bit more. I can't do nothing to get it back." He said, "All right, John, let's go home."

And that time he told me, "You want to help people like I do?" Then he said, "Tomorrow morning I meet you over there, the same place where I pray for you already. I pray for you, and you can do it."

But I didn't go that time. I go some other place and get drunk. And after maybe five, six months he came over to me and said, "I was trying to get you do something good. You didn't do it. But someone is going to do it. And you'll see," he said, "he will come over to your place some time."

Mike Nelson knew it. "I wanted you to be like him, but you didn't come. It is too late now. I can't do it over. You didn't get it, so somebody is going to get it and you'll see."

Mike Nelson got Jim White, a Cocopah from Somerton. He prayed for Jim White like he did for me once over there at little hill. That's how he made him the way he could help people.

Some years ago my wife Minnie, she got pretty sick. She lay there still and can't do nothing. I get her up and give her water and everything. For two years she was like that. She was sure sick and I was afraid I lost her. The White doctor could do nothing. Just said, "Stay in bed."

One day I come home and that man Jim White was there. And I asked him, "You can help her? You can do that?"

"That's all right," he said, "that's why I come over here."

I hadn't called him. He just knew it and so he came over here. "I'm here and I help her right away," he said. "Let's see her walk around again."

He prayed for us and then he said, "Minnie is going to be all right. Maybe you see her walk around with no stick some day."

And she did. Now she is walking around good.

Jim White is now the only medicine man who comes here. But he is old now and pretty sick himself. Mike Nelson, he wanted to teach me how to help people. He told me to come and I didn't go. Too late. He is gone now.

Jim White, taught by Yavapai medicine man Mike Nelson, gathers *etchitawa* (yellow powder) at Fort McDowell. 1977 photo by Sigrid Khera.

Chapter 22

◆

John Williams, My Life
(1904 - 1983)

I was born over there in San Carlos on June 15, 1904. When I was born my mother threw me away. They have a hole there where they put ashes and trash and old cans. And she threw me down there. My uncle's daughter, a little girl, she saw it when my mother threw me in there. But she didn't say anything. Then one old lady came by to get water. And she heard something make noise down there. Sounded like something is in that hole down there. She took the water up to the house and came back. Looked around, looked around. There was a roll of a skirt in that hole. She unrolled it and I was in there. That old woman took me out from the ashes. That was on a hot day, fifteenth of June. I lay right in the sun. If I stay a little longer down there, I don't live. They didn't cut my navel, yet. She cut it for me, clean me and put me in a cradle. They used to make a cradle pretty quick. She lay me in there.

My grandmother didn't know about me. But somebody told her then. She just came into the old lady's house and carried me away. And that lady didn't say anything. Later she told me, "Your grandmother didn't say anything. Just picked you up and went off. Your grandmother is sure a tough one, so I didn't say anything. Another woman I fight. Don't let her carry you away. But not her." After that I stay with my grandmother all the time.

I don't know what is wrong with my Mama. She threw me away as if I had been a banana. Later I asked her, "Why you threw me away, Mama?"

"Oh," she said, "I don't know you last a long time. When you came out, you look awful. That's why I threw you away." My mother had a boy before me. That boy looked pretty, she said.

But he died when he was about two years old. My mother thinks another woman witched that boy, and so he died. My mother used to play cards and she was winning all the time. Got money all the time. So one lady talked bad to her and the boy was gone right away.

"So you come out after a little while, and you look awful. That's why I threw you," she told me.

Everybody over at San Carlos knew it that my mother threw me away. Once I go over there to San Carlos and I meet the old woman who picked me out from the trash hole.

She said, "Hey, who is your mother?"

I told her my mother's name. (*Jakhwa*, ? -1913)

"Oh, one time you were down in the trash pit," she said. "I know you now, you are the one they threw away down there. Come on, I take you over there."

"No," I said, "I don't want to see those bad times again. I don't want to go over there."

"It's all right," she said. "You go with me and eat. Meet people and eat."

"All right." I go with her and eat.

"If you want to stay here for a few days, it's all right," she said.

"No," I said, "I go home tonight." And I come back home the next day.

I never stay much with my mother. Always with my grandmother (*Kohwah*, that's "buzzing sound") and her old man. They had killed my grandfather over there at the cave. So my grandmother married again. That man was my grandfather's cousin. Younger one. That's why I call him *nakwe* and he called me *wanna*. He called my mother *nood*, and she called him *naya*. His name was *Pelhame*. That means, "big feet." He sure was good to me all the time.

I don't know my father's mother, my *morra*. She got killed somewhere around Ash Fork where the railroad junction is now. She got killed when the White people sometimes killed Indians. Meet them and kill them. My father's father, he got killed above Prescott same place. But that was a Hualapai that killed him. Hualapai don't get along with Yavapai, and that was how my grandfather from father's side got killed. But that was before the White people were around. That time the *Wipukpa* get acorn and piñon in that country way up to Seligman, and the Hualapai see them and kill them.

When I was maybe six, seven months old, my grandmother and my uncle took me back to their old country. They left San Carlos. From San Carlos, first time they come over here, they go to Camp Verde. We camped there for a little while. From there they took me to Prescott. My grandmother was from Four Peaks, Fort McDowell. But her old man, my uncle *Pelhame*, he was from over there, Prescott. That's why they went back to that place.

A little after I was born, my father and my mother split. My father found another woman. Better looking. He went back with her to Camp Verde and then down to Fort McDowell. My mother got married to Jim Hunt. Way after me my mother had another boy. But he died when he was just little.

When I was just a little boy, my grandmother, she tells me everything.

"Don't get bad, don't get to steal, don't hate people," she said. "Be kind with the people all the time," she said to me. "That's what the God do to us. If you are a good boy, a good man and you passed away, he has a place for you over there." She told me that all the time. My grandmother had never been to school, nothing. But she talks like church all the time.

My grandmother never let me stay in bed long. She let me get up early. She told me, "When you get up early and do something around, then you never get lazy." She is right.

My uncle *Pelhame*, he was always good to me. When I was little, he always packed me on his back. He braided some strings, put it around me and carried me.

He made shoes out of buckskin, moccasin for me. When they make these shoes, they put a big piece in the front. All of the Yavapai moccasin had that. We call that piece in the front *nanyodjawadawa*. I don't know why they make that piece in front of the shoe. When I went out with my new shoes, run around to chase rabbits, I get caught in the brush all the time with that piece. The brush hooked me with that, and I fell down all the time. I got angry and cut that leather piece off. But then I hide my shoes all the time. I come in to the camp with my shoes, but when I come very close, I take them off. I laid my shoes way up in the corner and upside down.

My grandmother asked me, "Where are your shoes?"

I said, "Right there." Pretty soon she thinks something is wrong, and she picks them up. There is a hole in that thing. She whipped me! She whipped me, but the old man, my uncle, he said, "No, don't do that! There is only one around with us, and I don't want to hurt that boy. Just teach him how to do things. He will be all right."

My uncle, the old man, he never whipped me. He never talked bad to me. And he never wanted to see anybody whip me. My mother always whipped me. So he moved. He didn't want to bother with my mother. So I wasn't around much with her.

Sometime when I was little we stayed at Walnut Grove. *Pelhame* had a relative from the *Tolkepaya* side, and heard that man stays over there at Walnut Grove with his old lady. So we moved over there. Next my *nithi* ("aunt"— mother's parallel cousin) and her old man *Purgas'icha* hear we go over there, so they come, too. Next bunch coming was my relative from my father's side with his old woman and the kids. Mike Harrison and his mother and father *Okanya* (also *Oskannya*) came, too. And another relative of *Pelhame* moved in. All us people together there were relatives. Maybe twenty people together.

A White farmer, I don't know his name, gave us some land there. He plowed the land for us. Fenced it, too. The water was right there, so we made a ditch across and irrigate. We have lots of watermelons and squash and everything there. *Pelhame*, and another old man, Jack Jackson, did the planting.

We have no house there. Just use the wikiup, and use all the Indian stuff. When we moved in there, the farmer butchered a cow for us. So we have lots of jerky meat.

That farmer had lots of cattle, and we kids bring the cattle down a canyon where there is water. We ride the cows, too. One girl, she is older than us, she stays on the bucking cattle long time. But we younger ones fell off all the time.

There was a storekeeper there, Mr. Wagoner, and he told us that long before we moved in, White people built a dam above Walnut Grove. But they didn't build it solid. Just filled it up with cement sacks. There was lots of place to hold the water in there. But when it started to rain hard, the dam bust, and the people and everything below was washed away. [Editor's note: In February 1890, the Walnut Grove Dam on the Hassayampa River—some 30 miles north of Wickenburg—failed, and approximately 100 people were killed.]

They had a big pipe there for the spillway, and that pipe was still there when I lived there. Sometimes I used to play in that pipe in the summer time. It's cold in that tunnel. I went in there and played all the time.

White people were going to start a school there. My grandmother would have let me go to that school because we lived right there. That was the only time she would have let me go to school.

Lots of the White people sent their kids to school at Skull Valley. But my grandmother didn't let me go there. Kids in Skull Valley were rough. But in Walnut Grove, the kids all around there were friends. Our kind. They were White kids, but like our kind.

I was quite small then, and sometimes everything seems like a dream. I was too small that time to go to school.

We stayed there at Walnut Grove for two years. But then *Purgas'icha* my *nithi's* husband died, and their boy died. So we all left the place. We should have stayed there, but we left because they had died. *Purgas'icha* had kind of a heart trouble, I think. He worked in the field, and then he didn't feel too good. So he comes back and lies down under the shade. His old woman trying to cook. When she is through, she calls him to eat. But he lays there, and pretty soon he just shakes the head and is stiff.

We bury him there. The men made a hole pretty deep and bury him. The old man had been quite sick before already and he had told them to bury him. That's why they did it that way.

Purgas'icha was kind of a medicine man and he was like a chief when we lived there. And when he died, we all left the place.

For some time we stay up at Mayer. Camped around town. That time we live in Mayer they have a smelter there. They boil the rock in that smelter and it sure smells strong. I was a little boy and I had asthma pretty bad. When it is a cloudy and windy day it sure is bad. My God, it choke me. When the smoke gets me, I can't do anything. I can't breathe. I stay in bed covered with a blanket all day. I feel like choking at night when I sleep. Mike Harrison's father saw it and he said, "My child, I'm going to fix it for you. When I see you, you look bad all the time. I make you some medicine." Mike's father, he boiled a weed for me. He make some kind of a tea and I drink it four mornings. The choke is all gone. I just run around and I don't have it any more.

Some time we stay down at Congress Junction. There was some mining around there. Lots of people were washing the dirt to get some gold. *Pelhame*, he helped cutting wood, digging, putting in water lines.

And there were Mexican kids, too. The man from the mine gave us kids a tube, flattened at the end. Then he let us blow in the sand with it. Pretty soon we see something yellow in it. When we get it, we put it in a little perfume bottle. Then we bring it to the commissary and get some apple or banana. Sometimes that commissary man give us shoes or a shirt. Blue shirts cost 25 cents then. And he gave us this kind. He lines us kids up and gave it to us. Pretty soon he said, "All right, get some more." So we go and make some more yellow. Crazy Indians. That yellow was gold. We give lots of money away for an apple. That's why I say, "I'm just a dumb Indian."

There were lots of *Tolkepaya* around Congress Junction, and they camp all over there. They used to work in that mine. There were lots of trees, sycamore, in the washes, and water running high from the springs. Everything green around. We call that place *Localoca*. That means "Willow." But the White people suck all the water away and use it for the mine. Now there is no more water around the place. Everything is dead.

Smelter at Mayer, Arizona. Photo by Sigrid Khera, August 1975.

We moved around a lot. One time we stayed at a mine near Skull Valley. We call that place *Ahagua*. That means, "Cottonwood stay there all the time." There is just one cottonwood tree down there. One Mexican lady was having a little mine there. Her name is Maria and she calls that mine Santa Maria. That Mexican lady worked like a man. Worked all the time. Two, three boys working with her all the time. That woman was washing the sand, try to get the gold. They make a rail and put a cart on. Bring the dirt to the water with that little cart. Put the dirt in a round pan, put a little water in it, wash it, wash it, wash it and put all the dirt out. Just at the bottom there is a yellow stuff in there and they take it.

That time I was still good for nothing. Just a little boy. I don't work that time. I just watch people work. But my old man *Pelhame*, he worked there. Put dirt into that cart. Push it to the water. I don't know how much they pay him. But anyways, we stay there for a long time.

Ahaytikutoba (Black Canyon). Looking west from Sunset Point rest stop to the Bradshaw Mountains, where Yavapai John Williams' grandmother took him to live, to save his life from government boarding schools. Photo by Elias Butler, 2012.

When the other kids started to go to Indian school, my grandmother was hiding me all the time. She had seen lots of kids go to school and they got TB and died. "I don't want you to get TB and die." Then White people went around and got the Indian kids for the school. When they came around, my grandmother covered me with a burden basket. She put me in there and put lots of stuff on me and I was laying in there. Hot! I can't breathe much.

That's the way they did with Mike Harrison over in San Carlos. His father said, he will never let him go to school. Mike's brothers and sisters, they take them away to the school. Two sisters and two brothers. They were older than him. They don't know where they go, they don't know where they take them. And they never bring the kids back. Two or three years after they had taken them away, another man came around and tried to take Mike to school. But his father and his mother told him not to take away Mike. They told the man, four of their kids they took away and never brought them back, so they can't take this one.

My grandmother and her old man took me over to Black Canyon. We call the Black Canyon *Ahaytikutoba.* That means "The Water gets Together." The big mountain there, the other side where the lookout place (Sunset Point) is now, we camp there for a long time. There is a spring and we used to live there for a long time. At Black Canyon they don't work at any mine. Just stay there around and live like Indians. Get fruit and get deer.

In June when the saguaro fruit get ripe, we went down from Black Canyon to Cave Creek. We camped near a spring and there were always other people from Fort McDowell over there camping with us. Sometimes my mother and my grandmother wanted coffee. So they sent me over to Black Canyon to bring it for them. There was the store where we had credit. We bought stuff and my people worked for the storeman for that. I sure liked to go over there. We got that Eagle brand coffee and there was a candy tied to that can. For that one candy I run all the way to Black Canyon and back to Cave Creek. They tied a bag over my back and I ran along the hills. Start out in the morning and get to the store at noon. Come back in the evening. Sometimes my cousin, Yuma Frank's boy, came along. He used to camp there, too. We played all along the way to Black Canyon. Chase little rabbits and jackrabbits. Just to play with. Let them loose after we catch them. Also get little coyotes. You can get them easy. Just grab their tail and hold them at the neck. We don't kill the animals. Just catch them to play.

Over at Black Canyon, I had a little black horse, and I catch burro with it. There were lots of wild burros around Black Canyon. Some were black, some red, gray, piñon. I just play with them. Catch them and rope them. Make a pack saddle of wood. Just cross the wood. The burro kick around a while, then they stop. When the sheepherders came along, they traded them for guns sometimes. I got lots of guns then.

That time I wasn't alone. Way down at Black Canyon there lived White people. They had long hair. First White people I see with long hair. They were Mormons. Down at Black Canyon River lived old man Heckle. Old man Heckle got lots of kids. Lots of wives, too. There were lots of little houses around there. He got too many wives—just one man. I think they were about ten. And lots of kids. Some grown, some little ones. Some of them were walking, some of them the women carried. Lots of fighting with that many kids. There were about six or eight big kids. Grown ones, just my age.

We go and get burros down in the canyon. Sometimes we make a corral and run them in, close it. We get that curved knife (sickle) and cut lots of grass with it. Pile it in there like a haystack. We pack water a long way. But they have a big drum there. So we bring water in it. Make a big hole there and dump the water in. The burros stay there and drink the water. We ride the burros. If there was one which bucked good, we kept him. One of the Heckle boys was riding bucking horses at the rodeo shows in Prescott and Phoenix. He rides lots of times at rodeos. Always gets money. He is my friend. But I never see him for a long time.

In 1912 I stayed with my mother in Black Canyon for some time. Jim Hunt was postman over there. He rode the pony express. I guess he went to school a little bit, that's why he could read the names on the letters. He brought the mail from Mayer to Black Canyon. He got over there to Mayer early in the morning, got the letters and put them in the boxes. That time there were lots of camping prospectors around. So he rode to all those camps. Three days a week he made the round. Monday, Wednesday and Friday. He used to ride real fast and he used to look to all sides. I asked him why. He said, "One of these White soldiers might be around and shoot me. So I look this way and that way."

That year we came down here to Fort McDowell. We came on horseback from Cave Creek. We were looking for cactus fruit over there, and then we heard they are having a rodeo at Fort McDowell. So we come to Fort McDowell and we stay here for two or three weeks. We stayed over there where Mike Harrison lives now. Yuma Frank lived over there.

When we were down here, people used to play games all the time. At one place, couple of miles from where we stayed, they used to play cards. My mother used to go up there and play, play, play all day to sundown. Men and ladies all mixed together play. I get hungry and I pull my mother to get home, but she just plays on. When they go home at night, my stepfather had a stick to get rid of the snakes on the trail. When he hit a snake—shht—we just turn a flashlight on and go on.

That time, when I come over here first time, Yuma Frank's wife (Mary Mischa) is here. "Hey, your daddy is coming here and see you pretty soon," she said. My father used to work in the irrigation, taking care of the ditches. Take the boys over there and fix it. That's how he came back and forth here for the ditches all the time. "He get you pretty soon," she said.

"Ah, no, I don't like him!" I didn't know him, so I didn't care much. But one day he came on here, and "come on," and he puts me in the saddle of his horse and brings me down to his house. He stayed there with the other wife. But he had no other children. Only the two of us. But the first one had died before I was born. After that I know my father. And much later when I get laid off from work at Prescott, I come down here to Fort McDowell.

My grandmother and her sister had had one man. The same one. People were like this sometimes in old days. Two women stayed with one man. Tom Jones was the son from the other woman, my grandmother's sister. But the man, my grandfather got killed in that cave. Tom Jones' mother got killed in that cave, too. Tom Jones and another lady, two of them were from my grandmother's sister.

That year 1912 my uncle Tom Jones and his sister were with us at Black Canyon for a while. This lady was a little younger than Tom Jones and older than my mother. She is my *nathia*. In the morning she got up and get cactus fruit. Come back about noon. There was a cottonwood tree and we spread canvas underneath it. She lay down there and cover herself with a shawl. I thought she was asleep. My mother was cooking and she said to me, "Tell your aunt we eat." So I went over there. I touch her with my foot and she is just stiff. I take the scarf from her face and

278

it looks like something is wrong with her. So I run back to my mother. My mother comes and tries to get her up, but my aunt is all stiff. She is gone. Right there. Nothing wrong, nothing hurting her and she is dead.

In 1913 I was again with my mother (*Jakhwa*) in Black Canyon, and she died in there. My grandmother was not around when my mother passed away. She was in Prescott. That morning we were also going to go to Prescott. My mother said, "Go, and get the horses. We go and see your grandmother." She got up and cooked. She make tortillas and we eat. But then she told me, she wasn't feeling too good. She thought, she couldn't make it to Prescott that day, maybe she would wait a couple of days. Jim Hunt was going to go with me and look for the horses. She said to him, "No, don't go." And she said to me, "Just look at the horses and come back." When I come back, she was gone already. Just like that she died. So I lost my mother.

We bury her down there at Black Canyon. But White people dug her out and I heard they put her up in some museum in California. I don't know what they did with her. But she had lots of silver rings and bracelets and a necklace on her. When she played cards, she won that jewelry. So we put it on her when we buried her. That's why I think they dug her out.

My mother went away fast. I think someone witch her. Long time later Mike Harrison's father said something to me when I came to Mayer. "You people over there," he said, "You live at the wrong place. The man in there is just like a sticker. Dangerous." But he didn't tell me who it was. "I don't want to tell you," he said, "but anyways, your mother didn't die for nothing. Somebody did something to her."

So I said, "You tell me, you tell me who did it."

But he never told me. He knew, I'm going to get into trouble. So I don't know who did it. I sure got mad, but I can't help it. She is gone already.

After my mother had died, Jim Hunt took a wagon and went back to Camp Verde. I was alone and I had nobody to help me. I went to my grandmother in Prescott, and they take me over there to the ranch where they work.

Sam Jimulla, my mother's younger sister's husband, he worked at the cow ranch. He got me to work with them, and that's how I learned to become a cowboy.

Sam is the one who teach me to be cowboy. He told me, "When I tell you something to do it, you do it. So you learn something yourself. Nobody going to help you when there is nobody around."

I sure liked Sam. When he takes off and goes somewhere, I cry all the time. And when he comes back, he says, "I missed you, so I know I come back." Sam Jimulla is relative from my father's side, my *kinya*.

My mother's younger sister Viola I call *mira*. If she is the older I would call her *nathia*.

That cow ranch belongs to a Mexican lady. I help cutting corn and I feed the horses and pretty soon the Mexican lady said, "Do you want to ride with the people? I give you a job." That time I get 25 cents a day. She paid me a quarter for a long time. And after a long time she paid me 50 cents. And then she paid me a dollar, $30 a month, that's what they paid people at that time.

Sometimes we were at a ranch way back, the other side of Skull Valley. That time I don't talk English, just motion. I helped around there when they cut corn. Pile it, pile it, throw it on the wagon and bring it in. Sometimes they give me 10 cents, sometimes 25 cents. The man paid me like that. Next time I start working there steady. Help him pick potatoes, and he was going to pay me. But he said, I got no name. He said, my Indian name was kind of hard to say. Sometimes he called me Charlie, then Jim, sometimes "chief."

"But you are too small to call you chief," he said. "I give you my name." His name was John Williams. He had another name in the middle. But he didn't give me that. He said, "I give you my straight name."

My father's name is *Surrama*, Thomas Surrama (1865-1939). *Surrama*, that means "green split over." I didn't know they use that as his last name. But I never go round with my father for a long time. Later, when I came down here, my father wanted me to change my name to his name. "Too late," I said. "Everyone know my name is Williams. I can't change it now." Sounds like this wasn't my father. But I like Williams better anyways.

When we were at that Mexican lady, she called me with my Indian name *Kehedwa*. And when I come back to this lady again to work at the cow ranch, she called me Williams from there on.

But there was a Negro boy with that Mexican lady and he called me with my Indian name all the time. The Mexican lady, she had raised that boy. They had thrown him away—just like me. That Mexican lady had married a White man. Over there in Prescott in town, the lady came around with her old man in the wagon. They used to have a barber shop in town and the old man was going to get his hair cut. They stopped there. The woman stayed in the wagon. She hears something cry over there. She looked around, looked around, sees nothing. There was a little box laying there upside down. She picked that up and that little baby boy was laying in there. The mother maybe she don't like the baby, so she put him there and covered him with a box. So the Mexican lady got the boy. She went around and asked all those people in town. Nobody get that boy. So the Mexican lady took him over to the ranch and raised him there. There was a milk cow and she gave him milk and everything. They gave him the name of the Mexican lady's old man. His name was Joe Blyer. The White man gave his name to that boy. Same like with me. They sends this boy to school in Prescott. When he is old enough, he works as a cowboy. Worked with me. He sure worked good. Made a good cowboy. And he looked like he is a good cowboy. He is skinny and tall.

Kids when they grow, when they begin to be a man, the voice kind of changes. That time my grandmother told me to get up very early, and she let me holler very high. She told me, then I won't get a big, grouchy voice. We don't like that kind of voice. All our men can get very high up when they sing. When I was a cowboy, I holler like that. They heard it all over and they said, "Hear, that crazy cowboy comes down again."

That time, when I get up very early in the morning, my grandmother took the rocks where they put the pots on the fire. That kind she took, rolled in a corner. I sit there and watch and watch and watch those rocks until the sun comes up. "That's a rabbit," she said, "that's a deer." You know how the rocks look kind of gray. When you look at those rocks all the time, you see deer, you see rabbit easy. You see things good. That's what she did to me. Four mornings. That's what we used to do, us Indians.

When your voice changes, that time the old people work on you real strict. They don't let the kids lay late in the morning. They have to get up before sun up. Go some places and get wood and get water and bring it home. Then my grandmother had cooked something for me and put it away. "I got something to eat for you, right here. But don't eat too much," she said. When your voice changes, you don't eat much. Just walk around and move around. When I walked a long ways, and I come back, my grandmother said, "Yes, that's what I mean. That's what I want you to do. I want you to be staying like that all the time. If you happen to have a baby, if you happen to have a boy, if you happen to have a girl, teach them like I did to you. So they do the same thing like you."

My grandmother said, "If you lay there, lay in bed like this, some enemies will come around." When I didn't get up fast, she hit me right on my leg with a stick. I woke up and I was crying. I jumped up and walked away. From then on I watch when she is ready to do it again. Then I get up and walk away. But my uncle *Pelhame* said to my grandmother, "Don't hit the boy. I work hard and I carry him around, and I make him grow, so I am glad to see him grow now. I don't want nobody whip him. He is a boy, just like mine," he said. So every time I do something bad, I run to him. I know he lets nobody hit me.

When you change your voice, you don't use your fingernails when you scratch yourself with that. Don't take your hands. If you use your hands, you get lots of bugs in your head. My grandmother said, "They suck your blood, suck your blood, suck your blood, and you don't know anything." Same for the girls.

Also when you go to the water, you don't drink like that. I cut a little bamboo tube and suck water in there. If you dip your mouth in the water, they said, you are going to have hair grow in your face, and it turns your mouth black. "Don't get your mouth in the water," she said to me. Four mornings I must do that. I guess, White people dip their mouth in the water and then they grow wool all over their face.

Now the kids lay in bed for a long time. Then they get up and are cranky. Get mad and try to talk bad. "Silly thing you do," I said to my girl. Now they are going to have a Sunrise Dance for one girl from here. And my girl said, "They want me to go with that girl and dance."

"Well," I said, "that's all right. But you are laying too long in bed. When you are going to be in that dance, you have to be up a lot. Be lively and move around. If you get lazy and mean and cranky, you are going to make that girl the same way like you," I said. "I don't say, 'no, don't go to that dance,' but anyways, you are not doing it right. Get up early in the morning and do that, and you'll be all right."

Tom Jones, my uncle, he used to live up there in Prescott. He worked in Prescott, Mayer, all over. When he lost his wife, he went down to Clarkdale. And his boy, he worked there at the Clarkdale smelter. So sometimes we went over there. When I went there first, they don't give me a job. I was too young. Sometimes I help a little around and they give me 10 cents and I go over to the store and get candies. When I was a little older, they show me how to fill the cement mixer and I work there all right for some time.

I was pretty young when I started out to work for the city of Prescott. I start working for the city in 1922. Sam Jimulla worked in there first. That's why I got in. Me, and Tom Jones and Harry Smith, we work there. And then they want me to stay there and I work steady for the city for eleven years. I worked in the water lines. Put the pipes together. Fill the ditches when they put the pipes in.

That time we camped around the town of Prescott. Up there, where my cousin Lucy (Lucy Jimulla Miller, 1906-1984) has her house now, there was a spring there. We camp right there. One time when I come in after quitting time, my grandmother said, the old man, my uncle *Pelhame* went out and never come back for a long time.

I said, "All right, I go and look." And I went out, way up on the hills. It looked he was going up there to get some wood. He was laying there and there was some wood tied with a rope. Looked like he was going to pack it. He lay there and breathe all right, but he don't know anything. I take him home. For three days he don't talk, he don't drink water and he don't do nothing. Just stay like that. Then he passed away. This was my old man. And I sure missed him when he passed away.

I was raised around Prescott and I might not come down here to Fort McDowell. But the city mayor at Prescott changed office. One of the boys talked to me and said, "Hey, I just heard, they let you go! They don't want any Indians work for the city."

"Well, if they don't it's all right." The next day they let me go and I come down here to Fort McDowell. My father is still living then, and that's why I come down here. I stayed with my father three years. Then he died.

If they don't lay me off in Prescott, I might still be over there now. When they laid me off, I feel like I cry, because I like my job. I loved my work. When they let me go, I don't feel like I want to see Prescott any more.

Two weeks after I got laid off, I got a letter. I had a cousin here, and I used to work with him lots of times. His name was Quinna Harris (*Queena Harry*). I got the letter and opened it first. "Maybe there is a girl who writes a letter to you," he said. He reads it. "Hey, John, they want you to go back over there right away. If you want the job, you can go ahead and go now." But I wait till next morning.

That time I practiced driving fast. So I get up there to Prescott 9 o'clock. I go to the town hall and I see the city mayor who was running me off is coming in.

"Hahaha, John," and he put the arm around me. He sure stinks under his arm! "John, I want you to come back and work with me again." Pretty soon I said, "That's good, but I don't think I want to work."

"Well, John," he said, "we laid you off, and from that day to here we pay you the whole thing."

"Well," I said, "that sounds good. But I don't want to get fired twice. Once is enough."

"No," he said, "I pay you. And maybe your wage is up a little bit, too."

"That's all right, but I'm not coming back."

And I never did go back over there.

Later my mother's younger sister Viola came down to my place at Fort McDowell.

"Hey, John, they want you back over there. Come with me." She brings a car down here.

"No, I don't want to be fired again. So I'm not going to go back."

Viola said, "Come on!"

She put her arm around me and she was going to give me some money, too, to go over there. But I stay.

In 1933 I came down to Fort McDowell from Prescott. I was out of job and I was out of everything. I got no money, no shoes, nothing. I stayed with my father and my stepmother, so I had a house. But there was nothing to eat in there. I was plowing the field. Plowing, plowing all the time, and then I sit down on the ground and think. There I saw Mike Nelson way down on the road riding a horse. He was riding down this way. All of a sudden he stopped and came here to me.

Mike said, "What's the matter, John?"

I said, "I'm just tired and sit here. I was working all day. So that's why I'm tired and sitting here."

He said, "Look, John, you don't do that. I know what you did. I'm going to tell you."

I said, "All right."

He said, "You are here with your father. You got no shoes, you got no money, you got nothing. You are thinking you want to go back up to Prescott. That's what you are thinking. You are not tired, you are just thinking. You think pretty strong. You want to go back to Prescott. You think, when you go back, you wonder if he give me that job back again, that man. That's what you are thinking. But," he said, "tomorrow morning come down to where they have the sweat bath. And meet me there, early in the morning before sun up. All right?"

I go over there early in the morning. Well, I want a help. That's why I go over there. I wanted to see, I wanted to know what is going to help me. He takes me way up on a hill before the sun comes up. He gets onto a rock and sits right there.

"I'm going to pray for you."

"All right."

He said, "Get up on top of this rock and face this way." (To the rising sun.) And he said, "Don't laugh, don't think the other way. Just sit right there. I will pray for you." He put the hand on top of my head. Pray for me in Indian. And he said, "John, listen! I'm going to pray for you. You are going to be lucky. I'm praying for you for everything. Everything is coming to you. Don't say, you don't believe it. Just sit there. Everything is going to come to you easy."

And he sits on the rock and pray, pray, pray, pray. Then he took me over there and took me to the plow again.

But three days later, about evening, I see a pickup cross there and it stopped. Stopped and come round there to my driveway where I am plowing.

The man said, "What is your name?" I say my name and he said, "All right." Then he said, "I want you to help me. You know how to drive cattle?"

"Well," I said, "if you show me how to drive cattle, if you teach me, maybe I learn it."

"All right," he said. "But anyways, I'm not going to take you now. In two days, maybe three days, I come back for you and take you."

I said, "All right."

Then he asked me, "How much money you want?"

"I don't know," I said. "I'm not doing anything, yet, here. If you think it will help me, five dollar would be all right."

Verde River at Fort McDowell. Spectacular Great Blue Heron rookery in center. December 1982. Photo by Sigrid Khera.

The man writes a check on the hood of his pickup truck. He comes over here. "Hey, John," he says, "you know what? I made fifty dollars for you. What about that?"

"Well, it's all right. If you want me to stay over there and pay it back, it's all right. If you fire me before I pay it up, that's too bad."

"Well," he said, "that's too bad, but I think you'll make it. Do you know that Ann Porter's Saddle Shop?"

"Yes."

"Go in there and cash the check."

I said, "All right."

I go over there and cash it and get everything I want for work. Levis, two, three shirts, boots. And from there everything came out good. I wish Mike Nelson were around. I help him good!

I went to that cow ranch over there, and I stayed and stayed and stayed. I work there for over ten years. But then that man got kind of funny, so I got mad and quit.

Mike Nelson give me luck. That's what Mike Nelson did to me. When Indians pray, it sure is good.

When I was a cowboy, I work in the mountains and I run a horse in there like nothing. We worked out there with no house, nothing. We lay in the open. Got lot of fresh air. I made my own spring bed. Put forked sticks in the ground. Put long ones across and tie it with a wire. Put lots of brush across. Put my canvas and my sleeping bag over. Stay warm. Sometimes it rained, but I didn't care. Don't hurt me.

When I was a little boy, they told me, "Don't steal anything. Don't do anything bad. If you work for the White people, you don't do anything bad. Then they keep you, they like you." So I did. I work for a lot of White people. The first time they looked if I do anything bad. But then they don't look any more.

At the cow ranch, my boss Glen Moore, he just did that. One time they go to town. They want me to sweep all the house in the meantime. I did. I went in there and I found a twenty dollar bill. I put it on the clock there. They came back after a long time and they looked for that money first. I knew, they look for that. I don't say anything. Pretty soon, when we have supper I said, "Hey, Glen, I got your money right there. You left your money there and I got it. I put it over there."

"How you see it?"

"I don't know. Something looked like blue or green and I put it over there."

So he went over there and he got it.

"Hey, John," he said, "I don't know how I lost it. How I dropped it."

"I think, I know what you are trying to do, Glen," I said to him. "I know what you try to do. You want to see me steal that money. That's why you left that money there. But next time you leave it there, I just leave it. I don't touch it any more. I'm not going to get it for you any more," I said. "I'm not going to bother with it any more. I'm tired of it. You just trying to get me in the trap."

"No, no," he said, "I know, you are a good man, John."

Over there at Buck's Bar Ranch the same. Lean, the boss comes there and says, "Hey, come up there to my house. Take your beddings over there. Just stay around. We are going to town."

So I go to the barn and take my saddle off and go in there. There is a kitchen in the house. And there is the same thing. An open wallet lay there. I take it, and hang it up on the wall.

When they come back, I say, "What you leave money here for? I thought, you need money when you go to town. When you do that again, I'm not going to stay, I go home."

So they don't do that any more. I tell them, "When I want money, I just work for you and I get it. I'm not going to steal your money."

I have a wife. The first wife, I have. She stay at Fort McDowell, and I was cowboy over there at the cow ranch. And one time, I take a day off and come down to Fort McDowell. I want to get some tobacco. I used to smoke plenty, too, that time. I come back from over there and I stop at my house. The woman wasn't there, but my kid.

The little daughter. I stop there and she said, "My mother said, she wants to go away."

I said, "Well, it's all right. If she wants to go, it's all right. Let her go," I said, "nothing holds."

So after a little while—I was having coffee with my stepmother—I go and stop over there. And there is the woman in the house. Come out. She is kind of mad.

"Hey, I thought you work over there. You staying there alone. But I heard you got married, got another wife over there."

"Well, if you want to see where I was around, I can take you over there and show you. Where I have been around, there is nothing but rocks and cows. No people around there. There is no city, no nothing."

And she said, "That's what I have heard and I go away. This house here where we are in, some women said, this old rotten house is going to fall down and going to smash us and kill me. They say that, so I'm going to go away."

"All right. The road is right there. The road goes up and the road goes down. I don't know which way you want to go. So go ahead and do it."

"Well," she said, "I'm going to go out and have a good time."

"All right. That's very good," I said. "I'm working here. I don't make very much money. But I'm making a little money for you and for the little girl. But if you don't want that help, that's all right."

I went back to the ranch. Hugh was about ready to round up. So I used to go way up above that time. About evening I come down to the ranch. And the boss's wife said, "Come in! Hey, John," she said, "I got a bad news."

"What?"

"Your wife wrote a letter to me. She wants you tomorrow in the court."

I said, "All right, let's go there."

So she said, "I know where they are going to have it. So I take you over there. But you want the little girl with you?"

I said, "Sure."

So we get to the town early in the morning. Stop at the courthouse, right in front. That lady, my wife is in first. And we come in and the judge is over here.

"Hey, is that him coming over there?" he asked.

My wife said, "Yes."

"Come on, raise your hand up and say, 'don't lie, say right thing.' You can do that?"

I said, "Yes, sure."

"All right."

And my boss's wife, she come in and she said to the judge, "Don't talk to John first. Ask the lady first. She is the one coming to the court."

The judge said, "All right. Sit down there, John."

I sit down over there. He calls my wife.

She says, "John says, he works over there, but he got another woman over there."

"You sure?"

She said, "Yeah. So another lady has told me."

The judge ask her, "Do you have witness?"

She said, "No, but that's what they tell me."

And then the judge asked me, "Do you have witness, John?"

I said, "Yes. I got one. Not very many, but I got one."
I said, "Hugh, I've been with them 10 years. I go no place. I was working there where there is lots of rough country.

Lots of rocks and brush and cattle. I work in there. Ten years, I don't go no place."

The judge asked my boss's wife—her name was Ada. "Hey, Ada, you know John a long time?"

"Yeah, he is working there every day. Every day and every week and every month and every year. He goes no place."

"But he was alone?"

"Yeah, that lady there, he can't take her over there, because she does not know how to ride. And he is working around the mountain all the time."

"No other wife?"

"I don't think so," she said. "Nothing over there."

The judge said to my wife, "I think you are wrong. What you want to do with this divorce? You want to pay it all up by yourself? You have to, because you are the one who wanted to go out."

Then he asked me, "Do you want to help her?"

I said, "No. She want to go away, it's all right. But anyway," I said, "I have the little girl. But not her. If she wants to, she can pay all the divorce money. How much is it going to be?"

The judge said, "300 dollars." Then the judge asked her, "You pay all those $300?"

She said, "Yeah."

"Well, John," he said, "all finished for you. You can go home. This one here, I want to talk a little bit more. You just go and go out. Go to work again."

"All right."

And I went back.

About two weeks after—I heard she is going to have a good time—she goes up to Kingman. That's where she has an accident. Drunk driving. The truck hit her car. Cut the head off right here. She died right there. And pretty soon, when they have a funeral in Clarkdale, my mother's sister Viola she come down here. "Do you want to see her? Do you want to go over there and see her for funeral?"

I said, "No. Why? If she stay here with me and she gets killed, I go there to her funeral. But I have nothing to do with it." And I turned around and asked the girl, "Do you want to see your mother's funeral?"

"No."

We don't go over there. Well, the woman wants to go, so it's all right.

In 1937 or 1938 they were building Bartlett Dam. That time I was working at the cow ranch. We camped near this place for the roundup. So when I get through with the roundup, I went over there where they built the dam. They were making a spillway and drilling under the mountain. Then one boy came up to me and said two Indians got killed in that tunnel. That tunnel collapsed. He asked me, "Do you know who they are when you see them?"

I said, "Sure."

These two men from Fort McDowell who got killed were William Choka and Roy Dorchester. Quite a few men from Fort McDowell worked over there. After that no Indians worked in there. They got scared and quit.

When I quit at Buck's Bar Ranch, I went over to Seven Springs. And when I come back after three roundups, I get for the city of Phoenix to work steady at the water works. I start working for the city of Phoenix earlier in 1935 or '36. But only off and on. I work in there maybe one week, maybe three, four days. But the Indian foreman there, he let me go all the time. So when there is roundup time, I go back and work at the cow ranch. And that Indian foreman told the White boss, "John wants to be a cowboy, and that's why he quit the job." That's what he told the boss. But to me he said, the city of Phoenix is out of money. So they let me go. One time, when I came back from Seven Springs, the White boss got me. He told me, "You are going to work tomorrow morning?"

I said, "All right."

Then he told me "Why you quit all the time, John? I hear you quit for roundup when I got you in."

I said, "No, it wasn't that. He let me go all the time. He told me, the city is without money."

"Ah," he said, "tomorrow morning, before you work, come down here. We talk to that foreman."

That foreman was there and the White boss said to him, "Hey," he said, "you told me John was quitting himself for roundup. He didn't do that. He said you laid him off every time when I got him in. You said, the city has no money, that's why you lay him off every time."

And the White boss said, "We leave him on now. I don't care how long he works. But leave him on for that he gets his timing."

So I worked for the city of Phoenix steady for nine years and seven months. Then I got retired.

I worked for the city of Phoenix in the water department. Sometimes, when a pipeline leaked, I help them patch it. Sometimes I work overnight. That time we got only one premise pickup. That's the only one we used to drive around here. We used to haul rocks with it. Where there is a hole in the pipe, we fix it and pile up rocks. I put in eight hours work, and I don't take a coffee break. When I work, I work straight eight hours. Now they take it easy. Take coffee breaks and everything. Dumb Indian, I guess, that's why I don't do such a thing.

When I work for the city here, there was a big man, big shot. He was a Mexican. He was a supervisor, but he get me drunk all the time. That time the government didn't sell drinks to the Indians. That time we wouldn't buy that stuff. When it was around quitting time, he took me to Mesa or anywhere. He drink whiskey anywhere. And pretty soon, when I learn drinking, I don't stop any more. I can't buy it myself, but I get it from that Mexican.

I cared nothing when I was drinking. I didn't care if I kill the people or not. When a man gets lots of whiskey in his stomach, he is nothing. But he thinks he is a man and talks mean. They locked me up five times for drinking. The sixth time, the judge told me, "If you break probation five times, you are supposed to go in five years. I give you nine months straight. Just straight, that's all. But if you do the same thing like now, you know where the Florence (state prison) is."

So I go down there to the county farm. They were drying the stuff from the sewer there. Make manure of it. Let it stand and get it dry. Then shuffle it in a car and smash it there. Make it powder and put it on the plants. Watermelons, tomatoes, anything. I was in that county farm and there were lots of flies around. Dirty flies everywhere and it smells awful. When they give us the food, it is full of flies. There is a barn right there, and lots of flies in there. They come into our room just like bees. But some of the smart people I'm with, they get together like a club and said, "Let's talk to the boss to patch up the holes where the flies come in." A Mexican, a White man and a Colored man said that.

They say that to the judge, "We want a screen on the door, we want a screen on the window."

The judge said, "If you want anything clean, you stay home. Fix your house. Your own house. This here is a jail," he said. "You are in jail, and you are not free. You can't do nothing."

I was supposed to stay there for nine months. But I pray and pray, and pray, and I get a little help. I get out in 28 days. I am lucky. And I don't go back again there. Those flies down there woke me up.

Yavapai elder John Williams and Dr. Sigrid Khera enjoying Yavapai basket exhibit at the Heard Museum, Phoenix, Arizona. 1978 Photo by Carolina Butler.

Oral History of the Yavapai

Chapter 23

◆

Shelter, Food, Clothing, Hunting

We Yavapai live all around here. There were places where lots of us lived together. But it doesn't show much where we used to live. Looks like there is nothing, nobody. We don't make a rock house. We make a little house of sticks. And when we move away, we sometimes burn it up. My people know, they can't make it back soon. That's why they burn up that place. Everything is gone. I guess they don't want other people see their place. That's why they burn it up.

I see my grandmother do that lots of times. When we camp around Cave Creek, New River, Rock Spring, she makes that branch house, the wikiup. And when we start to move out, she pulls the sticks out and throws everything away. That's why White people think there are no Yavapai around. Because they don't find lots of things from us. They killed us all and they don't find things from us, and now they say there never were many Yavapai around. But there were many of us around and they had plenty to eat and plenty of everything. Yavapai country sure is beautiful and there is everything in it.

In winter the Yavapai went back to the mountains, to the caves. A whole bunch of them stay at one place. Built a fire in the cave to keep warm. My grandmother said, when they live in a cave, sometime they make a wall in the front. They put some rocks together, put mud on it, put a rock on it, put more mud on and another rock. Pack it tight and let it lay there. Maybe 2-3 days and it dries. Some of the small caves they use nothing in the front. Just build fire in there and get warm like that. But sometimes they put wall on the side to keep the wind out. The wind hits that wall and goes round it. That's why they make the wall like this.

Sometimes people use a brush house covered with dirt all around. It is like a wikiup, but they put dirt all around. We call that *watamarva*. That means "covered with dirt." When they make it, they put little, fine brush first. Then the big brush. Put it on, put it on. Put fine brush on top, and put dirt over it. When it rains a little after, people go up and temp [sic] it, temp it down. And when it gets dry and hard it seals just like cement. That house keeps cool in the summer and warm in the winter.

They have a hole in the roof to let the smoke out. But they make it open to the side, so the water don't go down in the house. Then they build that smoke stack, they put a log across and put others on top. But it is not too high, my grandmother said, maybe 6-8 inches. Then the smoke flows out good. If it is too high, the wind comes in there. My grandmother said, when they build fire, the air sucks the smoke out pretty good. But they don't change the direction of the hole. It is made tight.

They have a door at the side. In the wintertime they use a yucca weave. Make a flat mat and hang it to the door. They put a stick across the wall so they have a place to tie that curtain on.

I see people using that kind in Mayer. And I have seen lots of these mud houses around here in Fort McDowell when the old people live here. Good workers use that kind of house. It is pretty big, lots of people live in there. Maybe ten or more people live in there.

From Oak Creek Canyon all the way down to Tucson are Yavapai. These Pima wasn't around here then. They were way down in Gila Bend, Ajo, way back there. When the government built places here, then they get the Pima here. Then they put them up at the Salt River Reservation. So they are coming in, coming in, and now they grow right here. But this here is Yavapai country.

My grandmother told me, when the Yavapai used to camp at the Verde River down here, they get mesquite beans. The holes are still there where they grind them. *Oh'mukioh*, we call the place where the grinding holes are. And there is a little canyon close to where the Beeline Highway is now. That's where they liked to camp. There is lots of marked rock there. Sometimes they have a Crown Dance there. We call that place *wisalka apa*, "Great Bank." At that place my people make pictures on the rock.

In spring they live in those caves near the Needle Rock a little up the river. There are other grinding holes in those caves further up the Verde, near Needle Rock. We call this place *Ohyamsikanyova*.

This country here is my grandmother's country. My grandmother's grandmother's grandmother's. All this around here, Four Peaks, Saddle Mountain, Superstition, and on down to Needle Rock and Superior. There is a big mountain down there, that is kind of flat. We call it *Walganyena*. That means Pine Mountain. That's where my grandmother and her people used to go and get piñon and acorn. And another mountain over there. Looks like a man laying there and the nose is sticking out. We call that *Wi Bahudja*.

In the summertime when it gets too hot, they go over there to the Four Peaks and stay there. Up Superstition, too. And sometimes they go over to Fossil Creek and visit people there.

When they stay around the Salt River, they use that water. It is kind of saltish. Way up in the Salt River Canyon near Whiteriver, there are salty springs. Four or five going into the Salt River. So the water is not very good to drink. When the people want to drink it, they strain it. Let the water go through sand, make another pile of sand and let it go through that. Let it go through two, three piles of sand. At the end they can drink it. It is still kind of salty, but not too bad any more.

My people go anywhere. Just like wild sheep. That time my grandmother said, there were springs everywhere. There was still water around from the flood. That time the country was still kind of new. You can go any place and find water. Now the world is dry. No water no more now.

One old man talked about it how it is going to be when the White people are around, "Everything is going to be not very good life. All the trees are going to die. All the springs are going to dry out." He knew it right.

My people then live from anything. They always have food. Never have a bad time about food. And each bunch, when they stayed some place, they have a chief that leads them where to get food, and tells them to put it away (for storage). When they have more food, they call the other people to come and they eat all together. Have a good time.

There were lots of deer all over. When a man go out to hunt, the medicine man pray over him. Pray for that man. Then the man kill deer all the time. Never misses any. Never come back without one. And when the man comes back from the hunt, they pray for him.

When people have a dance, they make the boys dance. Four, five good boys. Sing over them, sing over them. Sing the deer song. Next morning they go hunting and they kill lots of deer. Sing the deer song. Next morning they go hunting and they kill lots of deer. Not little ones, big ones.

From top of *Wigidjassa* (Four Peaks), looking south to *Wigidjisawa* (Superstition Mountains). Photo by Carolina Butler, 2009.

My people, they hunt with bow and arrow. But bow and arrow don't go very far. You had to sneak up to the deer. Some of the people, they want to go right close. They put deer antlers on top of their head and tie it around. They look like deer and the deer comes pretty close. These young men, they sometimes know how to call the deer. Then they shoot the deer right in the heart. You have to be careful to hit the deer right. You don't hit them in the back.

Deer is hard to catch on foot. But lots of people here around do that. When they are hunting deer, they are walking along sometime and a deer jumps up. He runs away and they run after him. My people, they have some kind of a hammer, *nakesh* we call it. They put that on a stick with a string around to hold it. They kill the deer with that. Hit him on the head and kill him. Hold him at the horns and twist him up and get that little hammer and kill him.

My people used to be pretty strong. They kill a deer and pack the whole thing. Bring it home. Fetch the whole thing to the camp. My old man *Pelhame*, he do anything. When he saw a deer, he knock him down and carry him back to the camp. He was an old man, but he carries that deer home all right.

Once I killed a deer and my uncle asked me, "Why don't you bring it home?"

"Oh, it is too heavy."

"All right, I show you."

He tied the legs together, put the whole thing on a rock, pick it up and carry it away. He don't take the guts out. Pack the whole thing and bring it in. I couldn't make it. But that old man fetches the whole thing.

Mike Harrison's father the same way. Carry the gun with the deer and walk along.

Deer are different up around Sedona and here. Around Sedona and Jerome Mountain deer are bigger than in the Four Peak country. Same color, though. We call the deer around here *aquaka kwoyokopaya*. And the deer up around Sedona *aquaka wipuk*. People around here are also smaller. My grandmother always said, "*Kewevkepaya* are kind of small people, but pretty strong!"

When I was a kid, I had to watch rocks four mornings. Get up early and watch them. They say, you become a good hunter. See the gray and the brown things like deer. But when you are young and kill a deer, you are not supposed to eat it. Old people said, if you eat your deer, you get lazy and sleep all the time. Same with any animal we hunt. When a little boy hunts a deer or rabbit or anything, he don't eat it. Also if you see the animal alive and somebody else kills it, you don't eat it. They say, then you get lots of boils all over you. Maybe it is going to kill you. You get greasy hair. You are going to get lazy and sleepy. When a boy goes out hunting and see a deer and kill it, he don't eat it. But maybe another one, way over there, he don't see the animal getting killed, he eat it.

Only when they get married, then they can eat it all right. When you are married, you can do anything. You are grown, you are a man. Same thing the girls. The girls don't eat anything they see alive. Only after they get married. Some ladies, they can kill deer all right. Some ladies are pretty strong. Kill the deer with bow and arrow.

My uncle *Pelhame*, he made a bow and arrows for me. Use barrel iron and cut it like an arrow point. He uses bamboo for the shaft. Straightens it with a blue kind of rock. We call that rock *akhtaniwoi*. He cuts the rock and makes a groove on top of it. He makes the rock hot, then puts that bamboo in the groove and push it one way, roll it, push it down heavy, but not too fast. He gets it real straight. He made a sack out of hide to put the arrows in. We call that kind *nimbu*. You carry that bag on your left side, and you use your right hand to pull the arrow out of that bag. And when we go around, we don't take the string off the bow. You carry the bow and the arrow is on it. Always have it ready. And my grandmother said, "You just don't bring it inside the house. Leave it outside where you can get it. Right at the door above it or maybe on the side." We leave the bow outside all the time.

I always used to take that bow and arrows with me. One time the old people pick acorn. I was walking there to the spring with my bow and arrow ready. I heard something rattling. There was a big deer. That was in a canyon, narrow one. The deer comes like this and I am standing there and hit him right in there with my arrow. He just gets down. I tell *Pelhame*, I kill a deer over there. He went over there and the deer was laying right there. That arrow goes way in. I was about 10, 11 years, I guess. It was my first deer.

Antelope don't grow around here, Four Peak country. But there used to be lots up there in Prescott. When my people hunted antelope, they camped at Jerome Mountain, a canyon down there. They come down from there and hunt the antelope. When my people saw a bunch of antelope standing there, they get around them. Corral them. When the antelope see them, they run. The antelope see people over there and run, then see people over there and run. My people make a circle and scare them around. Those antelope run fast, but we tire them out. Then my people can go after them and knock them down, kill them. Then they pack them and carry them to the camp. Cook it. All the people are together and eat it. In that valley, there used to be lots of antelope in there. They are gone now. White people kill them all.

We used to live on quail. Shoot them with bow and arrow. That's the best meat we have. And when you have a little baby boy, you take a quail leg and scratch him a little. Then he sure can run fast. Like quail.

We hunt ducks with bow and arrow, too. When the ducks are in the water, and there is brush around, you can get right there. Ducks don't fly quick, so a boy can get two, three of them in a bunch.

Rabbits and jackrabbits, we catch them with a crooked piece of wood. It is kind of heavy at the ends, ironwood. And when you throw it, you can get anything. We call it *nyave*. That's the kind we use to kill rabbit and jackrabbit. Sometimes a whole bunch of Yavapai get together and chase the rabbits out of the brush. They don't use a net. Just that throwing stick. When they have killed them, they carry them home on a stick. Put all the rabbits together.

There used to be lots of javelina around, and we used to hunt that, too. When it rains and the grass is coming out, that time there are lots of javelina around. That time they are breeding.

We hunt and eat anything. But we don't use fish and we don't eat the beaver. Anything that lives in the water, we don't eat that. Up near Horseshoe Dam, I see lots of beaver when I was a cowboy. Those beaver put a dam on the river one time.

In old days, when the Yavapai come down here to the river to hunt, there is not much brush around. Just mesquite. They get beaver at the river. Beaver is hard to get, they say. But good hunters hunt the beaver, *hanyaka*, all the time. The hide is sure good.

Some people don't live around caves. They live in the brush house. So they sew the beaver hides together and put it over the brush house. When the rain comes, the water rolls over the hide. The water doesn't go through and in the brush house. Keeps people dry in the house.

I saw them one time use it and I asked them, "What you put that up for?"

"Well," they said, "that beaver stays in the water all the time. And when it rains, the water can't soak through the skin."

They hunt the beaver with the bow and arrow. Where the beaver make a dam, the hunter hides there, watch for the beaver. When they use the bow and arrow, they tie a string to the arrow. Tie that to a tree. When the arrow hits the beaver, it jumps. Then they have to pull it out with the string and kill it right away.

But sometimes the beaver goes down the water, and way down some place he dies. The hunter knows the beaver can't go up the river, they go down only. So next morning the hunter goes down the river and looks and finds the beaver dead somewhere. Skin the beaver and gets the hide. They need lots of hides to make a blanket over the brush house. Sew it together, sew it together.

But I don't see any beaver now. White people killed them all.

We cook that meat of deer and quail or anything. But we also used to dry meat. They dried the meat in the sun.

Maybe four, five days. You hang it on a tree and let it dry. Sometimes they eat it dry, just as it is. Sometimes they roast it on the fire. But you have to turn that dry meat over quick, because it gets burnt fast. But it sure tastes good. Rabbit we cook first and tie it together and hang it up to dry. They keep for a long time.

There used to be buffaloes around here, the other side of the mountains (McDowell Range), in the valley. I never see any, but some of the old people tell me. We call that kind *mathin*. They are bigger than cows, the horn is not too long, they say. Just small and turned. *Pakakaya*, he used to hunt buffalo. And another one, Dr. Siva, he told me, "I used to do that."

You can't chase the buffalo on the horse. You chase them on the horse and they turn round, put the head under the horse and throw you off. But these old men, they sure could run fast. Faster than a horse. They said, you can't chase them from the front. If you go in the front, they ride over you. You get them from the side. When the buffalo are running, they never turn. They run straight all the time. And the man runs at the side of the buffalo and kill it with a spear. We call the spear *basatohe*. They take a stick from a mulberry tree. Long one. Split it at the end and put an arrowhead in. Tie it with a string. Use deer sinew for string. Tie it, tie it and wet it good. It works like glue. Run on the side of the buffalo and strike him with the spear. Kill him.

People use a head of a buffalo. Make it like a crown and put it over the head. Put something on the body, too, and the buffalo thinks the man is another one. So the man can get real close. And when the man kills one buffalo, the other buffaloes don't go after him.

The men get the real fat buffaloes. They can tell the old ones. No fat! Not too round hip, kind of bony. That's the one they don't bother with. The one that is real slick, that's the one they get. When the buffalo is young and the hip is round, that's the one they try to get. They don't try to get the cow. They want to get more buffalo next time. It makes another little one.

When the men go to kill the *mathin*, the other people get up the mountain and watch. When the men kill some, they start smoke. Then the others know it. They go over there and bring the meat in.

We use the buffalo skin for a shield. When there is another man with bow and arrow, they hold that up so he can't hit them. When they use the skin for a shield, they don't tan it. They just put it in the water and stretch it on a frame. Put little sticks around and make it level. Put a little stick in the end and hold it with that. They also used that kind of skin for shoe. The sole is thick that way. Use deer hide for the upper part.

The one who is a good hunter, he gets lots of buckskin and he makes good buckskin clothes. Some hunters make clothes for their ladies out of cattails. Weave it from that. The lazy people use *hamsi'i*, cattail. But if you are a good hunter, you get your women good clothes.

When I was big enough to kill a deer, I save the hide all the time. My grandmother, she said to me, "Don't be lazy. Don't ask to borrow shoes or jacket. You have to make it yourself! If you don't make anything, your lady will have to wear yucca shoes." That's what they did if they didn't have buckskin. Make shoes out of yucca for the ladies. Sometimes also make yucca clothes. You get the strings out from the yucca. Braid it on the ground. Fit your feet around it. Weave it real tight. But those slippers wear out fast. That's why my grandmother said, "Don't do that. Make buckskin clothes. The good man gets buckskin clothes for his lady."

When they tan the deerhide, they first put it in the water. Let it soak I don't know how many days. Then they dig a hole in the ground, put the skin in when it is damp and cover it up. Leave it in there maybe three days. Then take it out, hang it over a post and scrape it with a rib. A sharp piece of rib. The fat comes off. Then they cook brain and the stuff from underneath the legpits, and smear it over the skin. Lay it in the sun for a while. Then roll it up and put it away. The grease goes into the skin. Then they put the hide in the water again and get it soaked good. Take it out and twist it, twist it, twist it. All the water goes out. Put it in the sun and let it dry. Then get a rock and pull the hide over it, pull it, pull it, pull it, all around it. Make it soft. The strong men do that. It comes out all white and soft. After that we smoke it with mountain laurel. Make it nice and yellow.

My uncle *Pelhame*, he sure makes good clothes and moccasin out of buckskin. For sole he use the skin from the neck of the deer. That's a thick one. Sometimes they use the skin from the horse or cow. When they kill a javelina, they use the neckhide for the moccasin sole. Pig hide is strong and they wear it a long time. And that time, when there is lots of buffalo around, they use that hide for shoes.

When *Pelhame* sew the moccasin, you don't see where the sole and the upper part get together. He sews it inside. So you think it is one piece. He used the deer muscle for the sewing thread. Muscle from the deer's neck. We call it *masmah*. You scrape the meat off the muscle and dry it. People used to sew anything with that. For needle he used the thin leg bone of the deer. We call that bone *chiaga*. We file it and make it kind of thin like a needle. Before White people come around, we Indians could do anything, make anything!

The women have a long rim on the moccasin. Fold it three, four time below the knee. But the men have a smaller rim. Make it single. In the wintertime, we roll the rim up. Like boots. We have a string to hold it up.

My uncle *Pelhame*, he also makes gloves from buckskin. Sew it, so that it is just like you buy it in the store. You can't see where he sew it. I don't wear White people's pants when I was a boy. I wore Indian pants. A strip of leather going through the belt. And the men, my grandmother said, they wear kind of chaps. They make pants like this.

Some women wear a long buckskin dress. It is heavy, but they use that. They paint on it. Make a design on it all around and it looks pretty. They use that red stuff from the rock, *kwedra*. It is a better paint than the White people have it. It don't come off, stays on all the time.

Antelope skins are thinner and softer than buckskin. They use these for making vest. My uncle, he used to make shirts with this kind.

A good man makes blankets from hide for his lady. Fox, wild cat, coyote, anything. They cut the fur like a string. Twist it, twist it and weave that. Make a blanket.

Sometimes they use the tail from the ringtail—*nameh* we call the ringtail. They split it and sew it together, sew it together and make it wide and make a blanket. My grandmother said it is sure pretty. When they use the fur, they take ashes and mix them with something. Put it on the fur and put the fur in the sun. That kills the bugs. Then they shake it and get all the bugs out.

The coyote hide they use for mattress. Coyote hide is for the ground. Put the hairy side to the ground and the plain side up. You lay on that and you are warm. If they make a blanket from cat hide, they do the same thing. Get covered with the plain side, leave the fur side up.

But sometimes they make a string out of wool. Hang up a stick and hang the wool strings on that. Get another wool string and put that through all the way. Make it flat like a Navajo blanket. They make it just big enough to cover the wife. Like a shawl. Only the ladies wear that. The men make it. A good man, they give him lots of wives, and he is the one who can do that. He can do everything. The men get the wool when they hunt the wild sheep and goat. There used to be lots of wild sheep and goat around in Black Canyon way up in the rocks. The wool is kind of straight. *Munimia*, that means "sheep wool." When they kill the sheep, they cut the wool off. Wash it with alder, with *tahsilga*. You put the *tahsilga* in the water and bubbles come out. They put the wool in that water and clean it, dry it on the sun. Turn it over, turn it over and make it dry. Then they twist it and make a string. When they twist it for a string, they use that little flat piece. I don't know how they call that disk, but I know my grandmother have it. That disk is out of wood. But a hard wood. They make a hole in the middle and put a stick through it. The wool is over here and they pull it out and twist it, twist it all day. Maybe four, five days. Put a little water on it. That's the way they get it tight. Men and ladies do that. *Hamesquirra*, that's how we call that string. They make different sizes of string. Sometimes they make it double. Put two together. And when it is a big bulk of wool string, they put it away and make a blanket. I never see my grandmother make a blanket, and I don't see *Pelhame*. But my grandmother showed me how they weave. She got the stick and hung it up. They call this loom *kwi*. *Chibewe kwi*, that means "blanket weave it."

Just showed me. And I don't know where my grandmother got the wool when she string it. But I see it. Fine, thin wool. She has the wool in the sack all the time.

I see *Pelhame* make a rope of horse mane. He make it sure pretty. He use white and brown and black. Make it all kind. He braid it, braid it, braid it. String it on a tree and wet it with water. Let it stay there for two days, maybe three days. And put water on it to make it tight. And when he takes it off, it just stays tight. Before they have horse, they use buckskin for packstring. They don't braid that. Just twist it and make a rope. We call that rope *sinawa*. *Hate sinawa*, that is the horsemane rope.

Everything is open to us when we first live here. Deer, rabbit, quail, antelope, everything. But when the White people come, they close everything and we get nothing. That's when Carl (Carlos) Montezuma takes some Indians from here and go hunting below Roosevelt Dam. There are many deer over there, and they killed lots of them. The rancher got them and he told them to come to court.

"All right," said Carl.

When he comes to the court they tell him, "You hire a lawyer."

And Carl says, "I don't take no lawyer, I am a lawyer."

Petroglyph of ancient hunter with bow and arrow, aimed at wild game, *Wipuk* (Sedona) cave. Photo by Sigrid Khera, December 1979.

He brings his own lawbook. So they open the court and he wins. He tells them, "This country here is my country. This deer here is my deer. That's why I kill the deer. God made me with those deer, and I am supposed to eat those deer. That deer don't belong to the White people. That's mine."

After that he gets the rancher fired, and that judge and the policemen. "You're fired now. Look for another job. Nothing in here."

In San Carlos the Yavapai got cow meat from the government. Thursday people called *Takoktalkepoo*. That means "the cattle, they put it in the corral." Friday they call *Aquaquadanehe*, that means "killing the cow." And that two days people come down and butcher the cattle. My father worked in the slaughterhouse. Then everybody got some meat. They got liver, kidney, anything. Guts, too.

They eat all the guts. They wash it good down at the river, make a fire and roast it, or sometimes boil it.

But before the White people come around food used to be everywhere. My people lived from anything around. They get mesquite beans, saguaro fruit, acorn, piñon, all those seeds. They gather those. Put some away for the winter, too.

People pray for everything. When they want things to come up good, they pray for that. And fruit comes up good, and get ripe and big.

When I lived with my grandmother in Black Canyon, we don't buy much flour or coffee or anything like that. We live on mesquite beans, saguaro fruit. When they take us to San Carlos, that's how we learned to make bread. Before that my people live on seeds. Seeds they grind and grind until they look like peanut butter. Then they don't drink coffee in the morning. Just mesquite powder in water and saguaro fruit and other stuff which they dry. They put it in water and drink it like juice. You don't cook it. Just put it in the water like that. But sometimes we warm the water. Put the pottery on the fire and warm the water a little.

Where there are mesquite trees, there are flat rocks with big holes in it. Three, four, five holes in a row. That's where the ladies used to pound the mesquite beans. But in old days, when my people come down here and get mesquite beans, the Pima sometimes come over and kill them, kill them.

In June we also come down here, Cave Creek, to pick the saguaro fruit. We use a long stick to get them down. My grandmother put three sticks of saguaro ribs together to make it long enough. Put a hook of greasewood on the end. Tie it together with buckskin. In the wintertime when we don't use the stick, we hang it on a big tree or rock. That keeps it straight. It rains on it, but that doesn't matter. But if you leave that stick on the ground, it gets crooked.

When they gather the saguaro, they drink the juice and keep the seeds. Wash them good and dry them in the sun. Then they grind it, grind it, grind it. Make it like peanut butter. They also make gravy with it. Put it in water and drink it. I drink that lots of times.

Saguaro seeds, mesquite, corn, we grind that and make gravy out of it. But first time the Yavapai get flour from the White people over there in San Carlos, they don't eat that right away. They level one place and put all that stuff in there. After a long time, they just make gravy with flour and drink that. They don't make yet tortilla. They don't know how to mix it. Just make a gravy.

When the White people were coming, the Yavapai had to move all the time. Four or five men looking around all the time. And when they went to sleep, four or five other men went on the lookout. Change around like that. In the morning they don't make fire. Too much smoke. They have a little something to drink. They put mescal in the water, cactus fruit and mesquite. Then pack everything and go. Get away up high where the mountains are rocky and stay there. Next night maybe they move again.

In the spring they get the mesquite down here. But they go where the brush is thick, and three, four men wait in the hills and watch. They don't dry the mesquite down here. Take it way up the mountain and dry it there. Same with the saguaro. They take it and go away, way up to the Four Peaks. Up there they dry it and put it away in a

Fort McDowell Yavapai Madeline Nelson with ancient Yavapai drinking cup and Kimberley Williams with ancient Yavapai olla. Photo by Sigrid Khera, February 1975.

cave. Dry the yucca fruit, *manat*, prickly pear, *hateh*, and put lots of it away. They don't take much with them. Just move all the time.

Prickly pear they pick with kind of a plier. Make that out of ash wood. We call it *sahdat*. When they pick the fruit, they put it on the ground and clean off the stickers with a little brush out of weeds. Put it in the burden basket and take it home. Then they make kind of a screen. Put sticks in the ground, put sticks across and put brush over it. Cut the prickly pear and take the seeds out. Dry the good part, the red one on that screen. Make it real dry. Turn it over, turn it over, turn it over. It stays sweet for a long time. We use that in the winter. But the seeds we don't use. Throw them.

When they get the fruit dry, they put it in a pottery olla. Put a lid on and seal it with pitch. That plant where we take the pitch to seal the olla, we call it *ahpihl*. *Ahpihl* grows down here. It's a small plant and the pitch is hard to gather. Get a little bit only from a plant. That pitch don't taste different. That's why we used that kind. Pine pitch has a taste, so they don't use that. When they have enough pitch, they warm it. Pat it, pat it, pat it until it's soft. Flatten it and put it over the mouth of the olla. Smear it on good, so no air gets in. Put the lid on that tight. Then the fruit inside don't get spoiled.

Long time ago, maybe 1920, 1921, I see something in a cave. So I go over there and take the rocks out from the wall. Take it out, take it out, take it out, and pretty soon I see lots of ollas in that hole behind. I don't know how many. I open some of them, maybe four, five. There is desert banana in it, prickly pear, mesquite, lots of it. Then I heard something in that cave. So I smear the

321

pitch on again, plug it and put the ollas back. I told my grandmother and she sure cried, "That's from the ones they killed over there."

There is a grass we call *sèléh*. It grows up high, Flagstaff, up near Superior. We gather these seeds and eat them. The seeds are small, tiny. My people, they gather around, gather around for these seeds. They put a burden basket under that grass and hit it and get the seeds out. Let them fall in the basket. My grandmother, when she brings that seed in, I'm just lazy and sit and watch. But she brings it, brings it, brings it. Sure hard work for my grandmother. That *sèléh*, that's the last kind that gets ripe.

There is another seed in the fall. We call that seed *màtták*. It's ready somewhen [sic] in September and my people gather it then. It's a tiny seed and it takes all day to fill a sack. But it is sure good eating. Grind it and it is just like peanut butter. My grandmother sure can grind anything and make it good.

Over there at Peeples Valley, they have that kind of seed, the *màtták*. One old man told me, the people were harvesting the *màtták* and the soldiers came just like that and killed the people. Without warning they came and killed them. Some of the people were out in the hills and they heard the shot. So they stay behind the hills and they don't move. When the soldiers are gone they go back. They see lots of people dead, scattered around. Then the Yavapai get some of their people from Kirkland. They tell them to come over. Then they drag the dead to a pile. Burn them.

Up at Yarnell Hill and up around Superior we also get acorn. My grandmother cooks acorn soup. Cook meat real well. Take a rock and put the acorn over the meat.

Pound it, pound it, pound it, roll it around and make it fine. Looks like ground beef with the acorn in it. Put it in an olla and stir it, stir it. Pretty soon put the soup in there. Tastes good that way. Not too saltish, just a little.

They used to go up to Payson for acorn. But when the White people come around, that way is kind of danger. Lots of tree and lots of brush over there. You can't see. So then they don't stay there much. They have men on the outlook. *Pakakaya* is an outlook boy, and another man *Walgtonamin*, "hair down this way." But sometimes White people come right up to them. Shoot, 'pang, pang' … and the Yavapai used to run like rabbits.

The people used to get salt from the salt mine near Camp Verde. We used to get it in a little chunk. Go over there and buy it. Some of the people get it from the Salt River. Where the sand is damp and kind of salty, they gather that kind, put it in something and carry it home. But that one, my grandmother said, it is kind of bitter. The one that is a good salt, that is in the salt mine at Camp Verde. An old man used to live at that salt mine, *Wikinya*, they called him. He is the one who stays there and owns the place. He is not a medicine man. He just lives there and so he owns the place. You bring him something, maybe mescal or sometimes treat him with a buckskin, sometimes with a bow and arrow. Give it to him and he cuts the pieces of salt and gives it to you. People can't go in and take it themselves. He don't want nobody around there. He sees people over there and he goes and tells them, send them off. Some of them, they are relatives. So they stay three, four, five days. But he don't want them to stay too long either. *Wikinya*, he is a pretty mean man, they say. Now there is no salt in there. White people take it all away.

Mescal, we get that any time. But it is best in the spring, when the young stalk comes out. We take it out with a sharp stick. Pound the stick with a rock, so it gets in (the plant) good. Get the mescal out with that stick. We pack it in the burden basket, a whole lot of mescal, and bring it down to the place where we cook it. We call that place where we cook mescal *matkama*. That's where they cook mescal all the time. They make a great, big hole. Put the rock in it. Make it solid in there. Put the mescal in it. Cover it all with grass. Cover all around with dirt. Put fire on. Let it cook two, three days, maybe four days. I help lots of time put the fire on. My grandmother wants me to do that all the time. Kids born in the summertime, that is the one to put the fire on. Then it cooks good, they said. The one who was born in the wintertime, they don't do very good. I was born in June, so they get me all the time.

When my people got together to bake mescal, each one make a little split in her mescal. And each one makes that split a little different. Then they know this one is theirs when they take it out after cooking.

The young people when they were just married had to learn how to cook the mescal. The old people let them dig their own hole and they let them cook it separately in there. That way the young people could watch the old people do it first, and then they do it themselves in that separate hole.

When it is all cooked it sure tastes good. They pound it on a rock for the wintertime. Then they put it in water and make juice and drink it. Put it in the water and soak it good. And walnuts, you wash them to get the black stuff out. Then put it in there and pound it with the mescal.

Walnut seeds, when they are mixed with mescal tastes like chocolate. We drink lots of it.

But over there in Bloody Basin, that's where all the people got together and cook mescal. The mescal is still there in the ground. Nobody take it out when they shoot my people. Same over in Prescott. Fossil Creek we call *Vialnyucha*. That's where they cook the mescal. They did that when they take them away from this country. There is still a pile there. I've seen the mescal in it. When I go back to Prescott, I ask my grandmother, "The people cook mescal, but they don't take it out. Looks like it's still in there." My grandmother cried. Same over in Prescott.

Before the White people come around, there is water running everywhere. My grandmother told me, when there was a little water running some place, the people switch it off and get it on the place where they plant things. They plant up in the mountains where there are springs. Up in the Four Peaks they plant before the White people come around. They plant beans, black beans. We call them *mariga*. They plant squash, *hàmté*. Corn, my grandmother said, that they plant more than anything. But that corn is not that big one, like the White people's corn. It is a small one, but it tastes good. It is white, red, blue, all colors. Sometimes they get blue corn from the Navajo. They trade it from there. Go down there and trade it for some buckskins. Squash is not very big either. It don't grow big, but it tastes good.

When the people plant things, they don't go to different places every time. They plant different things in the same places. They plant some corn in there now. The next spring they plant some beans. Next time squash.

When they work the soil, they soften it. Put water on. They take a digging stick and get it down deep. Hammer it down with a rock. All the way down. Push it back and forth. Make the hole big and round. Soften the ground all the time. Put water on the ground when they dig. Take an olla and pour the water on. Then the stick goes down deep.

They set the holes apart. When they have several holes, they make a little ditch between them. Put the water in the ditch. Maybe four, five, six days. Make more holes and put a ditch in between.

Some people when they plant corn, they soak the seeds in water first. My grandmother, she don't do it. Just put it in the ground, put water in and it comes up pretty good. Beans, they don't soak those before planting. Just put them in like that. My grandmother said, no matter how dry the beans are, they come up.

They plant the corn when it gets real warm. That's the time they do that. Up in the mountains, they do that late in spring. The country up there is cold all the time. When the tree leaves come out, they still wait a little. After that they plant. Then, when things are growing, they don't put too much water on it. Just enough to get the soil damp. If you put water too close to the plants, the leaves get yellow.

When my grandmother plant squash, she puts many seeds in the hole. When they come out, she pulls some out and saves some. The ones in the middle, that's the ones she leaves. Pull out the outside ones. These squash are wild. They don't spread like the White people's squash. The leaves stay small.

When weeds start growing, they pull them out. Women and men do that. People, all the people, never get lazy that time. When we live over there at Black Canyon, Hot Springs, my grandmother plants things all the time. My grandmother sure is the hardest working woman I have seen. When the corn comes up, my grandmother takes it and boils it. When it is green it is good. But some of it she dries. Grind it and make a gravy. Some of it she puts in the ollas. Seal it and put it away in a cave. Some of it they save for seeds. Plant it next year.

When the White people come they plant no more. Sometimes some squash. That's all. They don't stand still. No time. They move around too much when the White people come.

Over in San Carlos my people learn how to plant wheat and barley. The White people make them use the big ditches. And when my people come here to Fort McDowell they also use the big irrigation ditches. Every man had some land where he plants wheat and barley, corn, beans and melons, squash. Every family had the same plot every year. One man had one field and he kept it all the time. And in one night, maybe two, three people get water for their plots. There was a little box to let the water come in the field, a gate. When they opened it, the water ran in the field. When everyone had got water, they start all over again.

My father, he is the headman of the irrigation. They call him *aha mayora*, "water chief." There is no mud in the ditches then. People clear it all the time. Lots of people were cleaning the ditches. Always a whole bunch of people working. That time they get together and help one another.

They don't work for money. They work for themselves. But the little ditches which people got on their plots, they clean those out themselves. When they are not working on the big ditch, they are working for themselves on the fields.

When people start planting their plots in Fort McDowell, they don't put lots of water in right away. Just let it run in slow. That's how they soak the ground. We start planting corn in April, and it start coming up in May, June. In June it start coming into ear. After that they plow the land again. They plant corn two times. One in April, the other in August. That one comes out late in fall. We used the corn planter. Put the seeds in the machine and drop it on the ground. Drag the harrow over and get them covered. My father sure was good to plant anything. He had some good team of plow and he got a good wagon horse.

We plant beans with the late corn. Blackeye beans and pinto beans. They plant the beans at one spot. Maybe two, three rows together. And about late in the fall they are ready. We pull them out and pile it, pile it. Put it on the wagon, bring it home and thresh it. We thresh with a stone disk. People use a mule and pull that disk. It breaks all the leaves. There is a canvas spread out and they throw all the beans on it. Throw the beans up with a shovel. *Matzadeh*, we call that shovel. Throw it up in the air and the wind blows the leaves out. The beans make a big pile and they sack it.

When we cut wheat, we pile it, pile it, pile it. Throw it on the wagon and bring it home. Put it on a canvas and walk around, walk around, walk around. Get the seeds out. Then throw it up in the air and the wind blows the stickers out, and we just get the seeds. When the seeds are clear, we put it in a canvas bag. Put it on the wagon and bring it down to the mill. Some people bring it to Mesa, some go to Phoenix to the flour mill.

In 1911 the flood washed all the ditches up. Washed the old irrigation dam away. Then the agency comes around and says, "You people can have no more water now." The flood washed everything away and they don't help us to set things up again. They wanted us to get out. Go down to the Salt River Reservation. But my father said, "All right, we'll see." So people got together and they rebuilt it. No one helps us. We start a new ditch this side of the river. Use a hauler and bring the rock and the mud out. Make a new headgate. It is still there. Then we start a new irrigation dam. People get together and take loads of brush up there. Pile it, pile it and put rocks on top. Across the river in

Swollen Verde River at Fort McDowell, March 1978. Photo by Sigrid Khera.

an angle. Then they make the dam heavy and thick with moss. And when they pushed the moss down, the dam got thicker. They call this dam *taquok*. They do everything by hand. They have no machine.

Before the White people come around, the Yavapai used to make dams that way. When they saw a little water, they switched it off and got on their garden. And that's how they knew how to build that dam on the big river.

My people have everything, my people can do everything. Everything they need, they find it right there where they live.

There is a rock, kind like a glass. Black and yellow and red. Up in Sedona there is lots of this kind. People find a big piece of it and the men know how to shape it the way they want it, so they can cut things with it. That kind of rock is sharp, cuts easy. There is also a white rock and we make knives out of it. My uncle *Pelhame*, when he makes arrowheads out of these glass rocks, he does it with a little stick. Just push it, and chip off, chip off, chip off. He carried that little stick with which he works the rock with him all the time. He said, you can't file the arrowhead and knife from that kind of rock. Just cut it the way it is sharp. When people make the rock knife, they sometimes make a handle with deer horn. Make that deer horn wet and put the rock in. It fits tight. Sometimes make a handle out of wood. We call it *akquawa waje*, "rock knife." And when you cut things with the rock knife, it cuts straight. It don't twist the things.

My uncle *Pelhame*, he also made a knife from copper. When I was a young boy, we used to live in Prescott below Fort Whipple for a long time. And my uncle said he wants to go and see the place where they get copper.

I said, "Can I go with you, uncle?"

He said, "Yes."

So I saddle up my horse and follow him all the way. We come to a basin, but he leaves me right on top there. He left the canteen and the horses with me and walks down.

I said, "I want to go with you."

But he said, "No, you wait right here."

He leaves me there all day. He came back and I asked him, "You find the place?"

And he said, "Yes, still there."

He brought copper along. Then he put that copper in the fire and make it red hot. Put it on a smooth rock, a blue one, and pound it, pound it, pound it. Make a knife out of it. Then file it on a bedrock. Make it sharp. He wrapped buckskin around the handle and sew it with deer sinew. My uncle has that knife and use it for a long time.

We call that kind of knife *akwata aquqka*. That means "yellow knife." I see my uncle use it. He cut the deer with it. And when we eat boiled meat, he cuts that with the yellow knife. But it didn't get blue like copper the White people have. It didn't change color. Stayed yellow all the time. That knife is better than the iron knife. You put the White people's knife in the sun and it changes color. That's because it carries poison. But not our copper. The iron knife smells bad, and when you cut meat with it, it gives a funny taste to the meat. My people said, that smell gives you the TB. But the copper knife and the rock knife when you cut things, it don't smell. It's a good, clean knife.

The Yavapai around Prescott have this copper knife. The *Kewevkepaya* around here, they have a knife out of rock or bone. They use the javelina bone. Javelina bones are long and thin and stay sharp all the time. We call

331

that kind *wichiaga*. Deer bone is all right, too, but it gets dull pretty quick. We call that *aquaka chiaga*. You file this bone knife and it gets sharp. But the copper knife, some people from here, *Kewevkepaya*, they trade it with something. Buckskin or anything. Trade it and get that knife. *Kewevkepaya* and *Wipukpa*, they trade with knives and buckskin.

I don't think my grandmother knows where that copper is. She is from around here, Four Peaks. Just my uncle knows it, because he is from over there. My uncle didn't show me where the copper is. He might have been afraid I sell it to White people. Like over there at Jerome, one Indian, he knew where there is gold in there. This man comes up to a White fellow and the White man says, "You know any gold around?"

The Indian said, "Yes."

Yavapai olla from Sycamore Canyon. Photo by Peter J. Pilles, Jr., archaeologist, Coconino National Forest.

"Show me."

He gives him some drink and chewing tobacco. The Yavapai man like the chewing tobacco and show the White man the mine. For a little bit of chewing tobacco he shows him all that gold. That White man sure fools the Indian! That's why I say, White people, if they want to steal something, they sure can do it.

At Bloody Basin there is a place with dirt, red and sticky. We call that kind of dirt *kano*. That's the kind of clay we use for making pottery. There is that one place at Bloody Basin where you find that kind, and there is another one at Black Canyon and in the Salt River Canyon where they have Canyon Lake now. And there are lots of places around Prescott and in Kirkland, too, where you find this kind of dirt. Some people come a long way to get it and carry it home. Some clay is around here (Fort McDowell), too, but it is not too good, they say.

My grandmother, when she makes that pottery, she first puts the clay through some kind of strainer. She puts two sticks in the ground and puts brush across. Put the clay on it and pack it down, pack it down. Let the water run over it. Work it through and get the rough pieces out. Little rocks and hard pieces. Then she mix it, mix it, mix it all day and let it dry on a flat rock. Pretty soon wet it again and make it fine. Real fine, like silk. Some people mix it with the gummy stuff from inside the hedgehog cactus. We call that sticky part inside the cactus *mahligo*. I guess, that cactus juice makes the clay smoother. And when they burn it, it doesn't break, it stays together. Then she rolls one piece, make a coil. Roll it real good. Bend it around and put another roll on it, and another on it. People never make a pot out of one piece.

Yavapai jar. Courtesy of James McKie, archaeologist, Prescott National Forest. 2012.

You can make that pottery high or low, make it wide one place, narrow another one. Then she smoothes it with a little rock. Make it smooth outside. Make it smooth inside with a little stick, flat on the end. Smear a little water on it, too, to make it smooth. My grandmother, she really works hard to make just one pot. She works it over and over. Then she sets it in the sand and let it dry. When it's real dry, she puts the wood all around it and burn it. When you make these pots, you make them in a small fire. And when they turn red, you take them out. When the pot is ready, she takes it out with a bent stick. Let it stay until it gets cold. Then she puts water in. If the water stays, she keeps that pot. If it comes through, she throws it and makes another one. You can't patch it when it leaks.

I see lots of broken pottery and it is painted. I ask my grandmother, "Can you do that?"

And she said, "Oh, if I want to do this, I can do it. But I don't want to do it."

"Why, why?" I said, "Why don't you make it like this?"

"No, I don't want to make it. Too much work. I put some water in that pot and it is just the same."

The oldest people used to paint the pottery. My grandmother said, her mother and her grandmother used to do that. When they want to do that, they get the leaves from the Spanish bayonet yucca. We call that kind *manat*. They put the leaves in the fire and then twist it, twist it, twist it and get the juice in a cup. Then mix it with any color you want. Mix it with *kwedra*, that red clay we put in the face, or mix it with smooth ground coal. Mix it, mix it, mix it, add a little water and make a design. They use a stick for paint brush. Small ones, wide ones. That design when it dries, it stays. Never wears out like the White people's paint.

They make all sizes of ollas. Small ones, and real big ones. When it has a big mouth, they use it for cooking. Cook anything in it. Deer, rabbit, beans. They make the pot real thin. It boils quicker that way. The big pots they make thick. They use these for keeping the water. The water stays cool in there.

Pima and Papago (Tohono O'odham) and Hopi, they still make pots. But my people, they don't do that any more. When they take us to San Carlos, we stop everything. Some old people, when they come back from San Carlos, they still did it. Like my grandmother used to make them still and we used them as long as she was around. When her old man *Pelhame* was still around and they killed a deer or rabbit, they boiled it in that pottery. It tastes better that way. My grandmother said, there is no poison coming out from the pot. Not like from the White people's pot. That one gives food a funny taste.

We use the big ollas for storing the water. But you don't carry it in that big olla. There is another kind we use for carrying the water. We make a basket, just like an olla and put pitch around. The pottery we call *matethiwa*. But the basket olla we call *sùwá*.

We boiled the piñon pitch in a pot first. My grandmother said, if you cook it right, it stays for a long time on that basket when you smear it on. But if you cook it too much, it gets dry and crumbles off soon. So you put a stick in when it boils that you know when it is done. My grandmother made that sure good. She also put *kwedra* in it. Mix the pitch with *kwedra* and make it all red. Then smear the pitch all over the olla basket with a brush. Get a big bunch of grass and smear it with that. Put some pitch in the basket and put a hot rock in there, too. Roll the rock around, roll it, roll it, roll it. That rock plugs all the leaks. My grandmother showed me how to do it. But she said, the man, the boy, don't do that. She said, "Don't try to do that. That is not for the men. Let the lady do that."

You can carry water in that olla from here to Four Peaks to anywhere. You never lose water with that. I used to carry water a lot in it. We lived way up in the mountains and I carry the olla down to the spring, fill it with water and pack it home.

One time when I was a little boy, I carry that water in the olla and the handle broke. That olla fell down and split to pieces. I just stand there and cry. I stand there a long time and cry. Then my grandmother comes down looking for me. She sees that broken olla and she sees my crying. So she takes some cloth and wipes my tears off. "Don't cry," she said, "I'll make another one."

My uncle *Pelhame*, he could do anything. He gets a rock and another one, put dry leaves underneath. He holds the one rock and hit it with the other and the sparks come out. Fall in the dry leaves. He blow it, blow it and pretty soon the fire works. We call that kind of rock *ò'ótawe*. They have it around Prescott. They trade it for buckskin. You tan a buckskin and trade with it. Don't hit the rock hard for making fire. Just scrape it and a spark comes out and goes in the soft brush. A strong man can do that easy. That's what *Pakakaya* used when he started fire with the cholla. He hit the rocks and that cholla started to burn quick. That's what he did when he put lots of fires up when the Pima try to get him.

People used to keep a bit of rat's nest in a little sack to have dry weeds all the time. Hang that sack on the belt. When it rains and they start fire, they use a little bit of that rat nest. It sure is dry, burns quick.

When people want to keep fire for a long time, carry it with them, they take cedar bark. Roll it, roll it tight. Make it like kind of a stick and put that in the fire. They call that *o'okwidi*. That way they can carry fire for a long time. That bark burns slow. They carry it along, maybe when they go up Four Peaks some place.

When we were little boys we used to play with that kind. The fire lasts one day in that bark roll. When that fire bark stick burns up, we make another one. When this one all burned, get another one.

O'okaya, that's the pine stick we make fire with. You take a piece of dry pinewood, with lots of pitch in it. Pine or piñon. Split it in the middle. Make a hole in the middle, kind of a notch. And then grind it with another pine stick. But don't hold it too straight, hold it at an angle. When you drill real hard, powder comes out and gets hot quick. When it gets smoky, blow it, blow it and start fire with it. But that kind is a little slow to make fire. The rock striking is quick.

Before they take us to San Carlos, we still use the rock and the drill. But when we get to San Carlos, we get matches over there. That old kind of matches. You strike it and it sure stinks. We used that down in San Carlos. But my uncle *Pelhame* said, he don't use that kind very much, that White man's match. It stinks like a smelter and he don't like that very much. He uses the rock and the drill a long time. When they chase Geronimo he uses that. Gets fire pretty quick. And he uses it all the time back in Prescott.

Chapter 24

◆

How We Lived Together

We have no trouble before the White people are around. In those days there was nothing bad. Nothing to be afraid of. In those days us Yavapai were from here all the way down to Tucson. And *Tolkepaya* all the way down to Yuma. My grandmother said, there were sure more people over in *Tolkepaya* country than anywhere. And these here *Kewevkepaya* the same way. Lots of people here. But *Yavepe* and *Wipukpa* not that very many. They are in the middle. They live in Oak Creek Canyon, Sedona, Jerome Mountain, way on to Seligman, Peach Springs. *Wipukpa* and *Yavepe* speak the same. But the *Kewevkepaya* down here, they speak a little different. And the *Tolkepaya* speak a little different, too.

My grandmother speak *Kewevkepaya*. But I speak both, *Yavepe* and *Kewevkepaya*. And I always used to make fun of my grandmother. I said, "You talk like nothing!" She got mad!

Kewevkepaya are growing down here and *Tolkepaya* over there all the way down to Yuma. But we are not raised down here and around Yuma We are raised from the *Wipuk*, we come from Sedona. Us Yavapai are raised there and from there we spread out.

But when the people get together from different places, they have a good time. They kill a deer and they barbecue the whole thing. Eat it, drink mescal juice, have a dance, have a real good time. My grandmother said, "That time we are the happiest people in the world." But now, when they take us to San Carlos, and when they turn us loose from there, now we don't know one another.

Each bunch, they had a chief all the time. The chief told them what to do and the people did it. All the time they have a chief. There is the one, the head chief, and another one next to him. And when the head chief got killed, or died or something happened, the next one got it. That's the way we used to do. My grandmother told me my father was a chief. He is the same one who tell the people, "Don't kill the White people." My grandmother is cousin to some of the chiefs. She told me all the names of the chiefs, but I've forgotten. I know only of *Pakakaya* and *Kipilla*. *Kipilla*, that means "spinach." The one that grows on the river. But I think that chief was before they kill all the people in the cave.

There were some old men around, they tell people how to live right. We call them *bakwau*. *Bakwau*, that means "talking." *Bakwau*, that's an adviser. The chief would choose somebody to do that.

When I first come down here to Fort McDowell in 1912, that time one old man did that. *Koleonoteh*, Chickenneck was his name.

340

Every day Chickenneck got up on top of the *watamarva* early in the morning. Maybe 4, 5 o'clock. He tell everything to the people and the people listen to him. He said, "Don't fight, don't kill anybody. Leave them alone." He told them not to steal. He told them to live right. "If you don't live right, you may die," he said. "If you listen to me, you will get old like me." He tells the children not to get lazy, so the boys get out and hunt rabbits, deer and everything. And he said, "Don't kill the White people." He said, "If you kill the White people, they come in faster. They are like ants, like *jimul*. They are like water. So don't kill the White people."

Mike Harrison's father, that was another old man like that. He is the one who do that around Mayer. He just stands there and lots of people coming. Ladies and men, everybody.

He gets up early in the morning and tells everybody to get wood. And he told them, "When you work for the White people, don't get lazy. Move around, move around, or White people don't like you. Keep on working all the time." And he tells them, "Don't try to steal, don't try to kill people, don't try to hurt people. That kind of people they send over there to *Ahakasquava*, Florence (where the state prison is)." *Ahakasquava* means "White Cottonwood Tree." Yuma is another prison, but it gets too small so they move it over to Florence and make it bigger. "They put lots of people in that prison in *Ahakasquava*, that's why I don't want you to go in there. And those White people take you in there and hang you up. Put a rope around you and hang you up. Sometimes they put you in a chair (electric chair) and put something on your head. Put it on you and kill you. I don't want you to be that way."

I don't know how he learned those things, but anyways, he knows them. And that's the way he tells everything. But I just cover my head and go back to sleep. I was a little boy then.

The *Tolkepaya* got one chief, too. Up at Kirkland I see him on top of the *watamarva*, and he talks, talks, talks. Early in the morning he talks. And pretty loud, too. Tells them how to live, how to be good people, and trying not to fight.

I asked my uncle, "What is the one doing over there all the time?"

"He is the chief, he is the boss of everything around here."

When the *bakwau* speaks, he stands on the ladder, one foot a little raised. Sometimes he would talk about something that happened long time ago. Something sad. And sometimes tears come in his eyes. He would talk in the morning and sometimes also in the evening. Everybody listened. Everybody stops doing anything. Just listens.

They always told people not to get mad with their relatives, with their family. They said, "To look at their eyes bad, don't do that!" They said, "Don't kill people. Make friends, make relatives all over." They said, if you do that and there is another place and you go over there and camp, people give you something to eat. They do that the first time. And when they see you are a good man, you are a good help to them, they feed you all the time. You go out and hunt, get rabbit or anything and bring it home. Your relatives boil it and eat it. And when they go out and get something, maybe some mesquite or mescal, they save a lot of it for you. You are a good man. If you help nice, the people eat their thing, but they save some for you. Put some away for you.

But if you don't do anything for them, they don't feed you. If you are no good, they don't give you nothing. They eat everything away. In the evening you look at their mouth and it's all clean and they go to bed. Pretty soon you walk to another people. You get there and do a little bit at one time. After that they watch you. You walk out and they follow you. If you go and lay down in the shade and sleep all day, they know what you are doing. You come back and they don't feed you. They don't give you nothing.

And pretty soon your shoe is worn out. They know that! They know what kind you are. That's why nobody give you nothing. So you are going on, going on, going on. Pretty soon you come to a coyote trap. Maybe there is a rabbit in there, and you are pulling it out. Then that wood that holds the rock slips and comes down on you. You can't go up and you can't do nothing. That rock is right on your back.

That's what these old men said to the people.

That's what we did. When we visit relatives we bring something. My mother had three cousins here in Fort McDowell, *nedja*. That's why she and my grandmother come here after they picked saguaro fruit over in New River. They want to see their relatives. Then my mother brought dry saguaro fruit in a sack and bring it to all three of them. Give each one of them a sack. But my mother, she never stayed with the oldest one of these cousins. She said, "The wife don't like me, she don't care much about me. That's why I don't stay with them."

When the girls had their first monthly, my people make a hole in the ground and put hot coals in it. Put cedar leaves over it and let her lay on it. Keep her warm that way. An older lady, good in everything prays over her. One who is not stingy, don't get mad quick, works hard and good, runs fast. That lady prays over the girl, press her a little, sings four songs over her. Make her a good girl that way. But when we go to San Carlos, we don't do that anymore. The Apache do it different with their girls. Let them dance four days. We don't do like this.

We people have relatives all over, and that time relatives were close. I got relatives from *Kewevkepaya*, I got relatives from *Wipukpa*, and I got relatives from *Yavepe* and *Tolkepaya*. But they don't want us to marry our close relatives. We could not marry our first cousins. Not the first and not the second cousins. Maybe the fourth persons coming out. Maybe they can do that.

They say, they don't want close relatives to marry so no trouble comes out. When they are too close relatives that marry, we got no more relatives! My grandmother said, sometimes people don't look good. Kind of crippled. Their arm goes this way and that way, not straight. That what happens to kids when they come out from close relatives married. And sometimes when they marry their own close relatives, kids become midgets. We call that kind *panyudja*. That means "little, short men." My grandmother sees those midgets. That's why the chiefs don't like when people marry their own close relatives. They want to raise a good people. Good, healthy tribe. That's why they want to mix people. That's the way my grandmother told me.

There is a chief here and there is another chief over there and they make the same law. They don't let own relatives marry. Sometimes they just kill them when they do that. They hang them up on a tree. Both of them. The man and the woman. Shoot them in the stomach with an arrow. Shoot them down and kill them. My grandmother saw it. She told me this. But that time there were only Indians, no White people around.

Some of them they send away from here. Down to Yuma some place. Let them go there. They don't come back no more. They live down there at the other side of Yuma. They call them *Kewevkepaya Hauyam*, "*Kewevkepaya*, water washed them away." That's what it means. There is now lots of them down there, but we don't know them any more. My friend, he is a Cocopah, he comes up here some time and he sees me. He told me, "There is lots of your tribe over there. They talk just like you."

When I was young, I see an old lady here, and she has black marks right under the eyes. My grandmother had said, we never mark that close under the eye. We don't use that kind of marking. So I asked the old lady, "*Morra*," I said, "how you put this mark in there?"

"I didn't do that," she said. "They just take me away from here and put that on. They are people from way out west who take me away. But I come back. I don't know how many miles I walk. I come from almost Yuma or past Yuma some place. I walk from there and come back, come back."

These people didn't trail her, I guess. If they trailed her, they might have caught up with her. But she just runs, she said. Running, running, running, running long ways. She is dry, but she didn't give up. Some place there is little water. But long time there is no water. That time people used to put little rocks in their mouth, and then the mouth didn't get dry. She did that, and she never stopped walking. Some place she crossed a river, and then she saw the Four Peaks. When she saw that, she knew she was going to get home.

But when the Yavapai saw her, they aimed with the bow and arrow at her. "Who are you?" they called.

"Wait a minute," she said, "I am a Yavapai."

Her clothes were changed, that's why they thought she is a different tribe. But she said, "My mother's name is like that, and my father's name is like that, and they lived right here."

Now they knew who she is, and they give her a bath. Give her a sweat bath and clean her good. When something is wrong, sickness or something, they give the ladies a sweat bath. That's why they did that with her. They think there is some disease on her. They thought she sleeps close with those people down there west, so she might carry some disease, *hamalutha* (smallpox) or something. That's why they clean her. Boil a cedar and put it in a little pottery, and wash the girl good and clean with it. Put their own clothes on her, and burn her old clothes. From there she is with them again. But her eyes looked a little different because of the marks.

Kewevkepaya, they live here. But those who are raised at the same place, raised here, people tell them not to get married with each other.

These Yavapai here and Yavapai up there at another place, some of them have not been relatives before. Then these people here, they get a lady from over there, and they marry one lady from here to over there. Like when *Kewevkepaya* marry *Wipukpa*, they get relatives over there. And from there they get relatives all over.

Some *Wipukpa* and *Yavepe* come down here and get the *Kewevkepaya*. *Kewevkepaya*, they also marry people from around Hot Springs and below there. And then, when they want to marry, they come here and get a lady and take her with them. *Kewevkepaya* also go up to Fossil Creek. See the people there. If a boy from here, Four Peak country wanted to marry, he might get a girl from Fossil Creek. They are the same people but not too close relatives. When he gets a girl from over there, a boy from there might get a girl from here. Sometimes when the girls are grown up, old enough to get married, they come down here and get *Kewevkepaya*. The girls go all alone. *Kewevkepaya* girls, they go over there and marry *Wipukpa* boys. That way people get mixed.

When the young couple get together and want to marry, they tell the old folks. And if the old folk say it's all right, it's all right. But sometimes the cousins don't want that girl or that boy and they say, "No." And when the cousins say "no," they can't marry. Four, five close cousins may get together before the young people can marry.

Sometimes when a boy wants to get married, he asks his cousin. And his cousin asks the girl's cousin, "I want to get that girl for my cousin." Maybe the girl's cousin says, "no, no," then they can't do it. But if the cousin says, it's all right, then they can get married.

That time, when they see some people don't live right, they don't want someone from their side to marry anyone from these people. Like when the boy is not a good hunter or the girl is not a good worker. That's when the cousin don't like the girl to get that boy or the boy to get that girl.

Sometimes there are two girls, cousins, *baya*, and one is not very good looking. But the man, a good hunter, he go with this woman. The other lady is a good looking one.

She looks in the water and puts lots of *kwedra* all over the face. Looks in the water and mark the face all over with *kwedra*. She says, "I wonder why the man don't go with me. I'm better looking than her." But the other girl is a good worker. She gets prickly pear and saguaro fruit, seeds, anything. So the man get that good girl. The *baya* pretty one says, "Why he get this girl? She is an ugly one!" But good looks don't mean anything. My grandmother said, "If you don't do anything, they let you go. The lazy people, they let them go."

Maybe there is a man. Stout man, looking all right. But he use his cousin's clothes, vests, shoes, anything. He use the good clothes of his cousins and he goes over there some place and get married. But that boy's cousin, he knows that boy is no good, is lazy. So he goes over there and wants his clothes back. So the people over there, they know the boy don't work. They find out he is a lazy one, don't kill anything. They take the girl away from him. Let him go.

Sometimes people from here heard that there is a good girl over there at Fossil Creek. So they get together and make meetings, maybe five, six meetings. "All right, we get her!" They go and ask for that girl. So the women do lots of work. Get mescal, mesquite beans, seeds, anything to eat. The men get buckskin, take it and give it to the girl's people. The boy's people pile the presents, and the girl's people go and take a look at it. Look at it and then say, "Yes, all right." They don't touch the things, but the others know, all right we got the woman now. They buy the girl and she never runs away. They put lots of stuff for her, so that girl stays with the man a long time. She breeds kids from that man and they got lots of relatives all over now.

When the man is a good hunter, sometimes the mother and the father give the girl to him. But he don't get her right away. Just wait and wait and wait. They give lots of stuff to his people and they give stuff to them. He gives buckskin and meat, anything to the girl's people. After a year or maybe two years, the man stays with the girl's people and the girl with the man's people. So they get used to the families. Long time finally they get together.

When they are married, they still give the presents to the in-laws. That's what they did all the time.

Sometimes the in-laws have trouble. Then you know you have to do something for your in-laws. When the in-laws have trouble you help them. You fight for your in-laws.

But when a man is a good hunter, good for everything, the girl's family give him another girl. Give him his wife's sister. Cousins of his wife also. Give him maybe four, five girls, like Mormons. Like my grandfather. He had my grandmother and her sister, both.

When they marry, sometimes they go to the girl's people. But sometimes they go to the man's side. Sometimes they just change around. Go to the girl's family, then go back and stay with the boy's family.

Sometimes, when the young people stay at one place long, they want to go back over there. Then the old people give them something to take along as presents to the in-laws. Maybe shoes, or buckskin vest, mescal, dried prickly pear. They take it over there. And pretty soon this bunch over there did the same thing. Send something to these people here. So when the young people come back, they bring something along. That time they give lots of stuff to the in-laws. Always. Now they don't do that anymore.

My grandmother, she stays with her father when she get married. But sometimes, she said, young people just move out and stay some place nearby the old folks. They don't go away too far. Just around there. We just stay together all the time. *Manueh bajiyat*, that's what we call the people who stay all together. That means, "stay with them, stay with the children."

My grandmother, after my grandfather got killed in that cave, she married *Pelhame*. He was cousin to my grandfather, *chikawa*. *Pelhame*, he was younger than my grandfather. That's what they used to do. When a man died, his brother or cousin can get that woman. The next kin take over. The Apache are still doing that. The woman might be kind of old and the man is young, he still get that woman. Doesn't matter how the woman looks, her in-laws get her. And when a man marries his dead brother's or cousin's wife or wives, they call him *Assayowe*. That means "eagle get her." That time when they marry, they don't give anything to the parents. They have the woman already.

That's why when my grandfather, my *kwauwa* died, *Pelhame*, like eagle gets my grandmother. *Pelhame* is my grandfather's cousin. And that's how my mother always called him *naja* and he called her *nood*. *Pelhame*, he is half a *Tolkepaya*. His father was *Tolkepaya*, but his mother was *Kewevkepaya*. That's why his place was from over there in *Tolkepaya* country.

My grandmother told me, people used to have a dance all the time. But married men and women, when the man dance with another woman or the lady with another man, they separate right away. They don't wait. The husband leave his wife, the wife her husband. But some men, when they lose the wife, they get mad quick. They take a bow and arrow and shoot them down. Kill them. Kill the wife and kill the man. But now they don't do that.

Sometimes when a man has a wife but sees another woman, maybe better looking one, he tell his cousin, "You take my wife. I'm going to let you have her."

"All right."

Some of them say "no." But if the cousin says "all right," he gets the other man's wife. And the husband go and get the other woman. Pretty looking one.

If the cousin has a wife already, or maybe two, three of them, and he is a good hunter, that's all right. He still take her. But if the first husband has kids, girls, or boys, pretty soon the second husband goes up to them, "Hey, you go back to your father." The kids go back. The real father takes them away.

That Mike Nelson, they have a dance over there in San Carlos. Dance and dance and dance. That was when they were about ready to go home to Yavapai country. And Mike Nelson's wife having a baby soon. Then Mike saw that other woman. He dance with her and the lady want him. His cousin *Halkoyama* was sitting there. Mike said to him, "You want my wife? You can have her."

And *Halkoyama* said, "All right."

Halkoyama didn't have a wife. He took Mike's wife. My grandmother was right there when they did that. That lady went with *Halkoyama* all right. They stayed married a long time. And Mike got that other woman and they stayed married a long time. He got lots of kids from that other wife. But that first wife who went with *Halkoyama*, she just had that one little girl. She didn't get no more kids. And Mike said, "That is my daughter. She don't belong to *Halkoyama*. He can't make no baby!" And the girl knows Mike is her father. They live up in Camp Verde. She sometimes come down here to Fort McDowell to see her father.

My grandmother and *Pelhame* never call each other by name. In old days man and wife don't call each other by name. When they wanted to talk to each other, they said *nya eme*. Or sometimes the man would say *ichikuniwia*, "my cook" for his wife. But Sam Jimulla and Viola, they called each other Sam and Viola.

My grandmother and Sam Jimulla, they don't want to look at each other. They don't live in the same house. That time people don't talk to their in-laws. I tease my grandmother all the time. "There is Sam coming right over there, right over there!" And she put something over her and crawl in the house. He didn't come, but I just say that to see what she is going to do. I tease her a lot of time. I was a bad boy.

Close in-laws, we don't talk to them. Looks like they have no mouth. Like the lady, when she sees her father-in-law, she don't talk to him. Same about cousins. Men don't talk to the first cousin's wife. Never look at each other. You know why? My grandmother said, you get blind if you look at the in-law.

When I come here to Fort McDowell I never talk much with my first cousin's wife Rosie. But after a long time, when I was alone, she called me from over there to her house. So I go over and she fed me. That time I got nothing to eat. Drink, drink, drink. Just crazy. I drink my money up and I don't have any money for groceries. She knows I'm out of groceries, that's why she called me over and I eat over there.

My people sure used to be strict about close in-laws. They don't play and they don't joke with them. When they ask something, maybe like where they go, they tell them. But they don't stay there and keep on talking. But we sure have a good time with the far-off in-laws. With relatives from all over.

In old days when people got together, they have a good time. They sing and they play the fiddle, play the flute, play games. *Kwekioskesi*, that what we call the fiddle. Make it out of an agave stalk. Use horse hair for strings. The flute, we call it *taletala*. Make it out of bamboo. *Sakarakaamche*, he play that first. He play that, and one lady, a frog lady, she said she can make a better music. "All right," said *Sakarakaamche*. She makes "koah, koah, koah."

"Oh, not that!" said *Sakarakaamche*.

The flute, old people used to play that a lot. My mother's brother Tom Jones, he is a good one for playing that. When four, five of them play together, it sure makes a good music. Over at Mayer they play that all the time on Sundays.

Sometimes when people from different places got together, they play the pulling game. Make a rope of horsehair. Make knots in it. And when they pull the rope, they hold on the knots. Maybe eight men over here and eight men over there. Just the men play that, not the ladies. They always have an even number of men on each side. Some strong people on one side pull the people on the other side. Maybe *Yavepe* on one side and *Tolkepaya* on the other. A different tribe on each side. When they pull, they sometimes turn over and they lay on the ground, but they still hold on to that rope. Hold it, hold it, hold it. Finally they move on side, and the side that moves the other win. When they win, they get buckskin jacket, buckskin vest, shoes, anything.

And they play lots of games. Play *nòhówe*. That means "rocks in the dirt under." You take kind of soft dirt. Pile it, pile it, pile it, make four bumps. Put a rock in one. Then the other one don't know where it is and he must get that rock. He must guess. If he misses three times, he loses. If he gets it the second time, he win a little. When he get it the first time, he gets lots of things. Some pickers can sure pick right away. But some of them not. If the other one misses three times, you win. You get anything to win. Buckskin shoes, vest, blankets, anything. You take it from the one. Some of them lose everything, go home naked. They just have to work to make it again. Or win it back. My grandmother said, her father he always win. Never loses. He is a good one, she says. Little kids play it, too. But they don't bet nothing much. But the old people bet everything. When they get money in San Carlos, they bet lots of money. When the scouts get money, when they get paid, they play. Some of them win all the money. Some of them have no money. Go home and the woman quit them. But sometimes they bet the wife. That's what they do sometime.

And *itigoweh*. They mark four fields on the ground. Put ten rocks in here, ten rocks in here, ten rocks in here and ten rocks in here. They have three sticks with marks on it. Then they hold the sticks together and hit it right in the middle. The sticks spread out and you count how many stones they hit. The open between is the "water." And if your stick lands in the water you lose. And if one man hits your stick with his on top, he "kill" you.

Maybe five, six people play this one together. Men and women. My mother and Viola, all day they used to play that. They bet something, too. Money, handkerchief, shawl. Those people who lose all the time talk a little rough sometime. But people play on. Play, laughing, play, laughing. Never stop when they play. When they play cards the same way. Never stop.

Todoweh, that's another game. They make a hoop with grass. String it tight with soapweed. Make it pretty hard. Sometimes they string it with buckskin. Twist it real tight round the grass. Then tie two strings across. Make a cross inside the hoop with those strings. Make a line on the ground. Then one man take the hoop and another take a stick. A long stick. The two of them start running. Then the one rolls the hoop, and the other throws the stick. Throws the stick inside the ring. But if the ring roll this way, on top of the stick, the one with the hoop wins. And when both lay on the ground, the hoop and the stick, they measure it. Measure which one is the one closest to the line. The one which is the closest to the line wins.

Just the men used to play that game. Men running fast. But long ago, at my grandmother's time, there is one woman, a strong woman who runs fast. That one is the kind that play with the men, too. But when they take us to San Carlos and we come back from over there, the ladies sure are weak.

When I was a little boy, they play it in Mayer all the time. I did not play this game. I just watch them play, the old people. Now the road runs over that place where they used to play.

Todoweh, they also used to play that in a cave up in Sedona long ago. I never see them play there. This was long ago. It is not a deep cave. Just a rock ledge with a rock hanging over it. But it is gone now. That overhang come down. I don't know how they play it in there. It's a pretty narrow place.

And when the people still live down there in the Montezuma Well, they play that game. When the first chief down there died and they burned him, he went up to the sky, and he is the morning star.

There are also these many little stars together, and we call those *haneh churchura*. That means the hoop and the pole we use for the *todoweh*. It is up there in the sky now. *Haneh*, that's the stick, and *churchura*, that's the hoop.

All the Indians know the *todoweh* game. Yavapai and Apache, Yuma (now Quechan), Mohave, Cocopah. I don't know about the Pima.

My people, they joke and they play a lot when they get together. It is good to have relatives all over. I had relatives all over. Relatives from my father's side, they used to be all the way down to Yuma and all the way up to Seligman. And the ones from my grandmother's side, they were from here all the way down to Tucson.

My father is a bit *Tolkepaya*. My father's mother, she is half a *Tolkepaya*. And I have one grandpa from father's side, a *Tolkepaya*, Yuma Charlie. When I was a little boy, he give me money all the time. I see him over at Prescott. He works at the railroad. When he gets pay, he give me 15 cents, sometimes a quarter and I get me candies. Yuma Charlie had been in Yuma prison. And after that he came to Prescott.

Long time he had a farm down near Yuma. There was a Mexican and he let his horses graze in Yuma Charlie's fields. Yuma Charlie said to the Mexican, "I work hard, I get sweating and everything, plant things and raise them and irrigate. Don't put no horses in here no more!"

But the Mexican said, "You are sure lazy. You don't close the gate, that's why the horses come in all the time."

Charlie said, "Why is the fence down? I tie it and fix it a little while!"

The Mexican said, "You are just lazy. You don't close the gate well. That's why my horses knock it open and come in when they smell the grass. I don't open it!"

Yuma Charlie got mad. The Mexican did it again. There was some moonlight and Charlie could see the horses in his field. Charlie goes 'pang, pang, pang,' shooting the horses down. Close the gate and waits early in the morning for the Mexican to come round. "Hey, take your horses out now!" They were all dead. The Mexican went away.

Charlie was making some coffee and baking some biscuits and start eating when the police come in and take him. Put him in jail. There was an iron stake in the wall and a ring and a chain. They tie him with that chain. Get a chain between his feet and a ball in the middle. Chain him to the wall so he can't go no place. You can't drag that iron ball, he said. Too heavy. You pick it up so you can move around a little. But not very much. They never did say anything, they never did try him. They just put him in there and leave him there. About five years, something like that.

Notorious Yuma Prison. Photo by Sigrid Khera, 1978.

Yuma jail is pretty rough, Charlie told me. They sit right in there where the sun come up. And in the evening it is right there shining in the jail. There is heat in there. And they can't go nowhere. Stay there, stay there, stay there. Charlie always told me, "I tell you one thing, don't get bad." And when they let him loose, he never go back to his place. He is relative of my father, so he come here to Fort McDowell. He stay here and he is buried here.

When I move down here in 1930 my father has a little store. I came down from Yuma Frank's place to that store. And Chickenneck saw me first and he said, "This is my cousin!" He come and grab all of me. He called me *chikawa* and he almost cried. I kind of feel bad, too. He is my real close relative. Chickenneck was a real *Kewevkepaya* and my grandmother called him close cousin. He was one who got out from the cave with that bunch my grandmother come out. But he lost lots of family in there. So he wanted to kill that boy who show the cave to the soldiers. That boy showed the soldiers where the people live, and it looks like he kill them all. After the soldiers killed my people in the cave, they take that boy away. Send him to school. Let him loose when he is a young man. But when he comes back to San Carlos, people sure are pretty rough with him, my grandmother said. Hold him down, drag him around. Maybe ten, fifteen men drag him around. He was a *Kewevkepaya* from here and all those *Kewevkepaya* were going to kill him. They said, "You killed our people." He is my grandmother's relative, my uncle, *nakwe*. My grandmother said, "He is our relative, but he show us. Kill all of us. So I don't care much about him."

People were going to kill that boy. But there is one old man, *Wipukpa*, he told people to stop it. He said, "No, don't do that. I'm going to give my daughter to him. He is going to be my voice, my ear. I want him. I'm going to give my daughter to him." So he did. That old man is kind of stingy over that boy. He want him as his interpreter for English. So he give him his daughter for wife. He put him in the *watamarva* and lot of people watch him. All those *Wipukpa* and *Yavepe* watch him. That way nobody can do anything to him.

My grandmother said, if it wasn't the old man, nobody say anything, and Chickenneck is going to kill that boy. But Chickenneck never feel like giving up. He said, "He is my cousin, too, but I still feel like killing him, yet." And other people, too, they feel like killing him.

When Mike Burns was in Mayer, my uncle Tom Jones went up to his house with a gun. Four people have to hold my uncle. He is just a tiny, short man, but four people have to hold him. Finally his cousin said, "When I say you stop, you stop. You are my cousin. I don't want to see you in lots of blood. That's why I say, you stop now. Give me the gun. Please! Give me the gun."

He held the gun, and he got it away from my uncle. That time Tom Jones gave in, and he did not try to do anything anymore to Mike. He said, he thought of his father and mother and sister and brothers, and all of his relatives who died in this place. That's why he got mad.

Later Mike Burns come down here to Fort McDowell with his wife and kids. But people here are still rough with him. And they don't like his son. They don't like the son because the father showed the cave and all their relatives got killed. That time my father was boss for cleaning the irrigation ditches. He always send that man who showed the cave and his son the other way to clean ditches. Don't let them work with the rest of the people. If he do that, maybe someone hit them with a shovel.

Three boys the soldiers take them away from here. That boy who show them the cave, and another boy and Carl Montezuma. But I think those White people who got the boy who showed the cave and the other one, Francisco, I don't think those people treat them right. They don't learn them very much.

Francisco, they bring him to Texas or Mexico some place over there. Raise him there. When he is a man, he come over here for some time. He was pretty sick, so he come over here to see a doctor. He has some kids over there in Texas or Mexico. He stayed here two, three months. He stay here with his brother's son. Then he go back again.

He come here and we were working way over at the hills building a fence. We get paid for that, so he worked with us. He come over there to me and he said, "Hey, John." He said, "You take me over there and I know the place where they take me away. I can still remember the rock where I was sitting when they take me. My sister was on the other side of that rock. I was sitting up on the highest rock. They take me from up there, and they get my sister, too. But I don't know what they did with my sister. When they take me over there, I stay over there with the White people. But I don't see my sister any more." He said he got some cattle over there where they take him and he live.

When we worked at that fence we got pay. Francisco asked me, "Hey, John, you go to town?"

I said, "Yeah."

He said, "My grandkid, you take me over there."

I said, "All right," and I take him down with my truck.

When we get to town I get my groceries and I get meat. I wait for him and look like the meat get spoiled. So I go and I put lots of ice in there for my meat. Wait and wait and wait until sundown.

Then he come in there and he said, "Ready to go?"

I said, "Oh, yeah, it's a long time!"

And he said, "I'm ready, but anyways, I want to get a little tobacco."

I watch him and he get in the Chinaman's store and he get two boxes of chewing tobacco.

When he come back to Fort McDowell he said, "You unload my stuff." He say I shall do that at his brother's son's house. The shack is a little way off the road. "You take my stuff right to the door."

"All right." I take it up there and I look in the boxes. There was only two gallons of whiskey in it. That's all his groceries.

When I get back home, my father's wife asks, "What did he get?"

"I don't know. I see just two bottles of whiskey."

And my father said, "He pay you the gas?"

I said, "No, he don't pay me anything." My father laughed.

The one who showed the cave to the soldiers, he spoke Yavapai. But Francisco don't. They got him out from here when he was a little boy, so he forgot the words. He knows just a little bit, he said. Like *miowe*, "come on." And *mahamaka kamiu*, "how are you?"

"That's all I know," he said, "and I still remember my name, *Wadarudjima.*"

But Carl Montezuma he cannot say anything in Yavapai. All he remembers is his name, *Wassaja*, he said.

Carl's mother (*Tehilda*), she is a sister to my grandmother's mother. Carl is *maya*, first cousin to my grandmother. Maya, that means the kids coming out from two sisters. They call each other *maya*. I would call him *nakwe*, uncle. Carl Montezuma's father (*Uquiquequiva*) and mother died in that cave on the Salt River. And the boy who showed the cave, his father and mother died in there, too. His mother and my grandmother, they were cousins.

That cave at the Salt River, that's the one where people live in there a long time. But when the White people killed all our people in there and let them lay in there, we don't go back there any more. Only when Carl Montezuma go back there and get the bones, that's when we go there.

In old days, when somebody die in a camp, people don't stay. They move away from the camp. Break all the grinding stones and pottery. All the people who live in that camp move out. And when they leave the place, they flatten that house down and burn it. They put brush in the inside, that's how it burn easy. People don't use that place over. And that's why you see lots of broken grinding stones and pottery all around here. When people die, they break that in small pieces and throw it away. Move on to another place.

Up in Sedona they make a wikiup of cedar leaves. And when somebody died, they put cedar leaves in there, put them in there and make the house pretty solid. Put lots of wood in, too. Then burn the whole place. And after they burn it, they don't let it pile. Just like a fork and stick and scatter the coals around. Just like all the coal is gone again.

When a man died in a cave, they take him away and burn him. They don't go back to that cave where he died for a long time. When it is a good cave, they come back after some time and mark the cave with yellow powder. Pray four times. Mark it all around with yellow powder. Then stay there again.

When somebody had died, a year later or so they make a dance. They call that *papillo*. They tell people about it, and they again tell other people, and so on. So many people get together for the *papillo*. They get the relatives of the dead together, and that makes them feel better. It makes them stop thinking of the dead.

People put lots of things together for the *papillo*, and in the morning they burn it. But anyone who wants something out of that pile of things, he can get it. They give it to him and he keeps it. Sometimes it is a necklace, sometimes a skirt of buckskin. People who get that don't use it every day. They keep it, and only when there is a dance and people get together, they use it. Then they let everybody see they use it. When a lady died, her cousin, *baya*, get some things and they keep it just to remember. But all the other things on the pile they burn.

The Hualapai call that kind of dance and burning things for the dead *kor'uka*. One time when I was young I was over there, and I see all the things piles up. One man said to me, "Anything you want, take it out from here."

Salt River Canyon. Photo by Sigrid Khera, 1976.

We did that dance last before they send us to San Carlos. I never see it. When we come back, we just do the singing. I sing in there a few times. One time we had it here in Fort McDowell below the highway. But that time I don't get anything. They say, "You leave that alone. That's for the dead people. You're not dead, yet." I don't know who had died then.

My grandmother said, my people, they go some other place when something is wrong. But when they are going to die, they come back where they had been. They die there. Carl Montezuma the same way. He is in Chicago. He is a rich man, he is a doctor, a lawyer, everything. But he came back and he died right there where my corral is now. That's how the Yavapai used to be. He could have stayed over there in Chicago and died in his house. He has a good house with everything in there. But he comes here

(Fort McDowell) and stays in a cottonwood tipi. He lays in there and dies in there. I see him, when I come down from Prescott. That time I could not talk much English. I just sit there. He talks better English than the White people. So I am afraid and I never did say anything to him. My grandmother had said, "This is my first cousin. You go over there and see him." They come out from two sisters, they are *maya*. That's why she wants me to come down here and see him.

But I wasn't here when he died. He was real sick, I know it. I know, he couldn't live not too long. That time when I go back up there to Prescott, I start working cowboy. But after the roundup my grandmother said, "You want to go down there (Fort McDowell) and see him again? Go on!" She give me the money. I get the train ticket and go down here.

I come in the train to Phoenix. I know the people from Fort McDowell used to camp at some place in Phoenix when they go down there. So I walk over there. Ole Mason was there. I shake hands with him. "You come back over here? You have a car?" he asked me.

I said, "No, I come by train."

"All right," he said, "I'm going to go back to Fort McDowell tomorrow early in the morning. Come to my camp."

I said, "All right." And I asked him, "Do you think Carl Montezuma is still around?"

He said, "No, he is gone long time. About three weeks."

So when I come to Fort McDowell, I go over there where Charlie Dickens stayed. Nothing in there now.

Burnt up everything. And my father said, "He is gone long time. We put him over there (cemetery)."

My grandmother want me to come down here to see him, but it is too late now. I stay here this night, next day I go back. When I told my father, he said, "All right, tell your grandmother. I take you to Phoenix, get a train and go back."

I said, "All right."

He take me over there to the depot. I take the train and go back. And my grandmother is sure crying. "That's only one cousin I have," she said. "First one!"

She was too old to come down here. Too old, too old. Can't see, either. Can't walk too well, either.

Carl is her first cousin, she said. She had lots of cousin, but they died in that cave. My grandmother, she told me that over and over, "They killed all our relatives in that cave." She never let me forget that. My cousins, they run away when the old woman speaks. They don't like what she says. They don't want to hear it. They go to school with the White people. Now they are sorry they didn't listen to her.

I am thinking about my grandmother all the time. And when I think of her, I feel like I cry. I try to forget, but I can't. I have to think about her. She is the one who takes me around. Takes me around, takes me around all the time.

When she is old and I am working, I know what she eat and I always go to the store and get something for her. That's what I did for a long time. She is real old then. Maybe hundred, maybe two hundred years. Real old.

I heard, when people are ready to go, they eat real good. That's what she did. Before she don't eat much. Just a little bit. Drink some coffee. Sometime take a little water. Sometime she takes a little toast. I make a toast for my grandmother, and she eats just a little bit. She is kind of weak all the time. And one morning, that day when she is ready to go, I get up early in the morning. I make coffee.

She said, "I'm going to eat. I want to eat."

"All right."

I get up and cook. Roast some meat. I fry some potatoes. She eat that. She eat good that morning. She eat lots. And she talks. She kind of touch my head, "You know son, I want to sleep. You fix my place, I want to sleep."

"All right."

I put something on the place where she used to lay. And she is laying there.

Then I go out, shoe my horse. I shoe my horse and I go back in there and call my grandmother. It feels kind of funny. Her breath, when she sleeps, you always hear it. That time I don't hear it. Every time when I said, "*kolah*," she always said, "Yes." But she don't say it now. She just lay there. I come in and feel her arm. All cold. So I run to my mother's sister. She lives a little way off. I tell her, "My grandmother talks different now."

Viola just comes out and cry, "Maybe she leaves us. Maybe she is gone now!"

I said, "Yes, this morning she sure eat a lot."

Viola said, "Maybe she is gone now," and she starts running.

My grandmother is gone.

Notes

The Garland American Indian Ethnohistory series (118 volumes in the series) presented original documents on the history and anthropology of many American Indian tribes and groups who were involved in the Indian Claims action of the 1950s and 1960s. Much of this material was summarized in a 1,650-page document, House Report No. 2503, published in 1953, for the U.S. House of Representatives. These cases are public records on file at the Records of the Indian Claims Commission at the National Archives, Washington, D.C.

The volume pertaining to the Yavapai Indians is: Horr, David A., ed. *Yavapai Indians*, which includes: "A Study of Yavapai History," by Albert H. Schroeder, 22-354, and "The Yavapai Indians 1682-1848," by Alfred B. Thomas, 355-386, and "Commission Findings," 387-439.

In editor Horr's book the page number tells whether the source is Schroeder, Thomas or the Commission.

The abbreviation OSU is used here for the website: http://digital.library.okstate.edu/icc/index.html which includes some Indian Claims Commission proceedings not carried in Horr's excellent book. Oklahoma State

University (OSU) Library Electronic Publishing Center has digitized the Indian Claims Commission decisions. The Yavapai case is in volumes 15 and 21, Dockets 22-E and 22-F.

EDITOR'S PREFACE
1. Bourke, *On The Border With Crook*, 114.

CHAPTER 1. ARIZONA
1. Walker and Bufkin, *Historical Atlas of Arizona*, Preface.
2. *Ibid.*, 1.
3. Arizona State Land Department 2009 Annual Report.
4. Arizona State Parks.
5. Butler, unpublished manuscript on Orme Dam.

CHAPTER 2. INDIAN CLAIMS COMMISSION
1. Indian Claims Commission, Findings of Fact on Award of Attorney Fees, Sept. 17, 1969. OSU vol. 21, Dockets 22-E, 22-F, pp. 384-385, 396.
2. *Ibid.*, pp. 384-385.

CHAPTER 4. ANTHROPOLOGIST MEETS THE YAVAPAI
1. Butler, Nov. 13, 1973, letter to Dale Stuart King, Butler collection.
2. Nov. 6, 1973, Fort McDowell Tribal Council Minutes, Butler collection.
3. Butler, Apr. 9, 1974, letter to Fort McDowell Tribal Council, Butler collection.
4. Butler, unpublished manuscript on Orme Dam.

CHAPTER 5. ETHNIC IDENTITY, LANGUAGE AND TERRITORY

1. Horr, 401.
2. Horr, 423, 394.
3. Horr, 432, 433; Pilles, interview with Butler, December 2011.
4. Ortiz, ed., *Handbook of North American Indians, Volume 10: Southwest,* 5, 393.
5. Horr, 421.
6. OSU, vol. 21, Dockets 22-E, 22-F, pp. 384-385, 395-396.
7. Horr, 409.
8. Horr, 410.
9. Horr, 411.
10. Horr, 411.
11. Horr, 412.
12. Horr, 419.

CHAPTER 6. THE SPANIARDS SAVE HISTORY

1. Horr, Schroeder, 65, 66.
2. Horr, Schroeder, 78, 79.
3. Horr, Thomas, 366.
4. Horr, Thomas, 369.
5. Horr, Thomas, 379.
6. Horr, 413.
7. Horr, Schroeder, 34.
8. Horr, Schroeder, 31.

CHAPTER 7. PREHISTORY

1. Horr, Schroeder, 34.
2. Butler, unpublished manuscript on Orme Dam.

CHAPTER 8. POPULATION

1. Horr, Schroeder, 33.
2. Horr, Schroeder, 91.

3. Khera and Mariella, "Yavapai," in *Handbook of North American Indians, Volume 10: Southwest*, 45.
4. Horr, Schroeder, 49.

CHAPTER 9. YAVAPAI: TOLKEPAYA, WIPUKPA, YAVEPE, KEWEVKEPAYA

1. Horr, Schroeder, 27.
2. Khera and Mariella, "Yavapai," in *Handbook of North American Indians, Volume 10: Southwest*, 38.
3. *Ibid.*
4. *Ibid.*

CHAPTER 10. BORDERING TRIBES

1. Horr, 405.
2. Horr, 402, 423; Khera and Mariella, 40.
3. Horr, 403, 423; Khera and Mariella, 40.
4. *Ibid.*
5. Horr, 402.
6. Horr, Schroeder, 56.
7. Horr, Schroeder, 256.
8. Horr, Schroeder, 256.
9. Horr, Schroeder, 33.
10. Horr, 402, 411, 434.
11. Horr, 408.
12. Horr, 423.
13. Horr, 424.
14. Horr, 404.
15. Horr, Schroeder, 29.

CHAPTER 11. ANGLO-AMERICANS ENTER

1. Horr, 419, Schroeder 31.
2. Horr, Thomas, 281.
3. Horr, 398; Walker and Bufkin, *Historical Atlas of Arizona*, 17.
4. Walker and Bufkin, 20A; Horr, Thomas, 381.
5. Brandes, *Frontier Military Posts of Arizona*, 81.

6. Walker and Bufkin, 23; Horr, Schroeder, 107.
7. Walker and Bufkin, 22.
8. Brandes, 56-58.
9. Walker and Bufkin, 49, 26; Horr, Schroeder, 118; Nicolson, *The Arizona of Joseph Pratt Allyn,* 72, 154.
10. Walker and Bufkin, 25.

CHAPTER 12.   EXTERMINATION POLICY
1. Nicolson, *The Arizona of Joseph Pratt Allyn,* 6, 7, 9.
2. *Ibid.* Foreword xiv.
3. *Ibid.* Foreword xiii.
4. *Ibid.,* 68.
5. Horr, Schroeder, 38.
6. Khera, original unpublished Dec. 1982 manuscript on the Yavapai, *Souls on the Land*, 339.
7. Nicolson, *The Arizona of Joseph Pratt Allyn,* 76.
8. Khera, original Dec. 1982 manuscript, 312.
9. *Ibid.,* 313-314.
10. *Ibid.,* 314.

CHAPTER 13.   MISTAKEN IDENTITY
1. Horr, Schroeder, 266-276.
2. Speroff, *Carlos Montezuma, M.D.,* 443-448.
3. Iverson, *Carlos Montezuma and the Changing World of American Indians*, 6; Speroff, *Carlos Montezuma, M.D.*, 30-31.
4. Bourke, *On the Border with Crook*, 188; Waterstrat, *Hoomothya's Long Journey*, 3.
5. Bourke, 176-201.
6. *Ibid.,* 464.

CHAPTER 14.   BOWS AND ARROWS AGAINST PISTOLS AND RIFLES
1. Khera, original unpublished Dec. 1982 manuscript on the Yavapai, *Souls on the Land*, 309.

2. *Ibid.*, 349-351.
3. *Ibid.*, 352.
4. Horr, Schroeder, 277-287.
5. *Ibid.*, 115.
6. *Ibid.*, 38.
7. *Ibid.*, 277.
8. *Ibid.*, 40.
9. *Ibid.*, 283.
10. *Ibid.*, 277.
11. *Ibid.*, 278.
12. *Ibid.*, 279.
13. *Ibid.*, 284.
14. *Ibid.*, 284.
15. Horr, Schroeder, 281; Bourke, 170.
16. Bourke, *On The Border With Crook,* 199, 200.
17. Horr, Schroeder, 285.
18. *Ibid.*, 286.
19. *Ibid.*, 287.
20. *Ibid.*, 282.

CHAPTER 15.   UNDER MILITARY ORDERS FOR 40 YEARS

1. Horr, 400.
2. Brandes, *Frontier Military Posts of Arizona,* 75-80; Horr, 399.
3. Brandes, 27-29; Bourke, 166; Horr, 399.
4. Brandes, 70-73.
5. *Ibid.*, 53-55.
6. Horr, 400.
7. Corbusier, *Verde to San Carlos,* 17; Horr, Schroeder, 124; Khera, original Dec. 1982 manuscript, 357.
8. Brandes, 63-67.
9. Horr, Schroeder, 126.
10. Horr, 400.
11. Khera, original Dec. 1982 manuscript, 328, 331.
12. Horr, Schroeder, 125.

13. Horr, Schroeder, 124.
14. Horr, Schroeder, 124, 125.
15. Horr, 401.
16. Corbusier, 260, 261; Bourke, 216.
17. Corbusier, *Verde to San Carlos,* 263,
18. Bourke, *On The Border With Crook,* 217.
19. Heider, thesis, Fort McDowell 1955 field notes, 52.

CHAPTER 16. ONE MORE ARMED INVASION IN THE 20TH CENTURY

1. Heider, thesis, 1955 field notes, 18-20.
2. U.S. House of Representatives, Committee on Indian Affairs, Washington, D.C., 1911, *Memorial and Papers from the Mohave-Apache Indians of McDowell Reservation, Arizona, in relation to their Removal from McDowell Reservation to the Salt River Reservation, Arizona,* Butler collection.
3. Latimer, Joseph W., June 15, 1921, *The Rape of McDowell Reservation, Arizona, by the Indian Bureau,* Butler collection.
4. Khera, original Dec. 1982 manuscript, 9, 15, 16; Horr, 423, 413; Horr, Schroeder, 46.
5. Horr, 17, 18.
6. Supreme Court of Arizona, July 15, 1948, 196 P.2d 456, 67 Ariz. 337, Harrison et al. v. Laveen, No. 5065; "Editor's Last Lawsuit," Lem Mathews, Editor, Nov. 30, 1963, *Dunbar's Weekly,* Phoenix, AZ, Butler collection.
7. *Chicago Sun-Times,* "A Yavapai goes home to a struggle," May 3, 1976, 4, 26.
8. KTVK-TV, Phoenix, AZ, July 23, 1977, DVD in Butler collection.
9. OSU, vol. 21, Dockets 22-E, 22-F, pp. 384-385, 395.
10. *The Arizona Daily Star,* "Orme would destroy Yavapai tribe, study says," Sept. 24, 1981, A9.
11. *Scottsdale Progress,* "Casino raided," May 12, 1992, 1.

12. King, interviews by Butler, May 12, 1992, September 27, 2011.
13. *Arizona Republic,* editorial "The Fort McDowell pact," Dec. 1, 1992, A12.

Bibliography

Arizona Daily Star, (Tucson), p. A9, September 24, 1981.

Arizona Republic (Phoenix), p. A12, December 1, 1992.

Barnett, Franklin. *Viola Jimulla: The Indian Chieftess.* Sponsored by Prescott Yavapai Indians. Yuma, AZ: Southwest Printers, 1968.

Bourke, John G. *On The Border With Crook.* New York: Charles Scribner's Sons, 1891; University of Nebraska Press, Lincoln, NE, reprinted 1971.

Brandes, Ray. *Frontier Military Posts of Arizona.* Globe, AZ: Dale Stuart King, 1960.

Butler, Carolina C., all references are in her personal collection, Scottsdale, AZ.

Chicago Sun-Times, p. 4, May 3, 1976.

Corle, Edwin. *The Gila: River of the Southwest.* Lincoln, NE: University of Nebraska Press, 1951.

Courbusier, W.T. *Verde to San Carlos: Recollections of a famous Army Surgeon and His Observant family on the Western Frontier 1869-1886*. Tucson, AZ: Dale Stuart King, 1968.

Dunbar's Weekly, Phoenix, AZ, Last Edition, November 30, 1963.

Eason, Nicholas J. *Fort Verde: An Era of Men and Courage*. Camp Verde, AZ: Camp Verde Historical Society, 1966.

Heider, Karl G. Fort McDowell Yavapai Acculturation: A Preliminary Study, B.A. Honors Thesis in Anthropology, Harvard College, Cambridge, MA, 1956.

Horr, David A., ed. *Yavapai Indians*. A. H. Schroeder and A. B. Thomas reports and Indian Claims Commission Findings. New York: Garland, 1974.

Iverson, Peter. *Carlos Montezuma and the Changing World of American Indians*. Albuquerque: University of New Mexico Press, 1982.

Khera, Sigrid, ed. *The Yavapai of Fort McDowell: An Outline of Their History and Culture*. Scottsdale, AZ: O'Day Printing Corp., 1978.

Khera, Sigrid. *Souls on the Land*, original unpublished December 1982 manuscript on the Yavapai. Labriola National American Indian Data Center, Arizona State University, Tempe, AZ.

Khera, Sigrid and Patricia S. Mariella. "Yavapai."
In *Handbook of North American Indians, vol. 10: Southwest*, Alfonso Ortiz, ed., 38-54. Washington, DC: Smithsonian Institution, 1983.

King, David, Fort McDowell Yavapai, interviewed by Carolina C. Butler on May 12, 1992, and September 27, 2011.

Larner, John William Jr., ed. *Papers of Carlos Montezuma, M.D.* Wilmington, DE: Scholarly Resources Inc., 1984.

Latimer, Joseph W. *The Rape of McDowell Reservation, Arizona by The Indian Bureau.* Washington, DC: Hayworth Publishing House, 1921.

Nicolson, John, ed. *The Arizona of Joseph Pratt Allyn-Letters from a Pioneer Judge: Observations and Travels, 1863-1866.* Tucson: University of Arizona Press, 1974.

Ortiz, Alfonso, ed. *Handbook of North American Indians, Vols. 9-10, Southwest.* Washington, DC: Smithsonian Institution, 1983.

Schroeder, Albert H. "A Study of Yavapai History," report for Indian Claims Commission, pp. 23-355. In *Yavapai Indians*, David A. Horr, ed. New York: Garland, 1974.

Scottsdale Progress (Arizona), p. 1, May 12, 1992.

Speroff, Leon. *Carlos Montezuma, M.D., A Yavapai American Hero, The Life and Times of an American Indian, 1866-1923*. Portland, OR: Arnica Publishing, Inc., 2004.

Thomas, Alfred B. "The Yavapai Indians 1582-1848," report for Indian Claims Commission, pp. 355-386. In *Yavapai Indians,* David A. Horr, ed. New York: Garland, 1974.

U.S. House of Representatives Committee on Indian Affairs, *Memorial and Papers for the Mohave-Apache Indians of McDowell Reservation, Arizona.* Washington, DC: Government Printing Office, 1911.

Walker, Henry P. and Don Bufkin. *Historical Atlas of Arizona.* Norman: University of Oklahoma Press, 1979.

Waterstrat, Elaine. *Hoomothya's Long Journey 1865-1897.* Fountain Hills: Mount McDowell Press, 1998.

WEBSITES

http://digital.library.okstate.edu/icc/index.html
United States. Indian Claims Commission. *Indian Claims Commission Decisions,* 43 vols., 2005. Yavapai case in Vol. 15, Vol. 21, Dockets 22-E, 22-F.

SUPPLEMENTAL REFERENCES

Burns, Mike. *All of my people were killed: the memoir of Mike Burns (Hoomothya), a captive Indian.* Prescott, AZ: Sharlot Hall Museum, 2010.

Braatz, Timothy. *Surviving Conquest: A History of the Yavapai Peoples.* University of Nebraska Press, Lincoln and London, 2003.

Corbusier, William H. "The Apache-Yuma and Apache-Mohaves." *American Antiquarian*, Vol. VIII, pp. 276-284 and 325-339. Chicago, 1886.

Gifford, Edward W. "The Southeastern Yavapai." *University of California Publications in American Archaeology and Ethnology.* Vol. 29, No. 3, pp. 177-252. Berkeley, 1932.

Gifford, Edward W. "Northeastern and Western Yavapai." *University of California Publications in American Archaeology and Ethnology.* Vol. 34, No. 4, pp. 247-354. Berkeley, 1936.

Mann, Charles C. *1491: New Revelations of the Americas Before Columbus.* New York: Alfred A. Knopf, 2005.

Fort McDowell Yavapai Nation, Fort McDowell, AZ.

Yavapai-Apache Nation, Camp Verde, AZ.

Yavapai-Prescott Indian Tribe, Prescott, AZ.

Inter Tribal Council of Arizona, Inc., Phoenix, AZ.

Arizona State University Libraries, Tempe, AZ.

Northern Arizona University Libraries, Flagstaff, AZ.

University of Arizona Libraries, Tucson, AZ.

Arizona Historical Society, Tucson, AZ.

Arizona State Library History & Archives, State Capitol, Phoenix, AZ.

National Anthropological Archives, Smithsonian Institution, Washington, DC.

National Archives, Washington, DC.

Acknowledgments

First of all, I want to acknowledge the great human spirit of the Yavapai. To learn their history—what they have endured, their captivity for 25 years outside their homeland, being scattered—and to see their survival and to see their dignity is to be deeply moved.

I want to express my greatest admiration for tribal elders Mike Harrison and John Williams, smart, strong and bold, who wanted to set the record straight. They didn't want the Yavapai to lose their rightful place in history. Their tribal history, preserved here in their own words, is rare primary source material which will stand indefinitely. These two tribal elders from one of Arizona's oldest tribes, the Yavapai, achieved their goal.

I met the Yavapai people by chance in 1971, first at Fort McDowell and then others at Camp Verde and at Prescott, and have made lasting friendships. I want to thank them all for their friendship.

I want to express great admiration and appreciation for Dr. Sigrid Khera, anthropologist, who worked with Mike and John, for the enormous amount of work she did, under trying circumstances, from 1974 to 1982, on her study of the Yavapai Indians. Sigrid Khera, Mike Harrison and John Williams have passed away, but they left a lasting legacy.

My very special thanks and appreciation to the talented, successful, and accomplished individuals whose advance comments are on the book's opening pages. These generous individuals value history and value the importance of recording and preserving it. Please join me in telling them thanks.

Although I do not know all their names, I want to thank all those who assisted Dr. Khera during 1974-1982 as she worked to complete her manuscript on the Yavapai. I was with Dr. Khera when she handed her manuscript to Elizabeth Shaw and Marshall Townsend at the University of Arizona Press in Tucson in December 1982. They were very kind then and also later during Sigrid's illness. I am indebted to the unnamed manuscript appraisor who critiqued the original manuscript for the Press in a jaunty but excellent way. I later used many of his/her recommendations.

In putting together this book, I worked primarily with the research done by Sigrid Khera, as well as historians and anthropologists who preceded her, including Albert H. Schroeder, Alfred B. Thomas and E. W Gifford. I am grateful to them all for their discipline, organization and thoroughness of their work on the Yavapai. And I am grateful to all those in every ancient and recent period who took pen to paper and recorded their day's events which give us information on the Yavapai.

I was amazed by the outstanding work of the Indian Claims Commission. Its reports, findings and decisions were extremely useful. With my focus on the case of the

Acknowledgments

Yavapai, I was impressed by the Commission's knowledge, thoroughness and desire to hear from the Yavapai themselves.

I was delighted to discover that Oklahoma State University (OSU) Library Electronic Publishing Center digitized the Indian Claims Commission decisions into 43 volumes and made them easily available to all. I made much use of this website; see Bibliography. Thanks to OSU for this outstanding service.

It was a pleasure to work with my son, Elias Butler, photographer/journalist, on the photographs for the book, and to witness first-hand his talent, skills and professionalism. Likewise, Carla Olson did outstanding work drawing the maps and creating the book's website. I am very grateful to Elias and Carla for their excellent work and impressive additions to this book.

I could never name all the Yavapai from Fort McDowell, Camp Verde, and Prescott to properly thank them, but I must thank the families of Mike Harrison, John Williams, and Jim White. And I want to thank all who were in attendance at a March 18, 2010, Yavapai-Apache Nation tribal council meeting at Camp Verde, where I spoke to them about the planned Yavapai history book. Then-Chairman Thomas Beauty graciously expressed appreciation for Dr. Khera's work and other council members joined him with their own heartfelt expressions. At the end, everyone in the room clapped their approval. The presentation was later printed in the tribal newspaper. Thank you all.

I want to thank many who were so helpful in a variety of ways, from some reading and improving the manuscript, to others contributing needed information, and all offered always-welcome encouragement. These include Louise Alflen, Carolyn White and Paul Blakey, Kathy Block, Matthew Bokovoy, Elizabeth Brandt, Allyson Carter, Selena Castaneda, Catherine Cocks, Donna Collette, Lucinda Harrison Denny, Bruce Dinges, Christina Farnsworth, Alan Ferg, Bernard Fontana, Gwyn Goebel, Greg Glassco, Lorlotte Guehde, Janet Jones, Melissa Jones, David King and Jania, Debra Krol, John Lewis, David Madrid, Ekkehart Malotki, Patricia Mariella, Christine Marin, Joyce Martin, James McKie, Verna Monenkirt, Pamela Mott, Cornelius Nelson, Madeline Nelson, Sandi Nikula and Nik, Daisy Njoku, Judie Piner, Delores Plunkett, Gina Rappaport, Jennifer Rauhouse, Paige Rocket, Olympia Sosangelis, Robert Spindler, Barbara Tellman, Pansy Thomas, James Vint, Cynthia Wallace, Frank Welsh and Barbara, Kimberley Williams, Bob Witzeman and Janet, and J. Scott Wood. And thank you to anyone I may have missed.

I want to thank Karen Gray, my publisher, whom I met by chance. She has been the best to work with. She has been very kind and helpful, and also fun, plus she has an amazing memory. I am also very grateful to Jason Crye for his many publishing contributions.

I want to thank Sigrid Khera's three children, Susheila, Paul and Otto, for their dear friendship, for their help, support and encouragement. And very special thanks to my husband, Walker, and to our four children, Paul, Michael, David Elias and Christina, for their loving support and encouragement. And for their unfailing support and encouragement, thanks always to my siblings, Margaret, Elias Jr., Irma and Nancy.

Acknowledgments

Lastly, thanks, Mom and Dad, for teaching me to work hard because that's what I've done for this book. And loved it.

Carolina Castillo Butler

Oral History of the Yavapai

Index

Austin, Harry (1895-?), 95
Awila Quiva (Willie Hunt), 140
Axe, Sam (*Palkahavo*), 151
AZ (abbreviation for Arizona)
Aztec Empire, 46

B

Bakwaeguo (Skull Valley), 40, 81, 111-113, 114, 116, 257, 271, 273, 280
bakwau (adviser), 340-342
barave (lightning), 30, 182, 201, 202, 203-204, 230, 238, 252, 260
Bartlett Dam, 295
baskets and basketmaking, 79, 109, 117, 131, 133, 139, 151, 189-190, 249, 251, 257, 274, 299, 321, 322, 324, 336
Beaver Creek, 84
Beeline Highway, 122-123, 303
beer, 261
Bible, The, 225
Bill Williams Mountain, 40, 80
Bill Williams River, 40
Black, colored, negro, 140-141, 240, 245-246, 260, 298
Black Canyon (*Ahaytikutoba*), 43, 196, 215, 216, 275-277, 278-279, 315, 318, 327, 333
Black Mountains, 81
blackroot (*isamaganyach*, also *isamaganyatch*), 112, 169, 182, 183, 188, 191, 193, 205, 209, 223-224, 225, 230, 235, 240, 259
Bloody Basin (*Atasquaselhua*), 109-111, 116, 232, 325, 333
blue stone, 190, 210, 223, 224, 242
Blyer, Joe, 282
boundaries, Yavapai land, 36-44, 48, 50, 56, 96, 153-155, 160, 164
boundary line, 50, 153-155, 160, 164
Bourke, Capt. John G. (1843-1896), i, 73-74, 75, 86
Bowie, AZ, 91
Braatz, Timothy, 85
Bradshaw Mountains, 37-38, 54, 274
British, 60

H

I

J

K

O

P

R

railroad, 61, 149, 356
    See also trains
Ralphson, Tom, 236
rancherias, 40, 43
ranchers, 66, 80, 316-317
Reagan, President Ronald (1911-2004), 97
Red Creek, 81
Red Mountain (Mount McDowell), 31, 160, 161, 233
Red Rock country, 25, 28, 31, 39, 54
    See also Sedona, AZ
religion, religious beliefs, 30-31, 223-264
Revolutionary War (1775-1783), 60
Rich Hill, 61
Rim Rock (*Chokasiva*), 143
Rio Verde Reservation (1871-1875), 84, 85, 86
rituals, 28, 30-32, 223-264
Rock Spring, 301
Romsa (Peter Harry) (? -1975), 159
Roosevelt, President Theodore (1858-1919), 50, 89, 153, 154
Rosie, 352
Roy, Robert (*Marikoka*), 144

S

Sacramento, California, 60
Saddle Mountain, 104, 105, 106, 108, 109, 113, 260, 303
Sakarakaamche, 176-208, 209, 223, 224, 225, 226, 229, 230,
    235, 239, 240, 241, 251-252, 253, 254, 259, 353
Salmeron, Geronimo Zarate, 48
salt, 304, 323
Salt River, 4, 38, 73, 84, 96, 103, 104, 243, 244, 304, 323, 363
Salt River Canyon, 23, 27, 67, 74, 80, 82, 103, 111, 116, 304,
    333
Salt River Reservation, 92, 155-156, 246, 303, 329
Sam Jack (*Homutalva*), 159

Vialnyucha (Fossil Creek), 3, 54, 198, 199, 232, 304, 325, 347, 348
Voting Rights for Arizona Indians (1948), 95
Vulture Lode, 61

W

Wadarudjima (Francisco), 361-363
Wadjemodema, 213-214
Wagoner, a storekeeper, 270
Wahagsigiita (Prescott, AZ), iv, 54, 61, 68, 80, 83, 90, 106, 113, 116, 124-125, 127, 138, 141, 145, 154, 159, 161, 164, 165, 229, 232, 247, 249, 268, 276, 278, 279, 280, 281, 284-286, 287, 308, 325, 330, 331, 333, 337, 338, 356, 366
Walgtonamin, 323
Walnut Creek, 80
Walnut Grove, AZ, 269-271
Walnut Grove Dam, 270
Washington, DC, iv, 85, 89, 95, 121, 147-150, 151, 153, 154, 155, 157, 161
Wassaja (Carlos Montezuma) (1866?-1923), 72, 76, 92, 106, 161, 316-317, 361, 363, 365
Wasyumje, 231
watamarva (mud house), 302, 341, 342, 360
Watarammah (or Watarama), 93, 112
Waterman, Bill, 140
Watt, James G., 32
weapons
  bayonet, 119
  bow and arrow, 65, 79, 113, 125, 126, 128, 139, 176, 178, 180-181, 182, 184, 209, 211, 212, 216, 252, 306, 307-308, 309, 310, 312, 317, 323, 345, 346, 351
  club, 77, 79, 124
  gun, 116, 117, 118, 128, 138, 276, 307, 360
  knife, 123, 124, 178, 181, 231, 276, 330, 331
  pistol, 65, 77
  rifle, 65, 77, 97, 116, 138, 212
  rock, 216, 330
  spear, 113, 229, 311
  throwing stick, 113, 309

Y

Visit the book's website to enjoy color photos of places within the Yavapai Indians' ancestral territory and see the beauty of the land where they lived and roamed.

www.oralhistoryoftheyavapai.com

Sigrid Khera
1934-1984

Sigrid Bechmann earned her Ph.D. in anthropology from the University of Vienna in 1958. She came to Canada in 1959 where she met and married chemist Dr. Paul Khera. They had three children.

From 1961 to 1968, Dr. Khera worked as a researcher for the National Museum of Canada. In 1962-63, she did post-doctoral training at Yale University, New Haven, CT and later was a Research Associate there. She taught at: Southern Connecticut State University, New Haven, CT; Albertus Magnus College, New Haven, CT; Arizona State University, Tempe, AZ; University of North Dakota, Grand Forks, ND; and University of Alaska, Fairbanks, AK

During her academic career, Dr. Khera did field research from 1958 to 1980 and authored several publications. In co-authorship, she contributed the chapter on the Yavapai tribe's history and culture to the *Handbook of North American Indians, Volume 10, Southwest,* published by the Smithsonian Institution in 1983. Earlier, as editor, she had published *The Yavapai of Fort McDowell: An Outline of their History and Culture,* 1978. She left an unpublished completed manuscript on the Yavapai, *Souls on the Land,* December 1982.

Sigrid Khera, born in Vienna, Austria, died in Fairbanks, Alaska on July 28, 1984 at age 49. Her remains were buried at the Fort McDowell cemetery, Arizona, at the request of the Yavapai.

Carolina Castillo Butler

Carolina Butler took an activist's path. While giving her time to house, husband and raising their four children, she was a leader in a ten-year plus battle, helping the Yavapai tribe at Fort McDowell save their land. The government wanted to relocate the tribe for a dam. The dam went down to defeat in 1981.

She was a successful leader in two Maricopa County elections. First, working for a "Yes" vote in 1980 for the construction of several useful bridges over the Salt and Agua Fria rivers. Secondly, working to defeat in 1987 the $3 billion Rio Salado Project and a new property tax to pay for this boondoggle. She was a water activist, testifying numerous times to reform water policy.

Her activities have been included by various authors in their books, such as: *The Yavapai of Fort McDowell* (Sigrid Khera); *Empires in the Sun* (Peter Wiley & Robert Gottlieb); *How to Create a Water Crisis* (Frank Welsh); *A Life of its Own: The Politics and Power of Water* (Robert Gottlieb); *Verde Valley Lore* (Robert Mason); *Indians and Eagles* (Ron K. Schilling); and others.

Carolina is Mexican-American, born in Arizona. Her ancestors came to Arizona from Mexico in 1864. Carolina and Walker, her husband of 46 years, live in Scottsdale, Arizona, 30 minutes from the Fort McDowell Reservation.